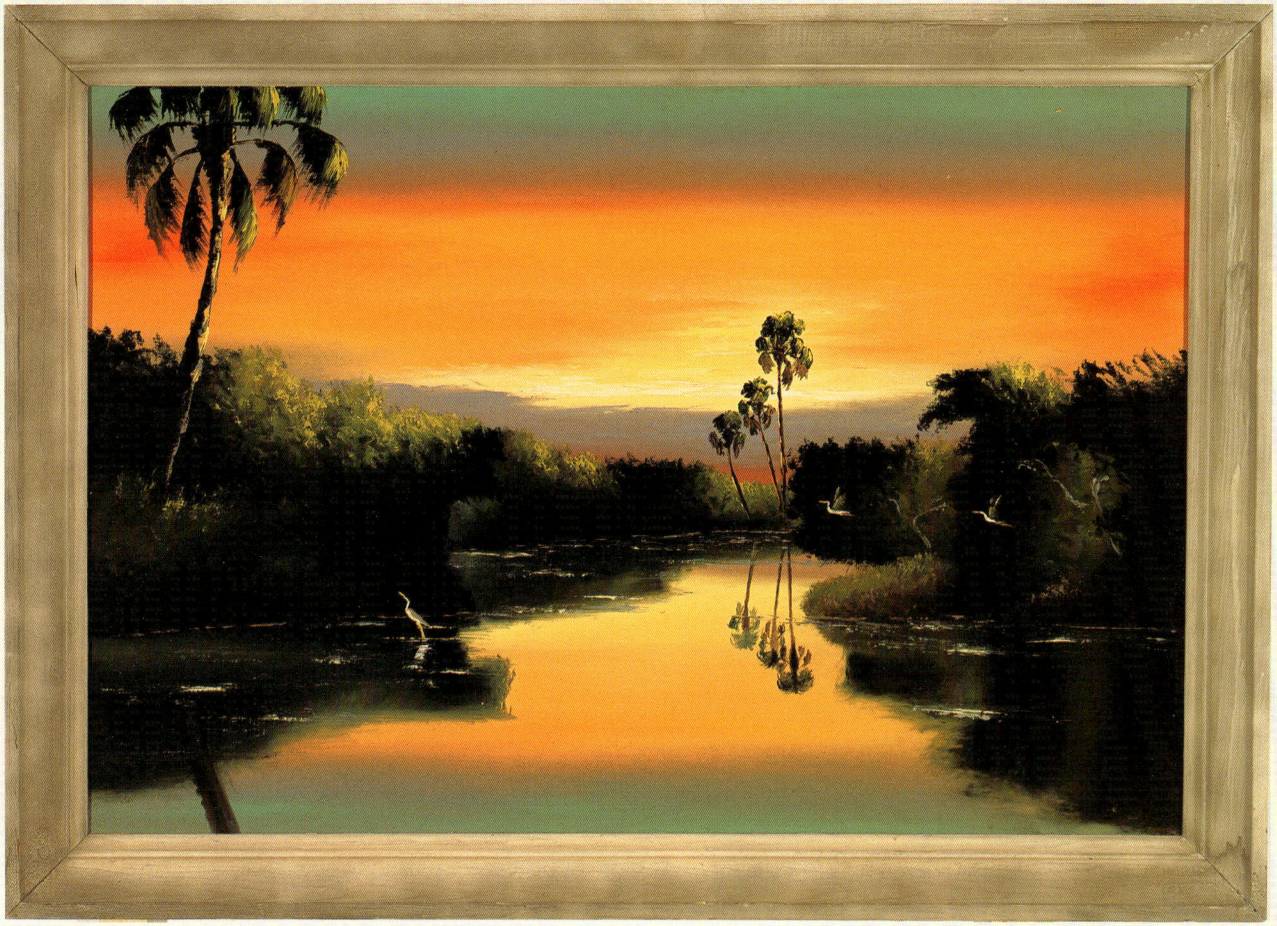

UNIVERSITY PRESS OF FLORIDA

Florida A&M University, Tallahassee   Florida Atlantic University, Boca Raton   Florida Gulf Coast University, Ft. Myers   Florida International University, Miami   Florida State University, Tallahassee
New College of Florida, Sarasota   University of Central Florida, Orlando   University of Florida, Gainesville   University of North Florida, Jacksonville   University of South Florida, Tampa   University of West Florida, Pensacola

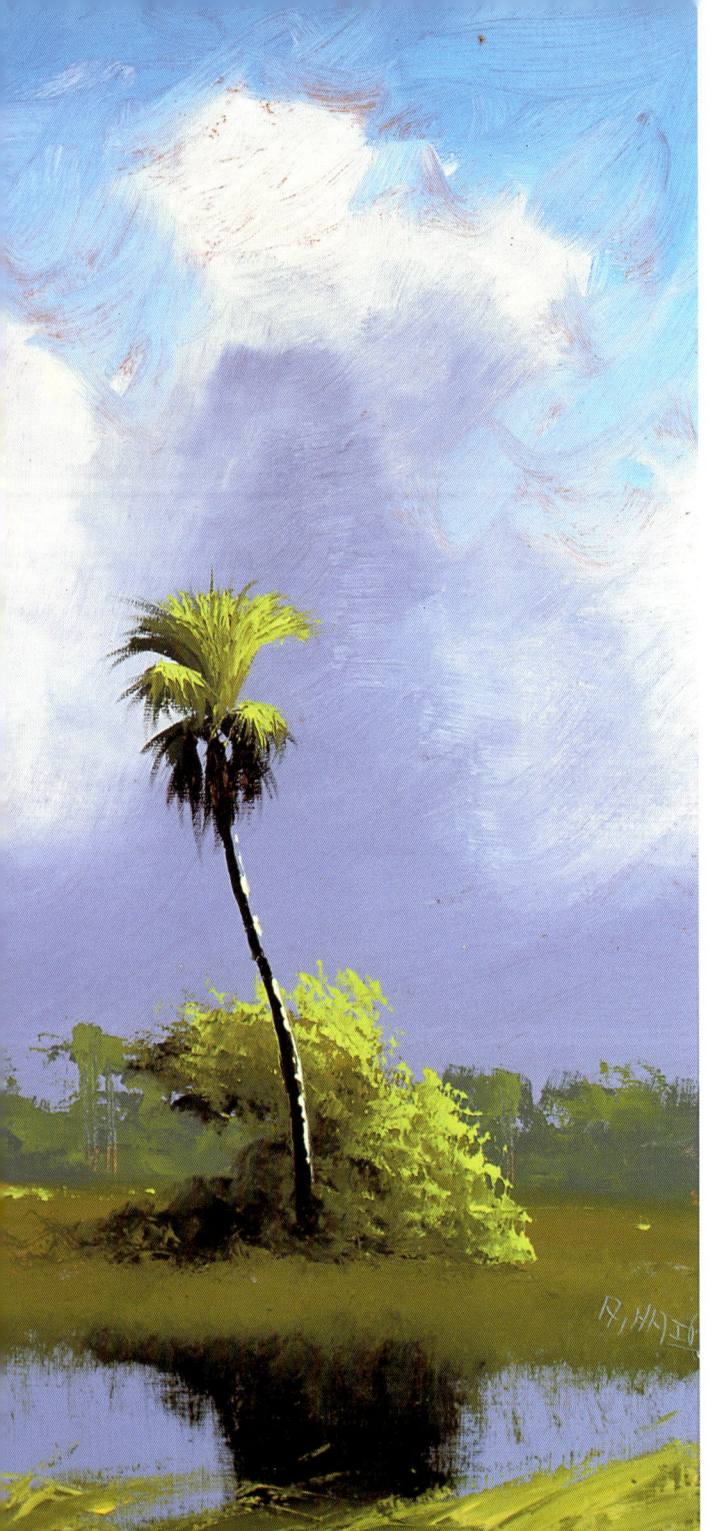

University Press of Florida

Gainesville · Tallahassee · Tampa · Boca Raton · Pensacola · Orlando · Miami · Jacksonville · Ft. Myers · Sarasota

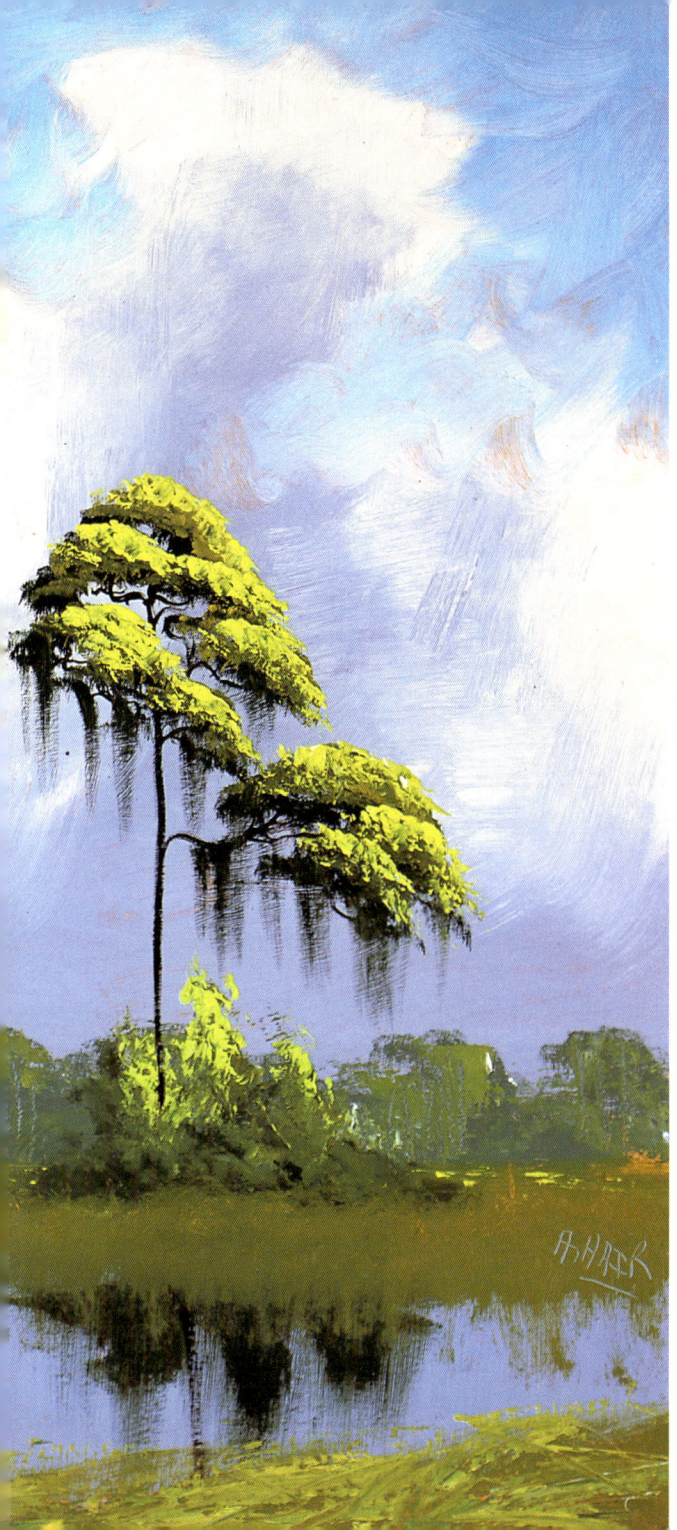

Gary Monroe

The
HIGHWAYMEN

Florida's African-American Landscape Painters

Page i, by Hezekiah Baker; pages ii and iii, diptych by Alfred Hair

29 28 27 26 25   15 14 13 12 11

Library of Congress Cataloging-in-Publication Data
Monroe, Gary.
The Highwaymen: Florida's African-American landscape painters / Gary Monroe.
p. cm.
ISBN 978-0-8130-2281-9 (cloth: alk. paper)
1. Landscape painting, American—Florida—20th century. 2. African American painting—Florida—20th century. I. Title.
ND1351.6.M66   2001
758'.1759'08996073—dc21   2001034077

The University Press of Florida is the scholarly publishing agency for the State University System of Florida, comprising Florida A&M University, Florida Atlantic University, Florida Gulf Coast University, Florida International University, Florida State University, New College of Florida, University of Central Florida, University of Florida, University of North Florida, University of South Florida, and University of West Florida.

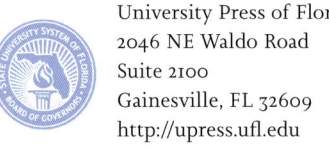

University Press of Florida
2046 NE Waldo Road
Suite 2100
Gainesville, FL 32609
http://upress.ufl.edu

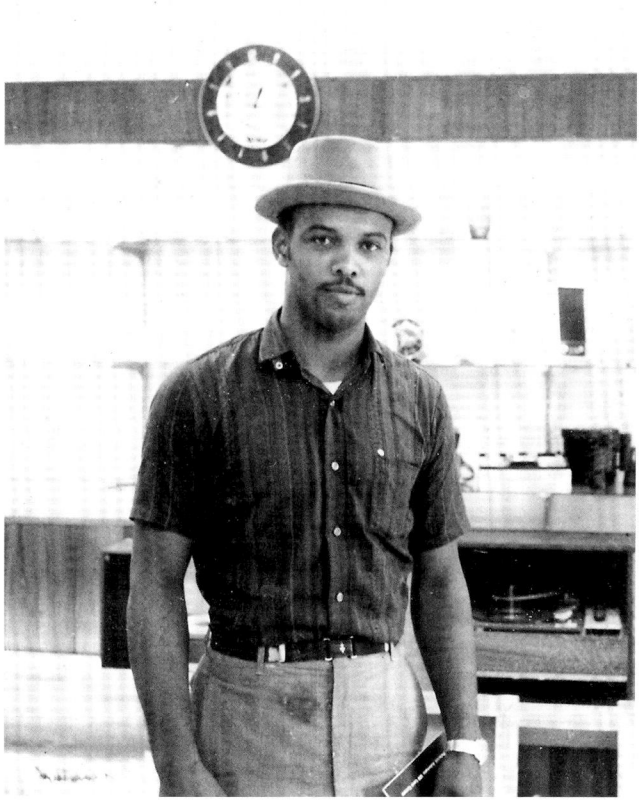

To the memory of Alfred Warner Hair
1941–1970

Acknowledgments

The paintings in this book are reproduced by the kind permission of the owners:

Henry and Julia Bosma

Rob and Julie Chaffiot

Geoff and Patti Cook

Don George

Tim and Eileen Jacobs

Gary and Teresa Monroe

Ty and Jean Tyson

Stephen and Lynn Werts

MY WIFE, Teresa Gurucharri Monroe, and our children, Mathew and Jessica, have long been accustomed to my traveling alone to photograph, and they extended their usual generosity as I spent many days and nights away from home to research *The Highwaymen*.

The willingness of the Florida Humanities Council to award a research scholarship to "a working artist" was especially encouraging and challenging.

This project owes much to the vision of Jim Fitch, director of the Museum of Florida Art and Culture, Avon Park. His trusting me to tell the group's story, especially as it relates to the bigger picture of his passion about "Florida's art tradition," has meant a lot to me.

I am grateful to the Highwaymen who invited me into their homes to talk about their past and their ideas. They shared some poignant memories, and I do not take their welcome lightly. I am indebted to Curtis Arnett, Hezekiah Baker, Albert Black, George Buckner, Robert Butler, Johnny Daniels, Rodney Demps, James Gibson, Isaac Knight, Robert Lewis, John Maynor, Roy McLendon, Alfonso Moran, Willie Reagan, Livingston Roberts, Charles Walker, Sylvester Wells, and Charles Wheeler.

Highwaywoman Mary Ann Carroll deserves special thanks. She took a personal interest in my work and was at my beck and call. Through her, I was able to become involved with the people whose lives I was researching. We had some remarkable times.

I received warm support from others who had knowledge about the artists' histories and about issues that I felt needed to be better understood. I appreciate the insights and expertise of Gladys Bennett, Henry Bosma, Gray Brewer, Don Brown, Rudi Cleare, Geoff Cook, Purcell Dixon, Mike Griffin, Kelvin Hair, Jack Hempley, Bob Hommell, Tim Jacobs, Zanobia Jefferson, Jerry Johnson, Gary Libby, May Belle Mann, Jim Murphy, Willie Pelt, John Phillips, Bob Terry, Jr., Trish Thompson, Sam and Roberta Vickers, and Ed Volonnino.

Tim Jacobs's energy, insights, and passion have made him a legendary collector among Highwaymen enthusiasts. I'm grateful for his assistance (and oftentimes insistence) throughout nearly three years of research and writing. Tim has taken more than 4,000 snapshots of Highwaymen paintings. His archive may well prove to be an indispensable resource to future researchers, curators, and writers. My friendship with Geoff Cook, another premier collector, has kept me on course, if not sane, during the escalation of interest in the Highwaymen paintings and the book.

I learned a lot about writing from my friends who read the manuscript at different stages of incompletion. Thank you, Rudi Cleare, Fran Ellison, John Guthrie, Len Lempel, Philip Lucas, and Mallory O'Connor.

Roberta Favis, professor of art history at Stetson University, consulted with me throughout the preparation of the essay. Her knowledge about the tradition of landscape painting proved critical as I developed my ideas about the Highwaymen's art.

My friend David Perry, editor-in-chief at the University of North Carolina Press, read the manuscript; his support and ideas guided me through the revisions.

Photographer Allan Maxwell went out of his way to ensure that the reproductions of the paintings for the book were excellently crafted.

The Tyson Trading Company in Micanopy, Florida, deserves recognition for having opened the only gallery dedicated to the art of the Highwaymen. I'm grateful to Ty and Jean Tyson for sharing their paintings and their knowledge about grassroots art. John Phillips, of American Fine Art and Collectibles, should be recognized for having aggressively bought and sold Highwaymen paintings and for fueling the resurgence and commodification of the art.

The people at the University Press of Florida were gracious throughout the publication process. Art director Larry Leshan's design surpassed my high expectations and my imagination, giving the viewer a terrific forum for experiencing the paintings. Production manager Lynn Werts "pushed the envelope" to produce a book worthy of the initial showcasing of the Highwaymen. Managing editor Deidre Bryan empathized with my editorial fervor, and her suggestions made for a much more readable text. I am especially glad to have gotten to know and work with the editor-in-chief, Meredith Morris-Babb. People like her have a way of making it seem that life is only as wonderful as it is challenging. Thanks for the tremendous challenges.

IN MIAMI BEACH, during its opulent 1950s and 1960s, more was definitely better. Photo studios stood along Washington and Collins Avenues, where vacationers lined up to have their souvenir pictures taken in front of stylized hand-painted backdrops, usually depicting palm trees and parrots. Along Lummus Park on Ocean Drive, the bases of real palm trees were painted white. Colored spotlights illuminated the trunks, yielding cake-icing hues blending with tropical balmy night skies. Across the street, the art deco hotel architects had all competed to see who could design the showiest facade to attract the most attention. Hotels were named after faraway places, places that people dreamed of or, more likely, had left behind. Ship motifs were very common—masts, streamlining, portholes. Cadillac fins grew bigger by the season. Fantasy came to life. "Kitsch" was part of the environment, my home.

So was the culture of South Beach, where elderly Jews of Eastern European heritage had established their old world mores. By the mid-1980s, their lifestyle fell prey to the redevelopment of the area as the trendy art deco district, hastening the disappearance of the Jewish community. I suspect that my delight and respect for the old South Beach parallels my interest in the history of a group of African-American artists who have become known as the Highwaymen. Both have fallen from grace, it seems, replaced by the new. Learning about the Highwaymen appealed to me as I remembered my childhood, when living in Miami still felt like being in a tropical village. Something more than "motel art" had to be behind these mass-produced and aggressively marketed Florida landscape paintings, which had at first seemed easy to dismiss as shoddy and formulaic.

With study, research, and conversations, I began to appreciate the art and the artists. I quickly realized that although the Highwaymen have recently garnered increased attention, the history available was composed of myths and vague tales rather than careful research. Since there was very little reliable information, I had to piece the story together from what I saw, heard, and read.

Gary Monroe

The Landscape as Dream

A copy of the universe is not what is required of art, one of the damn thing is enough.

REBECCA WEST

We didn't paint for perfection, we painted for color.

HEZEKIAH BAKER

T HE HIGHWAYMEN didn't exist, so to speak, until 1994, when art aficionado Jim Fitch assigned the name to an unknown group of African-American artists. Suddenly, thousands of the Florida landscape paintings they had produced since the end of the 1950s, which had been stored for years in Florida attics, were brought down, dusted off, and viewed with renewed interest. Until Fitch came up with the controversial (because of the bandit connotation) but nevertheless perfectly suited name for the self-taught painters, they remained unknown—unrecognized because they were black, according to Lincoln Academy High School art teacher Zanobia Jefferson. She is probably correct; in *A. E. Backus: Florida Artist*, by Olive Dame Peterson, there is no mention of these painters who had been inspired by Backus. But, according to the Highwaymen, anonymity was perfectly all right. Even if traversing the roads of Florida during the time of segregation wasn't dangerous enough, and if being young and carefree while roaming town streets with a stack of framed paintings wasn't suspicious enough, they certainly did not want to be asked to produce sales licenses and risk being jailed for solicitation. To them, time was money, and money meant more than sustenance. It was a way to keep score in their invented game of artistic entrepreneurship.

The majority of the Highwaymen came from a neighborhood called "Blacktown" in Ft. Pierce, Florida, and they attended Lincoln Academy High School. A few were from Gifford, Vero Beach's African-American neighborhood, twenty miles north of Ft. Pierce. Using a broad definition of the term, I identified twenty-six Highwaymen: Curtis Arnett, Hezekiah Baker, Al "Blood" Black, Ellis Buckner, George Buckner, Robert Butler, Mary Ann Carroll (the only woman in the group), Johnny "Hook" Daniels, Willie Daniels, Rodney Demps, James Gibson, Alfred Hair, Isaac Knight, Robert Lewis, John Maynor, Roy McLendon, Alfonso "Pancho" Moran, Harold Newton, Lemuel Newton, Sam Newton, Willie Reagan, Livingston "Castro" Roberts, Cornell "Pete" Smith, Charles Walker, Sylvester Wells, and Charles "Chico" Wheeler.[1]

They painted on inexpensive Upson boards (a product used by roofers), framed their paintings with crown molding, and marketed them around Florida from the backs of their cars, generally before the oils had dried.[2] They made upwards of 50,000 paintings; some estimates exceed four times this amount. They sold their paintings in the regions that fan out from Ft. Pierce: south toward Miami, north to the Daytona Beach area, and throughout the inland, making the name "Highwaymen" a fitting moniker.

The collective implied by the umbrella term "Highwaymen" barely existed in fact. The group was always amorphous; there was never a defined art movement based on their style. More than a decade separated the younger and older painters, while the ranks were filled over a dozen years. Today, nearly five decades after the start, some of the core group are barely, if at all, aware of the names of some of the peripheral Highwaymen painters.

the dream-state as a promise to be fulfilled . . .

The art of the Highwaymen may best be viewed as a vernacular art, art particular to a time and place. It is a stretch to position their paintings alongside acknowledged examples of "high art," although elements of the work easily lend themselves to such a discussion. Their lure is rooted in the wider culture, for their once-ubiquitous paintings are now part of Florida's identity.

Commerce is germane to the story of these emerging artists. Their unabashedly market-driven agenda challenges the notion of "pure art," while adding credence to the idea that art results from a collaboration between artist and consumer. It wasn't black people that whites were overtly supporting, but rather Florida as their home place. Yet the fact that the painters were black improved their prospects. The middle-class white consumers could see themselves as both patrons of the arts and liberators of the oppressed, while acquiring paintings that seemed to affirm their own status as landowners. As long as these young African-Americans retained the role of artist-as-entertainer, they were not threatening to their white customers.

Characterized by early critics as "motel art," the paintings reflect popular sentiments about Florida: the dream-state as a promise to be fulfilled. Highwaymen scenes had the essential ingredients with which to imagine the state: wind-swept palm trees, billowing cumulus clouds, the ocean, the setting sun. The intense and vivid colors of the images seemed otherworldly, just as an idealized Florida must have appeared to northerners. The Highwaymen's work became a popular representation of how Floridians wanted to see themselves and how they wanted others to see the state. Even if they did not originate the postcard image of Florida, the Highwaymen celebrated the ideal and helped make it stick.

The formulas for landscape painting that the Highwaymen absorbed have roots in the nineteenth century, when artists of the Hudson River school and their heirs created the first distinctively American school of painting. The fashion for landscape painting was broadly entrenched in the wide cultural currents of romanticism, which placed emotion over reason and celebrated nature over civilization. The taste for landscape painting emerged at a time when the pristine natural environment was increasingly challenged by development and the exigencies of the Industrial Revolution. With shifting beliefs and institutions, the American landscape itself was being transfigured by radical cultural changes. The race to be new was well under way by the twentieth century. Cities evolved and skyscrapers symbolized modernism.

During the early years of the twentieth century, while cities across America transformed their skylines, Florida remained relatively undeveloped, nurturing tourism and agriculture. In 1888, Henry Flagler's Florida East Coast Railway laid tracks in Jacksonville, and in 1912 trains were rolling into Key West. Along the way, grand hotels were built and well-to-do communities were established. The state had been mythologized from the start: in 1513 Ponce de León searched for the legendary Fountain of Youth, and nearly 500 years later Miami Beach was Florida's symbol of how modernity would enter the next millennium. Carl Fisher built that island-city on a dream and a scheme that would make it "the world's playground." Florida became a metaphor for escape.

Fruit grew everywhere. Residents and tourists enjoyed summer in winter. Florida seemed too good to be true: a developer's dream. But the great land boom of the 1920s was followed by an economic bust, and this was compounded by the hurricane of 1926. Though such hurricanes sobered speculators periodically, still there was no denying Florida's appeal. Floridians stayed busy domesticating a land that seemed distant geographically from the country proper—it even looked out of place on the map—as well as distinct with its subtropical flora and climate. Military training camps sprang up during World War II, contrasting oddly with their vacation-paradise backdrop. Later, discharged soldiers returned with their spouses and young families to settle in the Sunshine State.

The 1950s signified the end of the age of innocence and the start of another Florida growth spurt. Air-conditioning and mosquito control made the state more attractive for year-round living. During the Eisenhower era, citizens were focused on feeling good and "seeing the U.S.A. in their Chevrolets," with family

3

values intact. Tourists drove the length of Florida to rejuvenate body and soul. And those who came to the central east coast were ripe customers for landscape paintings.

At Cape Canaveral, just up the road from the site of the Highwaymen's humble beginnings, the explorations of space refined our understanding of the universe and changed the ways we thought about our world and ourselves. The Cold War was played out to the south, in Cuba, while a storm of civil-rights protest rocked the country and the Vietnamese War loomed. Highwaymen paintings offered a reprieve from the demands of contemporary life. And, consistent with the tradition of landscape painting in America, they offered the viewer a sense of spiritual transcendence through their presentation of nature.

a timeless world of breathtaking beauty . . .

Albert Ernest Backus—"Bean" or "Beanie" to his friends (and it appears that this included everyone who met him)—was born in Ft. Pierce in 1906. He painted from childhood and studied sign-painting techniques briefly in New York City during his teens. While making promotional materials, props, and scenery in Ft. Pierce's Sunrise Theater, he practiced landscape painting. At age thirty-five Backus joined the navy and served in World War II. An agent sold his paintings during his absence from Ft. Pierce, so he returned with money in the bank. Backus briefly joined a sister who lived in Miami, but he found the city too crowded. He returned home to Ft. Pierce and immersed himself in painting landscapes until alcoholism and cataracts got the better of him and his vision.

Backus had capitalized on the state's visual charms. His artistic treatment of the landscape was accessible and desirable, given the general public's clear enthusiasm for the representation of nature. The Chamber of Commerce could not have asked for a better ally. In appreciation of his art, Florida Atlantic University granted him the honorary degree of Doctor of Humane Letters in 1979. Backus died in 1990 and was named to the Florida Artists Hall of Fame in 1993.

Backus created a timeless world of breathtaking beauty. Around Ft. Pierce, where the tropics fade away and light and space seem exaggerated, he had to do little more than paint what he saw, to seduce a viewer. As his biographer Olive Dame Peterson puts it:

Backus is one of those rare cases, a nationally recognized artist who has spent his life searching out and recreating what is most distinctive about Florida: the sky, the sea, the rivers, and the back country where the changing light, the sudden bursts of wind and rain, the movement of clouds and birds are always rearranging the world. A Backus painting not only gives us a constantly renewed image of a definite place; it also returns it alive. There is a deep brooding quality about most of the paintings, as if behind the scene there is the presence of a mind, wondering perhaps how long the world it sees will last. (*A. E. Backus: Florida Artist* [Gallery of Ft. Pierce, 1984], p. 1)

Over the years many people, including fine painters, have come to relax in Florida's healthful climate and revel in its splendid environment. Among the landscape painters who accepted the challenges of Florida's topography and light were Martin Johnson Heade, Thomas Moran, Herman Herzog, Winslow Homer, George Inness, Louis Comfort Tiffany, and Eliot Clark. Clark's impressionistic paintings of the Indian River (the Ft. Pierce region) predate Backus's by two generations. These artists, unlike Backus, came to visit, not to reside and build their careers in the state.

A. E. Backus was a popular regionalist, but he was behind the times when he returned home after the war to continue his career as an artist. Realistic landscape painting had lost ground to self-reflexive art—that is, art examining itself. However, Backus was content living and painting in Ft. Pierce, where he enjoyed the respect of the citizenry. He flourished there; the region offered him endless delight. In turn, he painted the Florida that people loved, for the people who loved Florida. Backus, the ultimate regional artist, earned a reputation as "the dean of Florida landscape painting."

a new form of fantasy . . .

In 1954 Harold Newton, a young, self-taught black artist, met Backus, who had by then established himself as the area's most distinguished artist. Newton, who had drawn pictures since childhood and had a talent for representational painting, was persuaded by Backus to give up painting religious scenes (many on velvet) in favor of painting landscapes. With a sharp ability to copy anything, Newton made the transition. But without gallery representation or the ability to gain entry to that world, he had to peddle his paintings any way he could, so he took to the streets. This set the precedent for the Highwaymen, and Newton went on to become a role model for a small group of Ft. Pierce's youths.

Alfred Hair began taking art lessons from Backus in 1955 at the urging of his high school teacher Zanobia Jefferson. In 1957, he left Backus's studio, ready to be an artist. Hair was a charismatic young dreamer who planned to be a millionaire by the time he was thirty-five. He had learned Backus's ways of making

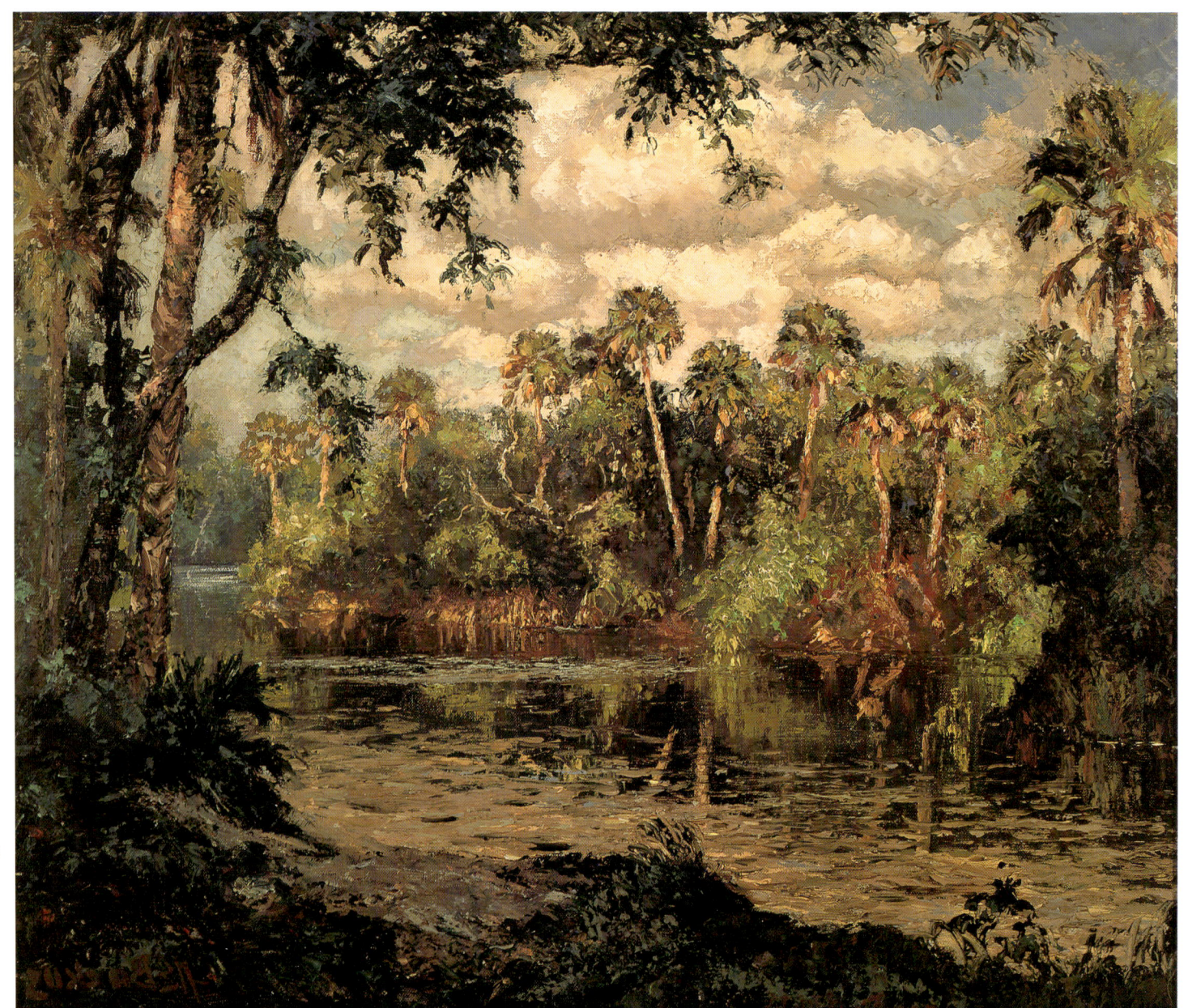

Albert Ernest Backus

predictable and pleasing paintings but knew that his work would never command high prices. Hair, always upbeat and likable, found that making and selling paintings came easily. He decided to make lots of reasonably priced paintings that would appeal to the general public. He charged an affordable twenty-five dollars for a large, framed landscape, an average day's wage for his targeted working-class audience.

Within a couple of years, friends of Hair and Newton noticed their success and learned from them how to paint. With practice, their crude paintings of the coastline and wetlands improved and became saleable; they were thereby able to avoid laboring in nearby orange groves and packinghouses, formerly their most likely source of available income. James Gibson, Roy McLendon, and Livingston Roberts were the first to paint with Hair. His energy propelled the fledgling artists forward. A cottage industry was forming.

Backus cared about the success of the young men who were informally under his charge, and his concern boosted their confidence. Though he was white and they were black, race seems not to have been a factor in their relationship. The aspiring artists would periodically visit Backus across the tracks in his home studio to seek advice. His door was always open, and he would cheerfully talk with them and often give them art supplies. According to Roberts, "Mr. Backus gave Alfred a stack of pictures [photographs] of paintings" and told him that they were a gift to ensure his retirement. Backus instructed Hair to base his paintings on these tried-and-true Florida images but to alter them to make the paintings his own. Furthermore, he encouraged all the artists to explore their own heritage in their paintings. But neither Hair nor the others worked introspectively. They felt no impulse to express their heritage, at least not consciously. Hair was on a mission of his own and zealously painted away, becoming known for working quickly.

The notion of speed is paramount in understanding the Highwaymen. It defines the ethos that drove them and is responsible for establishing their style. Hair led the way with roughed-in shrubs, "fast grass," and minimally established subjects. His imprecise but lively brushwork with slashed-in highlights became his trademark. Not a moment or a dab of paint would be wasted. A palette knife would "kick up grass" and, used in haste, could even pull the paint off the boards, leaving the surfaces raw in spots. This process left a distinct and surreal edge to the images.

Backus's protégé and manager, Don Brown, recalls his mentor constantly urging Hair and the other aspiring artists to "slow down!" But by ignoring Backus's advice, the Highwaymen became original artists. By unintentionally bastardizing the canonical pictorial strategies to which Backus confined himself, they created a new form of fantasy landscape painting.

The popular account of the Highwaymen story has portrayed Harold Newton rather than Alfred Hair as the story's chief protagonist and, especially, as a finer artist. Admirers of Highwaymen art align Newton with Backus. (This comparison, however, does not serve Newton well if a Newton painting is to be considered a poor man's Backus.) Newton may indeed have been a great painter, as his many fans claim, but the most compelling story about the Highwaymen is not about great painting. It is about young black friends who, as few others of their era have done, survived, prevailed, and left a legacy about their time and place. Furthermore, whether Newton and the others made fine art is a moot point, because their story challenges the standards of taste and quality as they relate to painting.[3]

Hair's persona was different from the romantic stereotype of the independent artist who possesses God-given talent. He embodied the generosity of Backus and the spirit of community that gave momentum to the artists. Through his own sensibilities and by empowering others, Hair was responsible for establishing a fresh approach to landscape painting and for showering the state with these images. Highwayman Isaac Knight says, "I appreciate Alfred's [paintings] more than Harold's." This feeling may have been a result of Hair's engaging personality as well as his art. Knight elaborates: "His personality is in his paintings; he expressed emotion. It's not in Harold's as it is in Alfred's."

Unlike Newton, Hair never aspired to be the best artist, just the fastest. James Gibson has said that Hair worked out and enlarged his biceps to be able to paint without needing to rest. He painted so quickly that he invented his own form of landscape painting *by chance*. A more suggestive than descriptive aesthetic is Hair's contribution to the genre. He could have replicated Backus's care in depicting the land with a quasi-luminist quality of light and detail, but for him being an artist was largely beside the point. Time meant money to Hair, and he opted for the trimmings that money could provide. His first goal on the road to riches was to buy a Cadillac. For this, he had to paint fast and paint a lot!

Hezekiah Baker, who became a Highwayman in the late 1960s, remembers Hair asking how long it took him to make a painting. Upon Baker's reply of "two to three hours," Hair gently commented that "I could make quite a few pictures in less time than that." Painting fast increased sales revenues, and the speed with which the artists painted determined their style. Speed freed them from working self-consciously and allowed them to paint exuberantly and confidently.

Hair's enthusiasm and diligence set the pattern. During the early 1960s, Hair had his wife, Doretha, and his in-laws helping him—"anyone who could swing a brush," quips George Buckner. Because those who followed Hair's model worked quickly and did not really understand the rules to which Backus strictly adhered, they didn't get *too* good. They became artists by default. He also employed framers and commissioned four salesmen, who also might be enlisted to paint. To Hair, a painting wasn't finished until it was sold!

George and Ellis Buckner entered the ranks in the early 1960s but preferred selling at Miami art shows to "running the road." (Ellis died of complications from diabetes in 1986 at age fifty-eight.) George sums up the brothers' experience: "We worked in orange groves, and Ellis said there's got to be a better way than this." George met McLendon and Newton, became interested in their work, and then told Ellis "everything I knew, which wasn't much about nothing." Ellis tried his hand, and soon afterward showed his brother "a wad of dough that would have choked a horse." George exclaimed, "You can't paint!" but quickly retired his picking bag to join the fold.

no "factory" existed . . .

Around 1998 a flurry of articles in travel and antiques magazines and in newspapers brought attention to the Highwaymen. They described an assembly line in which tree, water, and cloud "specialists" each contributed to the production of a single painting. The idea of a neighborhood painting factory has a nice media ring, but even though some of the group congregated at Hair's mother's home (and a few years later at his own house) to paint, that notion is inaccurate. Painting together was a common social function, a situation that has created confusion about Hair's method. A second painter might have added birds or otherwise developed part of another's work, but lending a helping hand was done to meet demand or done in jest. It was the exception, not the rule. Contrary to the assembly-line myth, no "factory" existed in which paintings were pieced together by uncaring hands. "We painted our own pictures," Roy McLendon says.

Descriptions by the participants in the communal painting bouts give a better idea of actual practice. Mary Ann Carroll was absorbed into the Highwaymen lifestyle after watching Harold Newton paint a royal poinciana tree and "make color come to life." She explains that typically the artists would have "tacked a board to a tree" or "nailed 1 x 4s against two trees to hold two to four paintings to work on." They could develop specific areas of several pictures at one time this way. Some of the artists often cranked out more than twenty paintings a day. It was quick and methodical. Hair increased speed and efficiency by tacking from ten to twenty boards in two rows. His production method was a response to demand; time was a commodity, and he developed a system to maximize his time.

Hair showed his helpers how to prepare areas that he penciled with rectangles and spheres. On these shapes they laid patches of colors that Hair would blend, build, and detail as he made his way through the lines of paintings. This system was direct and did not allow for much extraneous ornamentation, especially when business was most brisk. Radiating bands of yellow, orange, burnt umber, and blue would be blended to become skies. As he moved from board to board, he varied the paintings by, for example, adding a palm tree or ivy crawling up an oak's trunk. Each painting within a group varied, for Hair was impulsive, and, as evidenced by certain repeating symbolic elements such as his short, leaning, leafless trees, he was exploring his interior resources too.

With the demand for paintings escalating, Hair hired twelve-year-old Rodney Demps in 1965. His wife picked up the seventh grader after school and drove him to their home studio on Dunbar Street, where he quickly became an able understudy. His job was to prepare the skies. Thirty-five years later, Demps smiles as he reminisces about those afternoons: "After Alfred shellacked [primed] his boards, his studio was so bare, but a few hours later it looked like a jungle." He continues: "Alfred taught me how to mix a little cadmium yellow into white paint and make a flowing design across the boards to form [what would become] clouds. Then I'd blend a small amount of burnt umber—it made a grayish color—into the yellow areas. I'd mix thalo green into this and it would make turquoise; some blue would make the clouds jump out. . . . Alfred made those panels come alive. . . . He would just hit the board [with a palette knife] and it would come to life. He had a lot of talent, a lot of talent. He was gifted."

Hair's frenzy to produce paintings and realize his Cadillac goal was insatiable. He and the other High-waymen could each complete a standard-size image within an hour, sometimes two. This was fast but not necessarily fast enough for many of them. Gibson recalls Hair's advice to "paint slow when you get old," and the feverish times when Hair and his crew made forty paintings in a day. Friends and fellow artists would help Hair "out of a sense of duty" when they weren't busy working on their own paintings. "We did whatever needed to be done," Livingston Roberts recalls. Often a party atmosphere developed as the paint-ers worked through the night (Hair's favored time to paint), with barbecues aflame and beer flowing.

To maximize marketability, the artists framed the finished pieces with inexpensive crown molding (manufactured as floor, door, and window trim), which they usually coated with white house paint.[4] The frames were tacked together with small finishing nails but not glued; a painting was tacked into the back of a frame to secure it. A brush dipped in gold paint was dragged across the frames, "antiquing" them to make the paintings appear more valuable. Frames were occasionally painted brown or gray to complement the image showcased. The makeshift frames facilitated presenting the paintings for sale and hinted at how they would look if professionally framed.

The artist's signature was painted or incised with a nail, the end of a paint brush, or even the point of a palette knife, in the lower right corner. The paintings were usually signed with the artist's first initial and last name, as Backus signed his work. Full first names would have taken unnecessary time, and using the initial seemed more "professional." What sometimes appears to be a comma after the initial is a period done with characteristic flair. The paintings were never titled and very rarely dated. The standard sizes and thick molding of the frames allowed the paintings to be stacked without the surfaces touching, so they could be transported while the oils were still drying, unsmudged. Typically they sold before the oils had cured.

capturing imaginations . . .

The team spirit that grew out of Hair's studio largely accounts for the similarities in Highwaymen paintings. Carroll says that "we were borrowing strokes from another man's brush." Once Highwaymen got an image in their minds, "they just put it all together," Buckner adds. They inspired each other and learned to paint at their regular gatherings "by osmosis." Jack Hempley, a Ft. Pierce painter who preferred commissioned portraiture to uncommissioned landscapes, asserts that because blacks were denied a quality education, they had to rely on their "innate ability" to learn. He refers to gleaning knowledge and developing talent "through observation" as being gifts from God and adds: "We knew not to push above the white man; you had to be anonymous." The Highwaymen would threaten no one so long as they went unnoticed. Maintaining a low profile served as protective camouflage.

It would be tempting to construct a sentimental story or a common political agenda, but the facts do not support such a theory. All the painters were invisible at the start and, it seemed, destined to remain unknown. No one wanted the autobiographies of these young entrepreneurs. Obscurity proved a blessing, though; it fostered artistic surprise and an innocent vision of the land. Highwaymen pictures were distinctive and appealed to the public. Since the paintings had to focus on the interests of that audience, the artists could not afford to express the social or political views of American blacks, even if they were interested in doing so (which does not appear to have been the case).

Their brushstrokes were vigorous, and no politics were in evidence. This resulted in a transparency (the lack of a sense of the artist's presence) that, in turn, encouraged personal interpretations. Capturing imaginations was the Highwaymen's stock-in-trade. If they had injected current events into the mix, they would have found themselves out of work. Similarly, the Highwaymen did not paint street scenes, which ultimately worked to their advantage, for such scenes would too easily have elicited here-and-now responses. This kind of response would have turned the ethereal into the concrete and thereby would have limited the viewers' imaginations. Instead, a sublime sense of creation, empathy, and beauty worked magic. Viewers often personalize these generic views as site-specific, even though they usually are not. They are like looking through a picture window at one's own backyard; at the same time, they are idyllic and romantically appealing. Viewers are not outsiders looking in, as is the case with traditional landscape painting. The Highwaymen invited the viewer to enter the picture-postcard fantasies. The viewer is the *point* of the picture.

The early buyers of Highwaymen paintings may not have known good art from bad (indeed, they were often people who generally didn't buy art). But they "knew what they liked." So it was essential that they empathize with the land as rendered. Florida's beaches and palm trees don't carry the same metaphoric weight as mountain ranges and fruited plains. Unlike the majestic, near-to-heaven scenery found in the West or the Catskills, where the American landscape tradition was born, the Florida landscape was lush and primeval, lending itself naturally to a raw artistic interpretation.

While Backus's Florida landscapes are charming, they are executed in the more formal, polished style that people readily accept as "art." The same landscapes as portrayed by the Highwaymen have a temporal, transitory quality. This makes the interpretation of their images flexible and adaptable from viewer to viewer. Eliminating a grand, cathedral-like treatment of the landscape (as was fundamental to the genre), the Highwaymen minimized the aura of high art and thereby encouraged the viewers to engage with the paintings and extract meaning from them. Their imagery was instantly gratifying and perfectly suited for Florida's informal, fast-changing culture.

Because the Highwaymen marketed ideas—the landscape as dream, and as a sense of Florida—in the form of paintings, contributing to aesthetics took a back seat; they could just as easily have peddled chenille bedspreads at corner gas stations. They had a job to do while Americans eagerly invested themselves in the state and its new frontier, or at least in a painting of it. Inadvertently, the Highwaymen helped to establish a significant, shared vision that fostered the building of contemporary Florida. They reshaped reality into illusion. The audience for Highwaymen paintings co-conspired to turn that illusion into another reality—modern Florida. This "mass conspiracy" was born, innocently enough, in the studio of A. E. Backus.

they unconsciously expressed their own values . . .

During his formative years, Backus painted out-of-doors in the impressionists' *plein air* manner to capture the feeling of the land. But as he moved into the studio, his paintings became increasingly influenced by modern European systems of perspective for rendering classical versions of reality.[5] He began to carefully lay grids and sketch his images before committing paint to canvas; the rigid substructure made his works increasingly generalized and romantic.

The Highwaymen learned to paint without the aid of a sketch because most of them never could render well. Baker points out that "painting is not about drawing." This inability worked to their advantage. It fostered the idea of *drawing* the landscape with paint, the process that is rudimentary to their aesthetic. The Highwaymen rarely painted "on location." They painted at home and, through memory and imagination, created images that were emblematic and enigmatic. They worked in their yards, "like shade-tree mechanics," Carroll offers.

They approached their boards with only bare indications in mind of one of a handful of scenes. These mental pictures may have been partially derived from Backus, but they provided little more than templates. Of course, the interpretations of these archetypal landscapes differed with each artist's hand, and each iteration varied. While painting, the artists would inevitably individualize their images, more subliminally than intentionally. And, as Buckner points out, "a lot of trial and error" went into the early paintings.

A remarkable commonality distinguishes early Highwaymen paintings regardless of which artist painted a scene. The artists painted only the essentials and in an essential manner. Nonetheless, each artist's style is discernible. McLendon's brushwork often adds an agitated texture to his subjects. Baker's touch is similarly choppy but more abstract. Roberts's work is defined by detail and glowing light, while the Daniels' scenes are dreamy. Black's images are minimal and bleak. Carroll stands apart because of her vibrant color sensibility. Gibson's paintings are characterized by woodcut-like qualities of line. The Buckners practiced an elegant interpretation of the land through arcane compositional techniques.

Roberts explains that the images he and the other Highwaymen painted were always with them because they had seen the places throughout their lives: "You know what it looks like; you can picture it in your mind. It never leaves you." Knight knows that the palm tree adjacent to an oak tree in his panorama of the south fork of the St. Lucie River is an accurate portrayal because he grew up nearby and drove across the bridge looking at this view "every workday for thirty years." Carroll says that their "mental snapshots" of views of the land were their own, that the Highwaymen "were not working in a copycat manner of Backus. We had different experiences."

The Highwaymen did not consider themselves fine artists who worked for art's sake—purists might say that they created art for all of the *wrong* reasons. Their greatest achievement was in creating a seamless blend of art and commerce. As they rushed to get paintings out and meet demand, they unconsciously expressed their own values through their bold, sure, and energetic style. Having grown up in Ft. Pierce, where they played as children, fished as adolescents, and came of age, they painted scenes with insiders' eyes. Their affinity for and familiarity with the land made their images convincing, and their painterly treatments, coupled with the empathetic interpretations with which their audience identified, made the landscapes especially desirable.

The Highwaymen were, in a way, Backus's alter ego. Where Backus looked at the landscape, the Highwaymen *saw* it. Backus rendered wondrously by carefully attending to the intensity of the light that floods central coastal Florida. He could monumentalize a swamp. As a mature artist, Backus followed a route that offered security but diminished creative returns; the Highwaymen, with nothing to lose, ventured down another path. Hair's irreverent regard for tradition led the way.

By abandoning Backus's love of traditional form, Hair and his fellow artists freed themselves from the rules that circumscribed his compositions. Fortunately, the conventions that they avoided for the sake of saving time and increasing production were unnecessary to appeal to their clientele. Although the artists in Hair's circle were out to please the customer, they did not paint with a specific buyer in mind. Most of the Highwaymen worked away, knowing that the paintings would find appreciative owners. Once they found their customer base, they couldn't afford to experiment; they would have risked losing sales if they had altered their tried-and-true images.

Whether by the light of the sun (at sunrise, midday, late afternoon, sunset) or the moon, Highwaymen landscapes possess a made-for-me appeal. Florida real estate was booming in the 1960s, and bankers, insurance agents, and real estate brokers were among the Highwaymen's best customers. Their offices were convenient stops as the Highwaymen sold their paintings "from door to door and store to store." In a bank, for example (having received permission from bank officials), an artist would spread out a selection of paintings in the lobby, without uttering a word. Bank patrons would unfailingly approach and buy.

By making a game out of business, the Highwaymen pushed their unique aesthetic to its limit. They became, ironically, more mainstream than Backus, whose picture-perfect renditions were out of reach for the folks who purchased Highwaymen paintings. Sales soared during the 1960s. Typically, most if not all of an artist's inventory at any given time (usually ten to twenty paintings) sold on a single sales venture— usually a day trip. The Space Coast, north of Ft. Pierce, was a busy area, and tourism flourished along the Treasure Coast, down the southern seaboard. Offices and hotels were springing up, with lots of empty walls on which to hang paintings. Clienteles were established, and the affable Highwaymen were consummate salesmen. Bartering was perfectly acceptable, and they even traded paintings for medical attention and cars. Curtis Arnell says, "People waited for us to come by."

The other artists readily acknowledge that Al Black was the best salesman, selling the paintings of several other Highwaymen as well as his own. His sales pitch still rolls off his tongue:

> "Good morning, I'm Al Black, one of the artists from Ft. Pierce that do the Florida Landscape. I want to know if you would be interested, if it wouldn't take up too much of your time." Most of the time they would let me bring the pictures in and I would start naming them one by one. "This is a royal poinciana tree. This is a sunset in the glades. This is moonlight on the Indian River. This is a backwoods marsh scene. This is Indian River Drive. This is not one of my best paintings, but it's one of my best decoration pieces."
>
> If a housewife looked interested in a certain painting, I'd tell her: "Ma'am, you got good taste; that's the most expensive of them."

The Highwaymen designed their images to be irresistible decor accessories. When blue-green fabric covered sofas in living rooms and "Florida rooms" throughout the state, that year's crop of paintings was made to complement the fashionable color. Brown-based monochromatic paintings were produced during the 1970s when earth tones were popular.

The artists hammered away at every conceivable subject they thought viewers would find attractive: seascapes, backcountry glades, and river settings. Diptychs and even triptychs were made on standard boards that were cut in halves or thirds. Close-up paintings of hibiscus flowers offered another choice. Rustic images, such as wooden fences, shacks, sailboats, and cattle, occasionally found their way into the paintings, but modern elements like cars and motels were avoided, and human figures were rarely included. Besides locating the images in the here-and-now, such subject matter would have required additional painting time and therefore would have necessitated increasing the cost of the painting.

Birds and water were staples in Highwaymen imagery, as they are ever-present in Florida. The constant presence of birds invites debate over whether the artists had any symbolism in mind. Gibson says he painted cranes merely to provide contrast against the dark skies of his night scenes. But Black claims to have composed three birds to represent the Trinity, with another bird separate from the group to represent his own fall from grace. Every year, in memory of Alfred Hair, McLendon touches up the bluebird and the cardinal that Hair painted on the outside of his mother's house, at the beginning of his career.

the high arts and popular culture . . .

The Highwaymen may help to bridge the gap between the high arts and popular culture, removing the aura of elitism from oil painting and sparking interest in the visual arts. Their wet-on-wet brushstrokes and rushed palette knife markings produced visual and psychological excitement. Like vistas seen from a car window, their landscapes had a fleeting, half-realized sense of reality.

Without time for laborious technique or interest in painting details, the Highwaymen found their strength as colorists. More self-conscious artists would tone down the sun-drenched Florida landscape, fearing that accuracy would look unrealistic, but the Highwaymen often intensified colors to the point of flamboyance. The hues heightened the emotional effect of the paintings.

Johnny Daniels, born in 1954 and the youngest member of the Highwaymen, started out making frames for the group. "I asked the Lord to show me how to paint," he says, hoping to improve on the fifty cents he was paid for each frame he made. He agrees that Highwaymen are colorists: "It's not that we paint better, it's that we learned color." Daniels believes that because the artists rushed and did not concern themselves with details, the colors expressed their values and mind-set. The Highwaymen's language of color was instantly understood by the purchasers of the paintings, who appreciated its lively, emotional effect.

making a steady living . . .

Though she reared seven children as a single parent while working as an artist, carpenter, and church musician, and despite her considerable output of paintings, Mary Ann Carroll laments not doing more as an artist. She was one of the few who had a car in the early 1960s and drove other painters to their preferred sales locales. They in turn bolstered her confidence in her painting and encouraged her to persevere.

Carroll says that the Highwaymen "started as a rumor," and that all the artists had both desire and raw talent. Most of them had liked drawing pictures when they were children and had wanted to be artists, but as adults, family and making a steady living came first.

Some of the artists had other careers or took day jobs when necessary. Hezekiah Baker, for instance, left the group to sell insurance and real estate to appease his wife, subsequently painting only sporadically. In retrospect, he would have preferred to dedicate himself to painting. Upon his wife's death in 1999, Baker closed his popular Ft. Pierce restaurant, House of Food, to pursue his dream of being a full-time artist.

Even those who were latecomers had the true Highwayman spirit, no matter how peripheral their position in the group. Isaac Knight, who painted avidly as a Highwayman for about a decade, has considered painting again now that he has retired from his job at Grumman Aerospace. He ponders the idea of parking his car by the beach after church service and bringing home a few hundred dollars by selling his paintings as he did years ago—not because it might be lucrative but because "it was a lot of fun."

James Gibson is among the few Highwaymen who has always painted for his livelihood. His early, stylized images were simple conceptions of little more than a palm tree and radiating sunlight against rolling surf, with draped moss framing the scene. To further simplify the process and hence produce more paintings, Gibson made monochromatic night scenes. He claims to have once made 100 of these paintings in a twenty-four-hour marathon. Gibson, who was less influenced by Backus than others were, matured as an artist without losing the edge that set apart Highwaymen paintings. His palette became high-keyed, the brushstrokes gained confidence, and the scenes grew expansive. Gibson and Harold Newton proved to be the group's most prolific painters.

For much of the time, Cocoa was home to the Newton brothers, Robert Lewis, and Sylvester Wells. The Newtons (Harold, Sam, and Lemuel) established their own clientele and seemed to distance themselves over the years from the Ft. Pierce–Gifford contingency. During his long career, Harold's wanderlust spirit kept him on the move: during the 1970s, up to Daytona Beach, then inland to Sanford, and then to Bradenton; he finally returned to the east coast, settling in Palm Bay. Works on canvas board, done in the mid-1950s, mark the beginning of his artistic development. These paintings are coarse in comparison with those that soon followed, setting Harold's style in motion. His early Upson board works show the influence of Backus's technique with the palette knife, which Newton brandished aptly and energetically. He used a broader palette and the colors became brighter in the 1980s, when he switched to painting on Masonite. Details became refined and delicate in his later brushwork. The later paintings, which follow Backus's example, were more representational than his earlier ones, and their realism increased their marketability. His brother Sam's later works perfect the craft of the pretty landscape painting, while Lemuel left the scene entirely.

Robert Lewis recalls meeting the Newtons one day in 1969—while the brothers were working on a row of paintings tacked along the side of a shack—and surprising them with his ability to paint. He had graduated from college with a degree in art education, then had a brief stint as an illustrator with the Boeing Company. During and after his Highwaymen period he taught art in public schools, recently retiring. Lewis "learned through repeated practice, and prayed before painting." He and Sylvester Wells remained on the fringe of the collective. Although Wells made his living as a painter for a while—preferring "drifting to going into places to sell his paintings," says Lewis—he eventually settled in Tennessee to preach the gospel.

In 1966, Willie Reagan began painting with George and Ellis Buckner and Alfonso Moran in Gifford. Reagan's interest in painting lessened as he became increasingly involved with public school teaching. Looking back, he recalls with amazement "painting on Monday, Tuesday, and Wednesday, framing on Thursday, and selling on Friday and Saturday . . . sometimes on Sunday." Moran, who had made frames for Backus in the 1950s, "got us going and even gave us supplies," remembers Buckner. Moran drifted away from painting to pursue his more lucrative skills at pool and poker. Others with wandering spirits included Willie Daniels. He left the region to work as a truck driver and laborer and, occasionally, as a painter.

At another geographical extreme, Robert Butler lived inland at Okeechobee. His association with the east coast artists was brief, and his subject matter and style differed from theirs. He portrayed heartland settings dotted with cattle and other local fauna, designed to appeal to the region's cattle barons. Now he is marketing his how-to technique kit to amateur painters on cable television's QVC channel.

Charles Walker, although living in Ft. Pierce, was also a loner. He specialized in wildlife imagery; his unspoiled Florida is of another era, "before man was messy." A brother-in-law of fellow Highwayman Livingston Roberts, he learned to paint painstakingly and comments that both his subject matter and his more devout religious convictions differed from the group's, selling him apart. Nevertheless, being considered a Highwayman is not a distinction that he shies away from, even though he did not often sell his works from his car and had little in common with his artist-neighbors.

By the mid-1960s, most of those who would be known as Highwaymen had joined the ranks and were making more money than they had ever imagined. During these banner years, many of the artists lived extravagantly, drove expensive cars, and socialized about town. Hair painted flames on the sides of his 1958 Ford, and Newton adorned his car as well. Hair owned several cars, including some for his salesmen's use.

The 1960s were truly a charmed time for the Highwaymen. Looking back, the artists cannot recall any problems, even when they were selling to strangers on the streets (which they did less frequently than soliciting at businesses). Racial integration was beginning in Florida during the early 1960s, and the ease with which they worked seems astonishing, since the Jim Crow laws that relegated African-Americans to second-class citizenship were being tested everywhere.[6] Across America, angry blacks were taking to the streets in protest. But in spite of mounting racial tensions, Highwaymen—single itinerant merchants peddling paintings throughout segregated Florida—drove their cars down rural roads without incident.

Their practiced sales approach and deferential charm disarmed potential customers, and one glance at a painting, its oils shining and fresh-smelling, created a positive connection between seller and buyer. No Highwaymen reported (nor likely suffered) physical or verbal abuse during the thousands of trips they made through south and central Florida. The artists were on their way to being on top of the world. With money in their pockets, they radiated confidence.

twenty-nine years old, strikingly handsome, married . . .

The Highwaymen lived well during the 1960s. Their dreams were coming true. But on the night of August 9, 1970, in Eddie's Place, a Ft. Pierce neighborhood juke joint, Alfred Hair was shot dead. He was apparently caught in a romantic triangle, though the preferred account portrays him as an innocent bystander who was in the cross fire of a barroom brawl.[7] He was twenty-nine years old, strikingly handsome, married, and the father of six children. And he had bought a Cadillac, his first goal as a young artist.

Bean Backus, and Zanobia Jefferson were among those who eulogized Hair at the packed funeral service in the Friendship Baptist Church. Today, his cohorts remember him affectionately, speaking more of his character than of his art and acknowledging that it was his infectious personality and drive that made the Highwaymen successful.

Things changed after Hair's death, though the Highwaymen continued to work through the 1970s and '80s. Hezekiah Baker summed up the feeling for most of the group: "There was nothing to shoot for after Alfred died." The fever pitch dissipated. There seemed no reason to rush. Some artists drifted away. The movement continued, but the "organization" was falling apart. As ringleader, Hair had had the organizational skills, but, more important, the presence that had given strength to many of the painters. Carroll says that "people flocked to Alfred. He looked out for others."

beside the point . . .

Livingston Roberts looks back through hardened eyes and says, half to himself, "I wanted to be a good painter, one of the best." Self-effacement, possibly culturally instilled, is a common attitude among Highwaymen. But it may be that they, like some critics, formed opinions with faulty criteria. The Highwaymen had no point to make. Their paintings were never intended for gallery display, but as versatile wall hangings. They may have considered their paintings to be as replaceable as shower curtains. But that is not to say that these painters lacked critical judgment. To the contrary, they challenged each other and strove to do their best as they critiqued each other's work at their customary get-togethers.

Hezekiah Baker says, "It was like they [Newton and Hair] were learning from each other . . . to boost sales." It was to all the artists' benefit to work cooperatively. Some paintings certainly were more resolved than others, but the artists most valued the fact that all of their paintings were created to be sold; they intended to sell as many as possible, regardless of the paintings' relative quality. But the artists didn't know how good they were.

Roberts bemoans that "you couldn't be the best with Backus around." A "strange feeling" got beneath his skin, and that of others, from having Backus as artist-idol. He muses, "Something beautiful I never seen before . . . you feel something." He is talking about the Backus aesthetic. Backus may have been the perfect role model, but his art is not the best standard of excellence by which to judge the Highwaymen. Constantly comparing themselves to him, the painters were unaware that in departing from his methods they

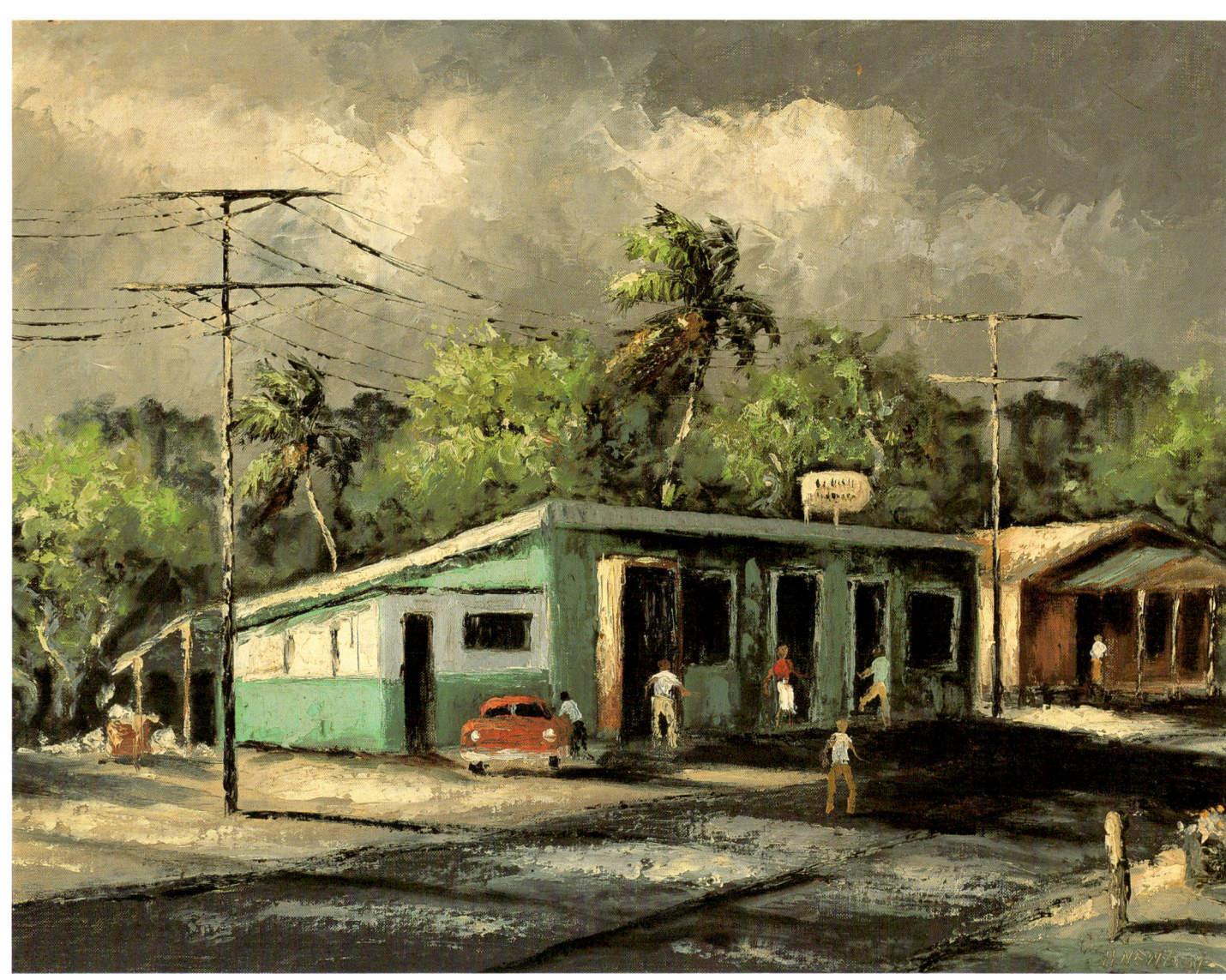

Harold Newton

EDDIE'S PLACE

had created something different and, by some critical standards, more interesting. Carroll tries to dismiss the comparison to Backus by pointing out that he had a waiting list for paintings and the luxury of taking his time, whereas the Highwaymen had to feed families and pay bills. This was true, but it is also beside the point.

The mid-seventies brought a national economic recession. Having reached the moon several times, NASA was handing out pink slips. "Ph.D's were pumping gas," comments Cape Canaveral worker and art collector Tim Jacobs. The end of the Space Coast boom might have been the first reality check for the Highwaymen after Hair's death. "People just stopped spending money on luxuries," says Willie Reagan.

By the 1980s, social realities were taking their toll on the Highwaymen. The recession ended, but many new competitors appealed to Floridians for their disposable income. Florida was going corporate, and the Highwaymen's art was beginning to look passé. Disney World was the iconographic symbol of the new age, as Florida fell prey to the homogenizing effects of mass culture. Family-owned tourist attractions lost favor, and the interstate system made it easy to pass them by. A gas shortage had affected the American psyche, too; people zoomed straight to their vacation destinations on the interstate rather than meandering along the state roads through the little towns where the Highwaymen sold their wares. Clearly, the times were changing, and the Highwaymen's market was shrinking.

Around this time, Al Black, who had been aggressively selling paintings since 1964, became too zealous in his dealings. Most opportunistic of the artists, he was allegedly skimming money from sales, changing names on paintings, and getting paid up front for paintings that were never to be delivered.[8] As a result the artists were often met with animosity while making their sales rounds in the mid-1980s. In addition, the authorities began enforcing nonsolicitation laws and asking to see occupational licenses, which the Highwaymen were unable to produce.

"to become like Backus . . ."

In an attempt to regain their success, the Highwaymen tried to emulate A. E. Backus. As Curtis Arnett says: "To mature as an artist was to become like Backus." Although this approach may have served briefly to rekindle sales, it also had a damaging effect on the nature of Highwaymen's art, effacing that which was uniquely theirs. Some of the artists drifted away from painting. Most of those who continued soon had too much time on their hands. They practiced and took their craft too seriously. Without the carefree energy that had guided them along effortlessly, the new images lacked spirit; the moment of shared recognition with the viewer was lost.

The style that characterized the Highwaymen's unpretentious beginnings—the plainly conceived, colorful, wind-blown look—was disappearing by the 1980s anyway. Instead of being raw and immediate, the new works were indeed merely decorative. Stretched canvas was used in an attempt to fit their paintings into new upscale condominiums. The artists increasingly looked to slick postcards and magazine photographs for inspiration, and some were just copying Backus's paintings. Newton's works, especially, began to resemble Backus's; painting this way offered him a technical challenge he was equal to—and, of course, proven marketability. Authorship was never an issue with the Highwaymen; they saw appropriation as simply a way to stimulate sales.

No longer naive painters, most of the remaining artists labored on images that often resembled those in technique books. As they began following established color theory and using grids, instead of trusting their own instincts, the power of their work continued to decline.[9] Their former *alla prima*, slapdash approach, in which underdrawing was ignored in favor of a quick and intuitive response, encouraged intimacy with the subject. But as their work became planned, this intimacy vanished. The artists didn't realize that their early paintings were appealing because they were unpretentious and honest—the kind of honesty that comes from living, and painting, in the moment.

an artless art . . .

Al Black started painting when Alfred Hair died, having waited "out of respect for Alfred" and because he was too busy making a one-third commission, sometimes more, from selling the other artists' works. When he did start, he followed Hair's principle of minimal detail. It was quick and easy. Black's spartan quality takes to the limit the basics of Hair's art and the Highwaymen phenomenon: The painter is transparent and the paintings are replicable commodities; no value is placed on making masterpieces; but somehow the result is a painting that invites the viewer to participate. And this is Hair's legacy: the practice of an artless art.

Rather than describing the land with skill-bound realism, the Highwaymen's spontaneity facilitated capturing the essence of the land in the way that a pencil sketch may realize an artist's ambitions for a painting. A pureness and spiritedness came through in the early works as the artists lost themselves in the physical act of painting rapidly. These early images were stripped of artifice and completed in the viewer's mind's eye. Understanding painting this way runs contrary to the conventional response in which the viewer merely appreciates an artist's interpretation of an event or subject, or is awed by an artist's technique.

The run-of-the -mill paintings may be the ones that best represent the Highwaymen. The painters who remained at the periphery of the movement, those who did not have much of an effect on the nature of the art, may have been the ones who were truest to the group's intent. For example, John Maynor, Cornell Smith, and Charles Wheeler made relatively few paintings, and their works are devoid of personal viewpoints or techniques. Such perfunctory works would be perfectly illustrative of the Highwaymen manifesto, had one existed.

The paintings first glowed in the silver-gray light of black-and-white television sets in the 1950s. As the years went by, the hues were muted by cigarette smoke and climatic elements, while the images themselves went out of fashion. They were removed from the walls of people's homes. Many were left at thrift stores, sold for pennies at yard sales, and thrown out along with yesterday's newspapers.

Scratches on many of the paintings, inflicted when they were tossed in a corner of the garage or attic, form part of their patina, their scars of survival. It matters little if spots of raw canvas were caused by an artist rapidly wielding a palette knife or by paint-eating insects. Holes in boards that were tacked onto the sides of buildings or to trees—the Highwaymen's easels—become part of the process and the image.

Some paintings were not even signed by Hair or the other artists working alongside him. So many paintings were being completed at the peak times that they were often rushed into salesmen's cars before the artist had a chance to sign them. This anonymity speaks volumes about the Highwaymen's lack of artistic ego.[10]

the land ad its depiction . . .

As the paintings have come out of retirement, they have enjoyed a new burst of popularity, as well as critical attention that they never received in their first life. Two categories are clear: the pleasingly accessible images by Harold Newton and the more dynamic, less formal ones by Alfred Hair. Although both men made exceptional paintings and earned a special place in the Highwaymen story, each represents a different approach to painting. Newton was a traditionalist who could paint masterfully. To a degree, his art is more aligned with the Hudson River school and luminist paintings than with Highwaymen imagery. He could imitate Van Gogh's brushwork and effect photographic realism. His versatile abilities awed the others.

Newton's technique rivaled that of Backus, whereas Hair challenged Backus's fundamental notions about the land and its depiction. While they are impressively elegant, the more realistic landscapes by Newton and Backus may seem less satisfying than Hair's lyrical expressions and, by extension, the majority of Highwaymen paintings. This, of course, depends on how one values painting, whether primarily as a means of demonstrating one's skills or as a means of revealing a personal vision.

Newton, who died in 1994 at age fifty-nine (he painted until disabled by a stroke about a year before), was an independent personality and had not been as affected by Hair's untimely death as most of the other artists. Newton's paintings are qualitatively different than the majority of Hair-influenced paintings. Black recalls that Backus recognized Harold Newton as a great artist, adding, "If it's a Newton, it don't have to have a name to be identified." His sense of light, depth, and surface coalesce beautifully in his enchanting landscapes. On the other hand, Black adds, "Alfred could paint as good as he wanted and as fast as he wanted." Hair showed how speed and quality could coexist beneficially. Painting fast was a prerequisite, not a deterrent, to Hair's art. He simply "threw paint" on his boards to miraculously achieve images that are more about being alive than about the manipulation of plastic values.[11]

Both Newton and Hair explored the *act* of painting. Newton, says Gray Brewer, a collector and acquaintance of the artist, painted with "a pocket knife, a spoon, and his thumb." His amazing facility produced paintings in a style that is simultaneously fluid and formally astute. Newton more than any of the Highwaymen lived the romantic notion of the artist developing patronage, painting when moved to paint and unconcerned about public taste. After establishing a popular reputation, he enjoyed that luxury to some extent.

Instead of patrons, Hair had connections. Though he always took his paintings on the road, he increasingly found customers coming to his door as well. Ironically, for one so commercially oriented, Hair (and those who worked closest to him) painted without trying to figure out what the customer wanted. This attitude helped to lead him even further from conventional imagery. He would alter his paintings throughout the process. "Let your mind wander," he would advise. His imagery took shape as he painted. He did not carry a sketch pad or use a camera. His split-second decisions about gesture and color were guided by the ephemeral qualities of Florida light and the dynamic, ever-changing effects of Florida weather. He advised others to observe nature, as if "the truth lies beyond the horizon," remembers Purcell Dixon, a Hair apprentice.

Ego gratification was not part of Hair's equation; self-affirmation was. Hair's philosophy took precedence over his art, which was, after all, a ticket to ride. He wanted everyone to have a painting, not simply because it meant more money in his pocket, but because he wanted to share his zest for life; friends often received paintings as gifts from Hair. He seemed to value the spreading of his paintings like seeds, everywhere.

the glory days were glorious . . .

It would be unrealistic to say that the American Dream came true for all of the Highwaymen. However, by becoming artists they rose above societal expectations and the hard-labor occupations that awaited them in Ft. Pierce.

The glory days were glorious, but none of the artists ended up wealthy, though several still paint for a living. Many live as they would have lived had they had menial jobs in racially polarized Ft. Pierce; the difference is that they are struggling artists instead of laborers. The rest of the group met various fates. Some enjoy comfortable lifestyles and have sent their children to college. Some found solace in devotion to God; only a few fell prey to drugs and alcohol. Many were never caught up in the artist's lifestyle but instead had full-time jobs. Others came and went.

Bound together by hard times and by their shared past, the Highwaymen exhibit fondness for each other and the early days. Roy McLendon smiles as he explains that his artistic roots go back to drawing in the dirt with a stick as a youngster; he straightens up proudly as he recalls the days and nights that he and his friends spent painting in Hair's backyard.

Whatever their fates, an identity informs and separates the Highwaymen's paintings from the banal formulaic pictures that are made far away from the locales that they pretend to represent, or by eager painters who try to technically capture the Florida landscape. Every member made a contribution, painted with passion, and expressed a personal view while contributing to a collective vision, all of which constitute a fresh art and a remarkable story. And, as Mary Ann Carroll says, "It was an honest dollar for an honest day's work."

Facing page: Willie Daniels

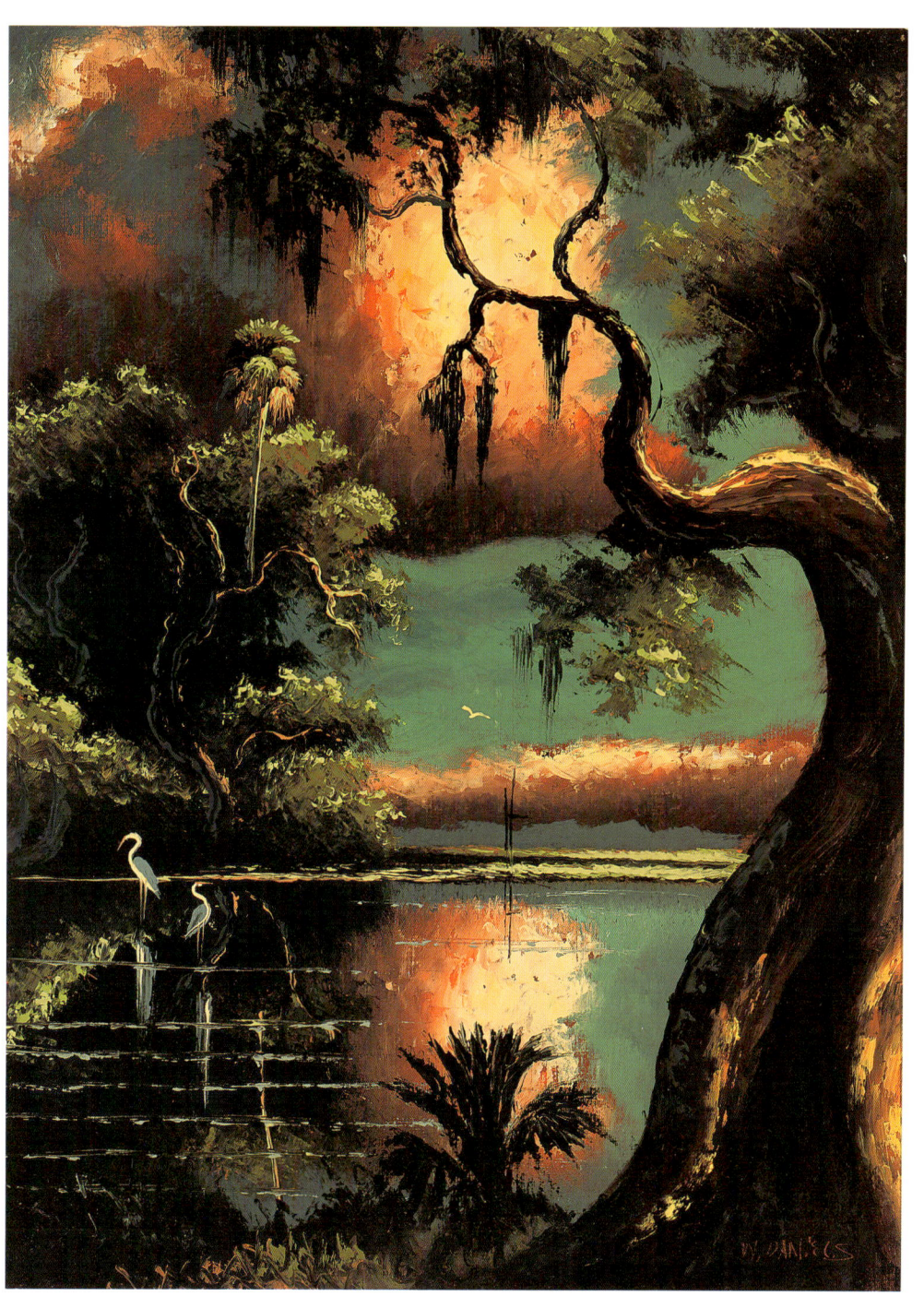

The Plates

1 . Charles Wheeler

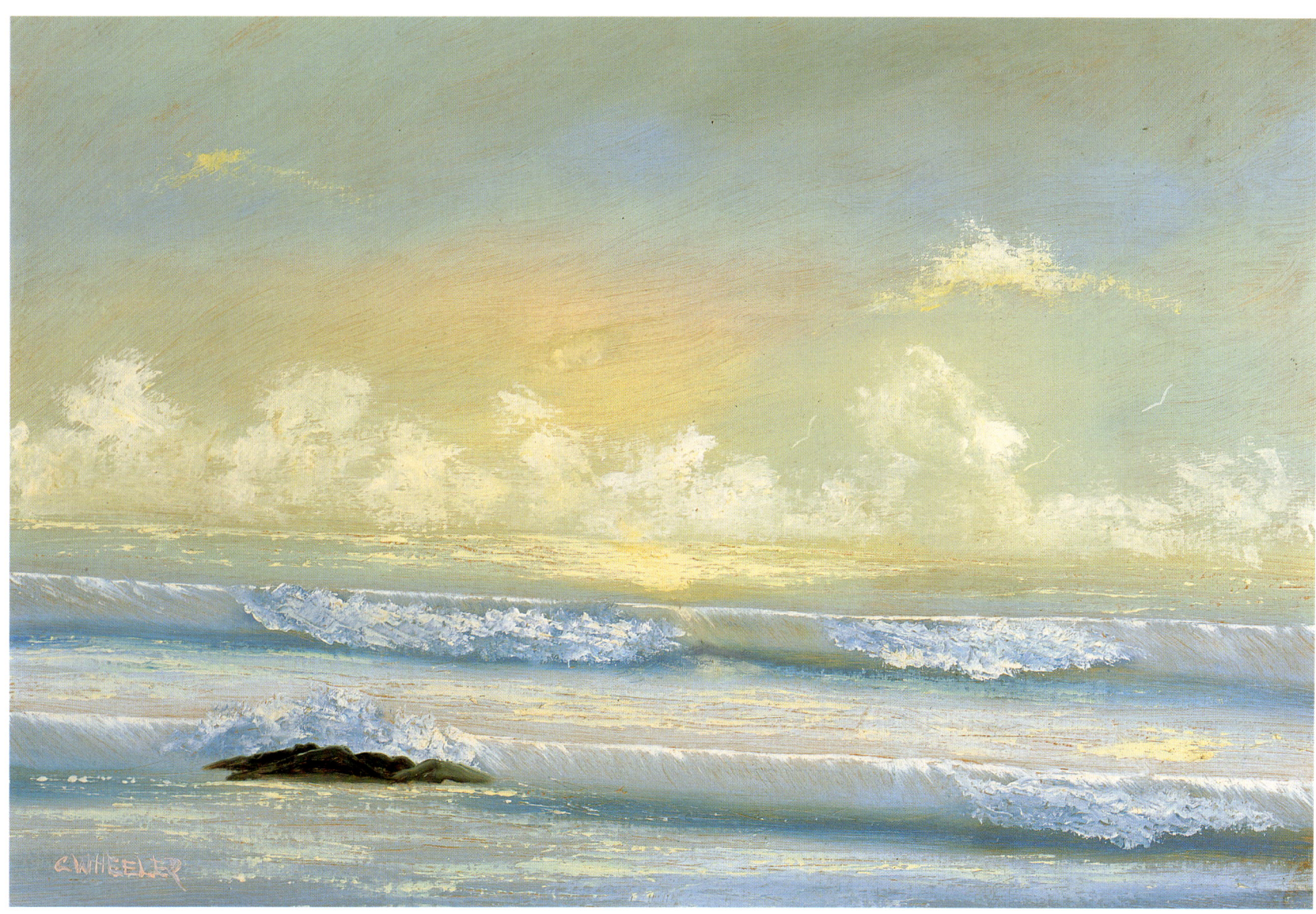

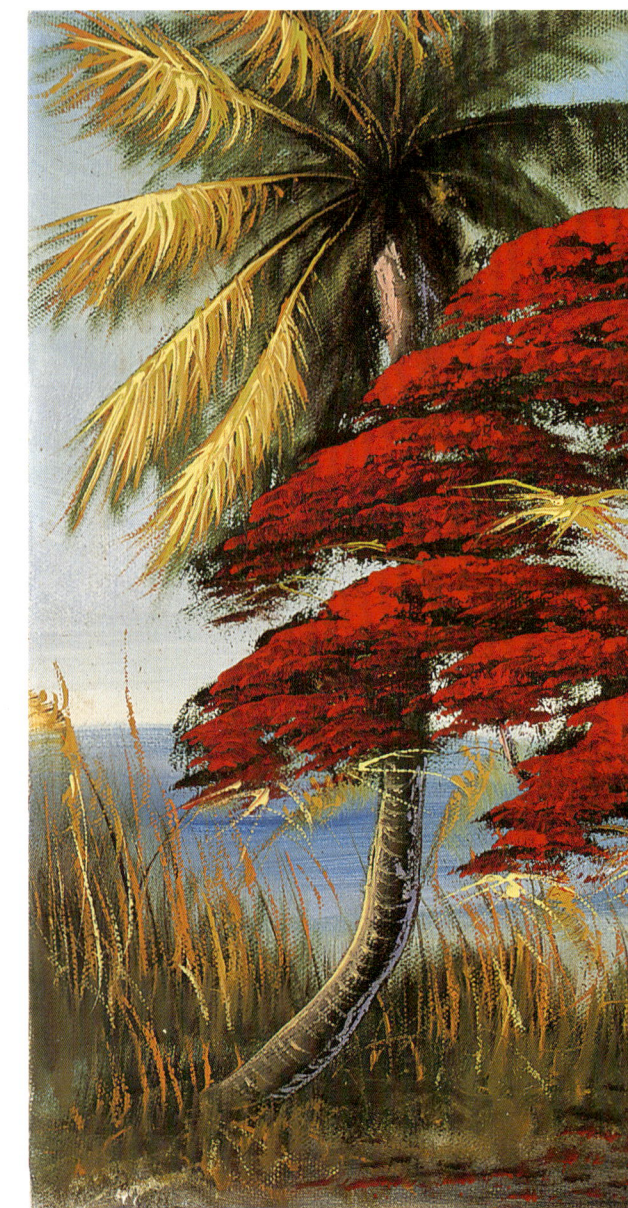

2. Johnny Daniels

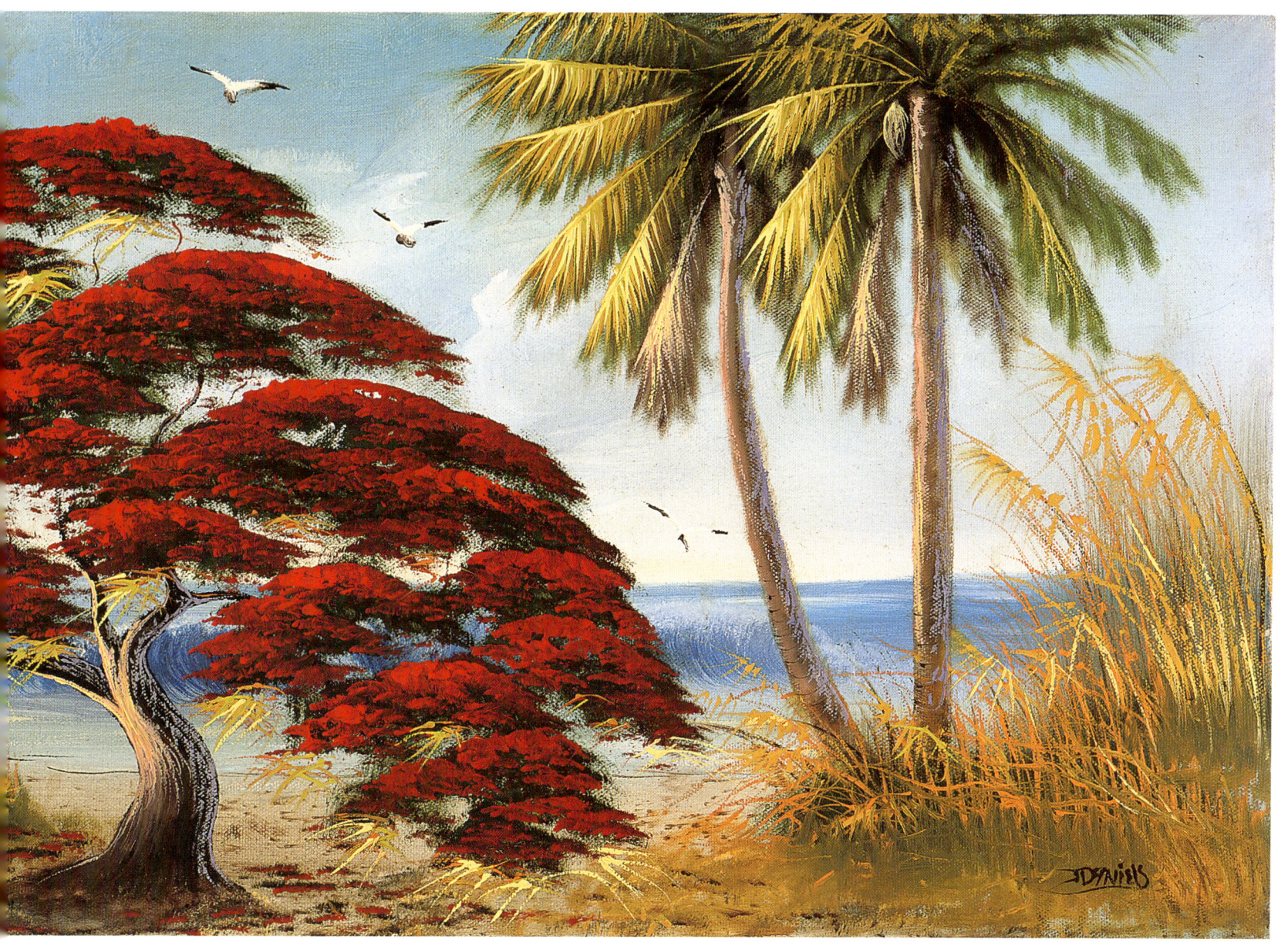

3. Alfred Hair

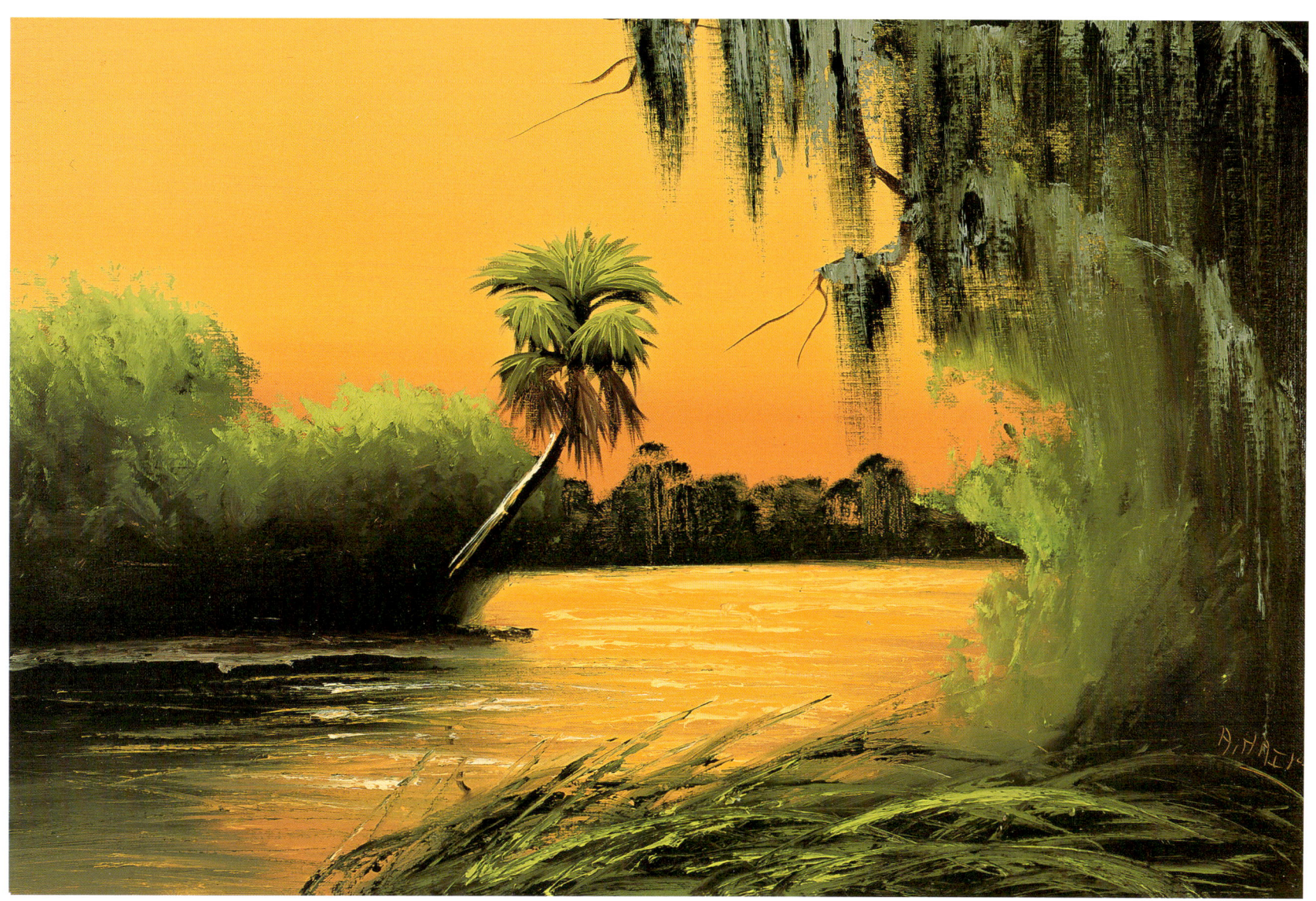

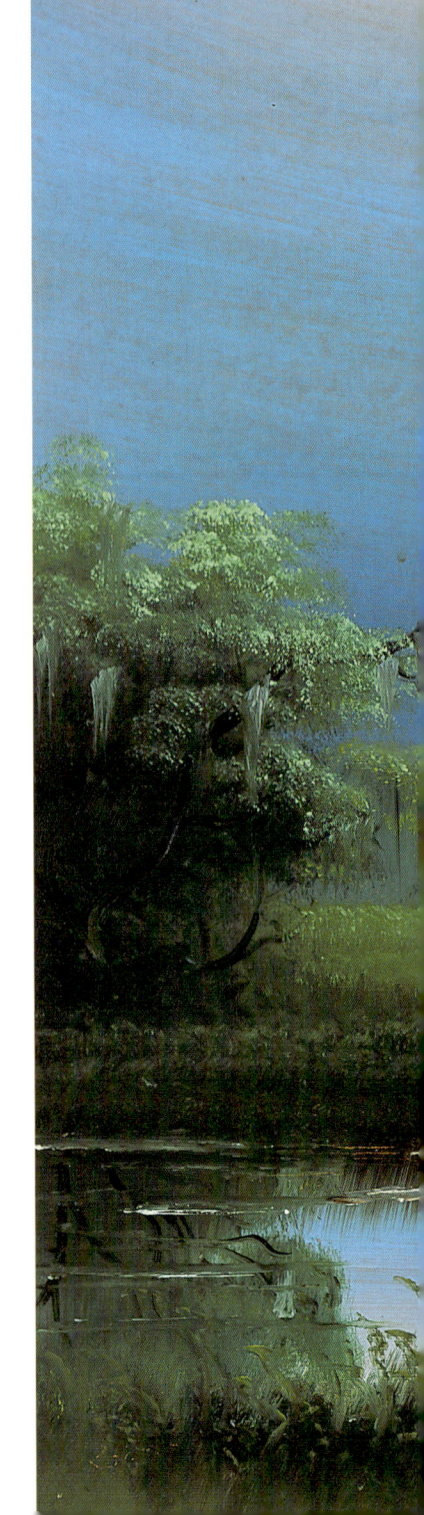

4. Al Black

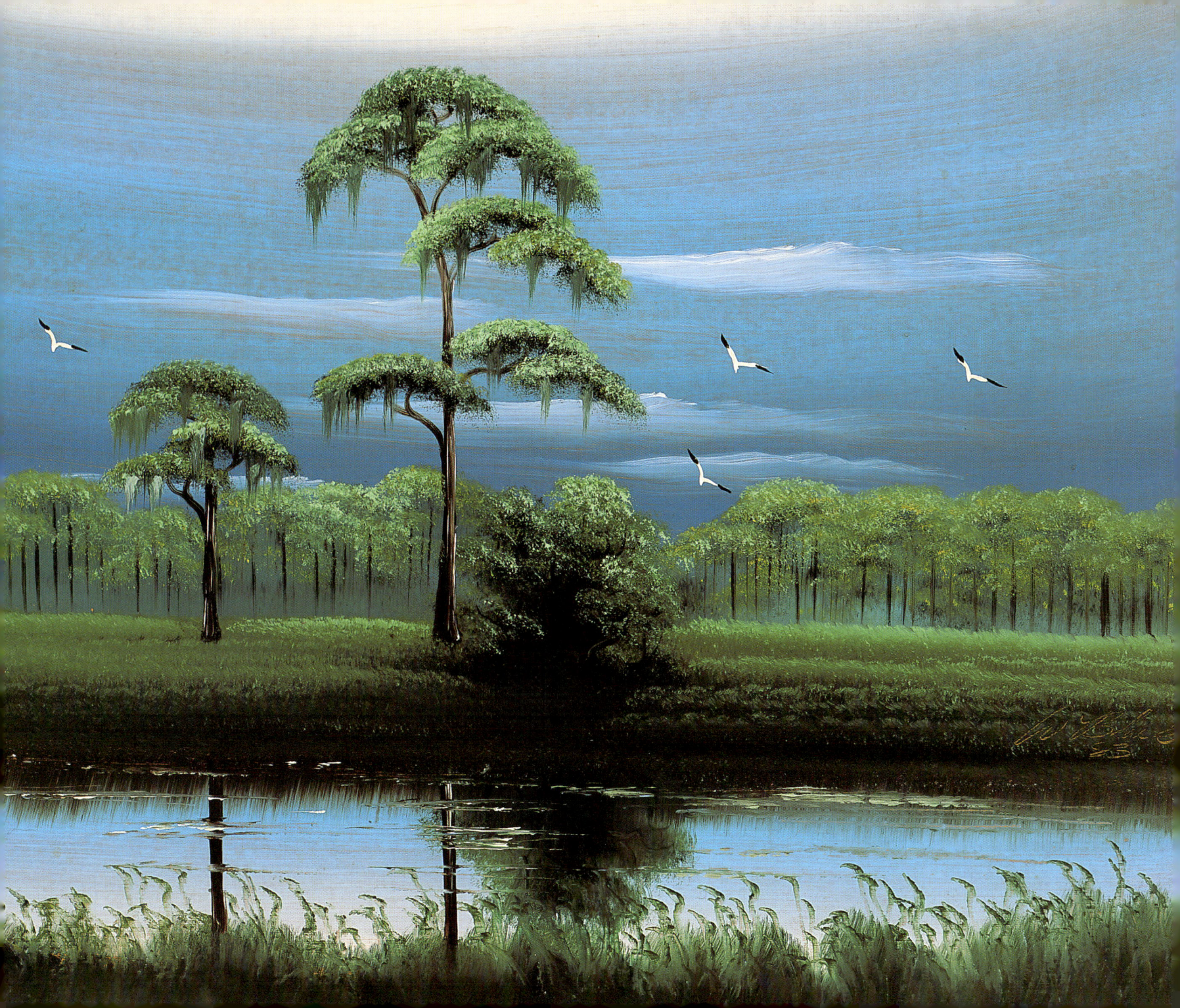

5. Harold Newton

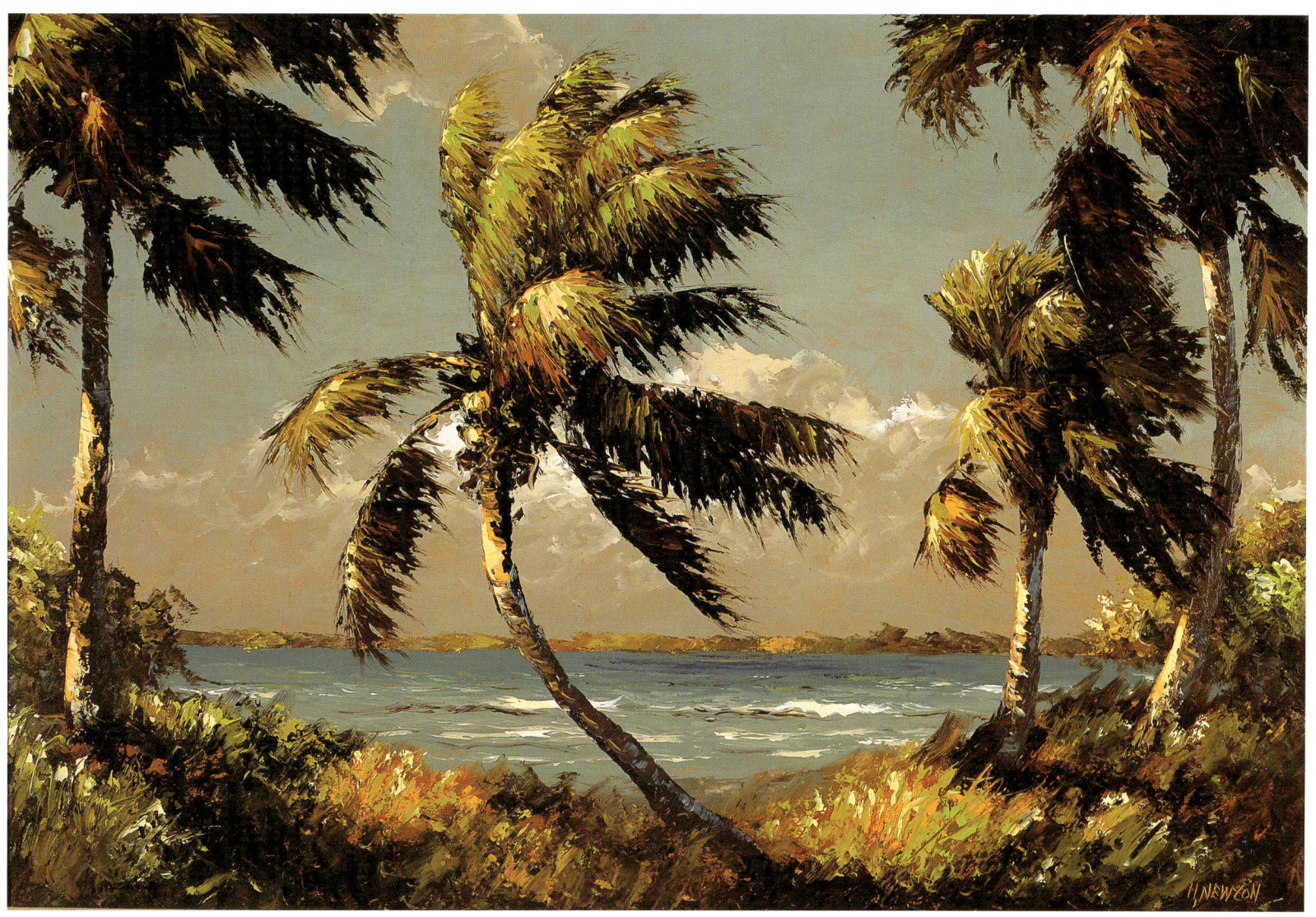

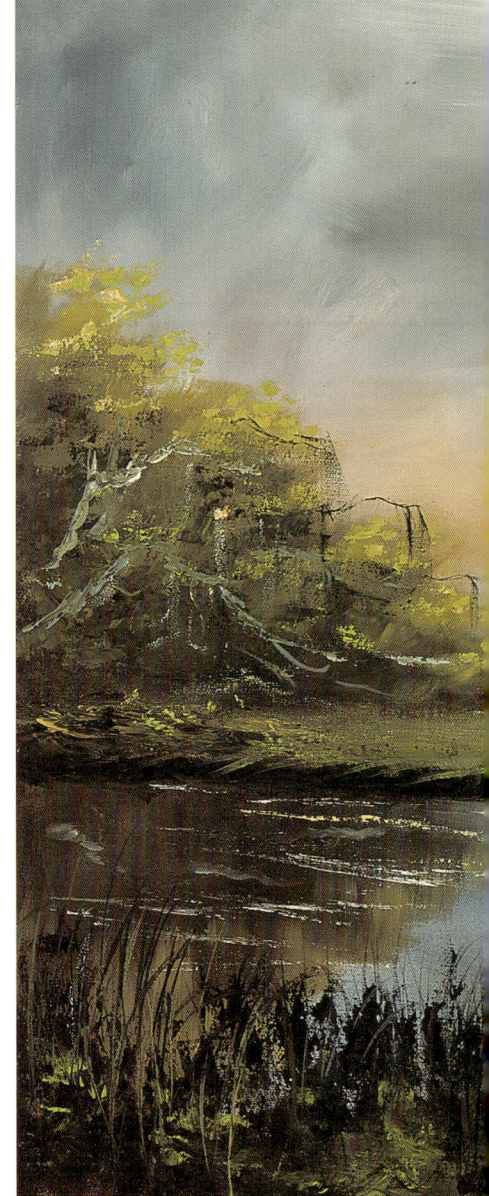

6. Robert Lewis

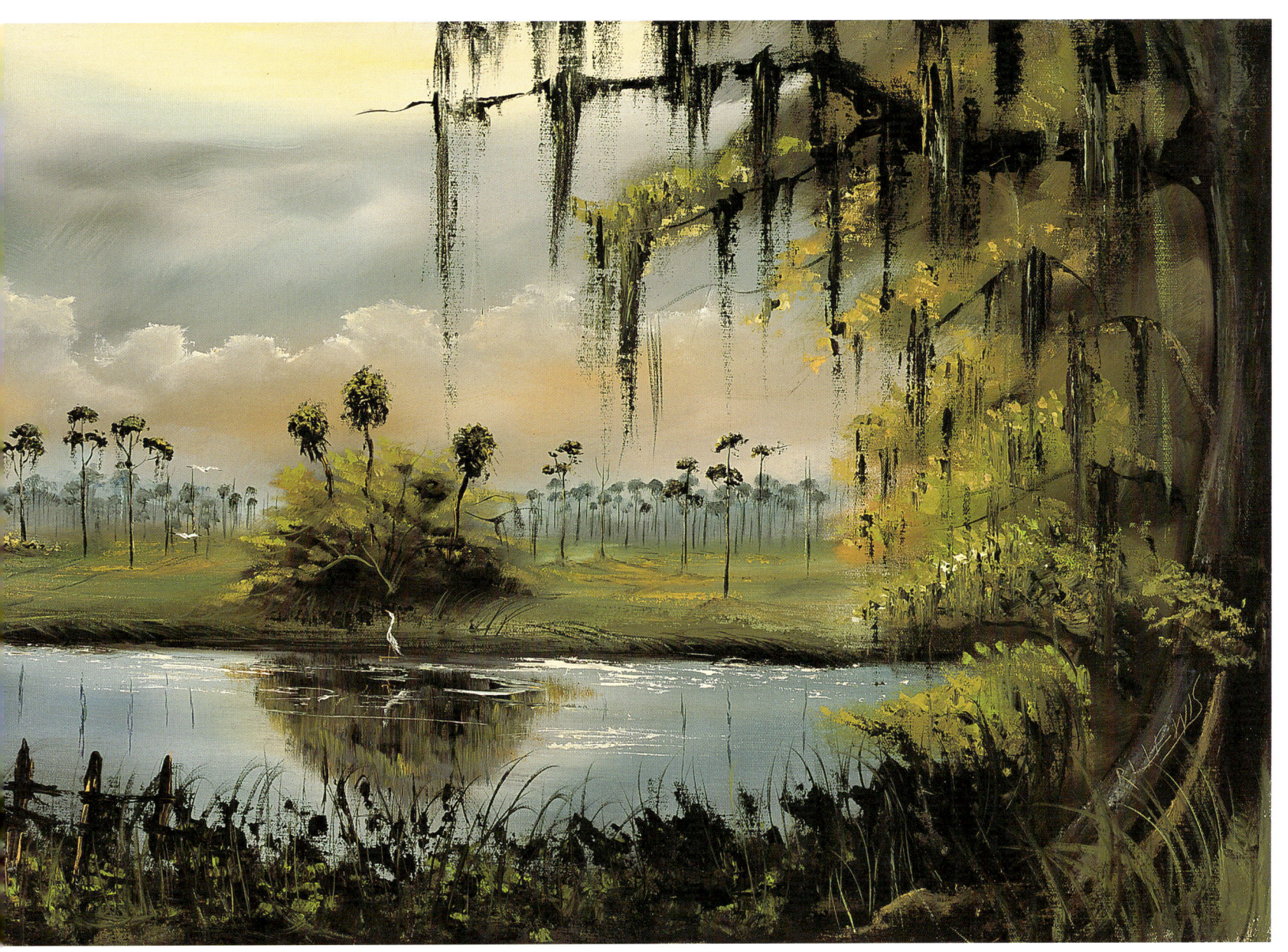

7 . Sylvester Wells

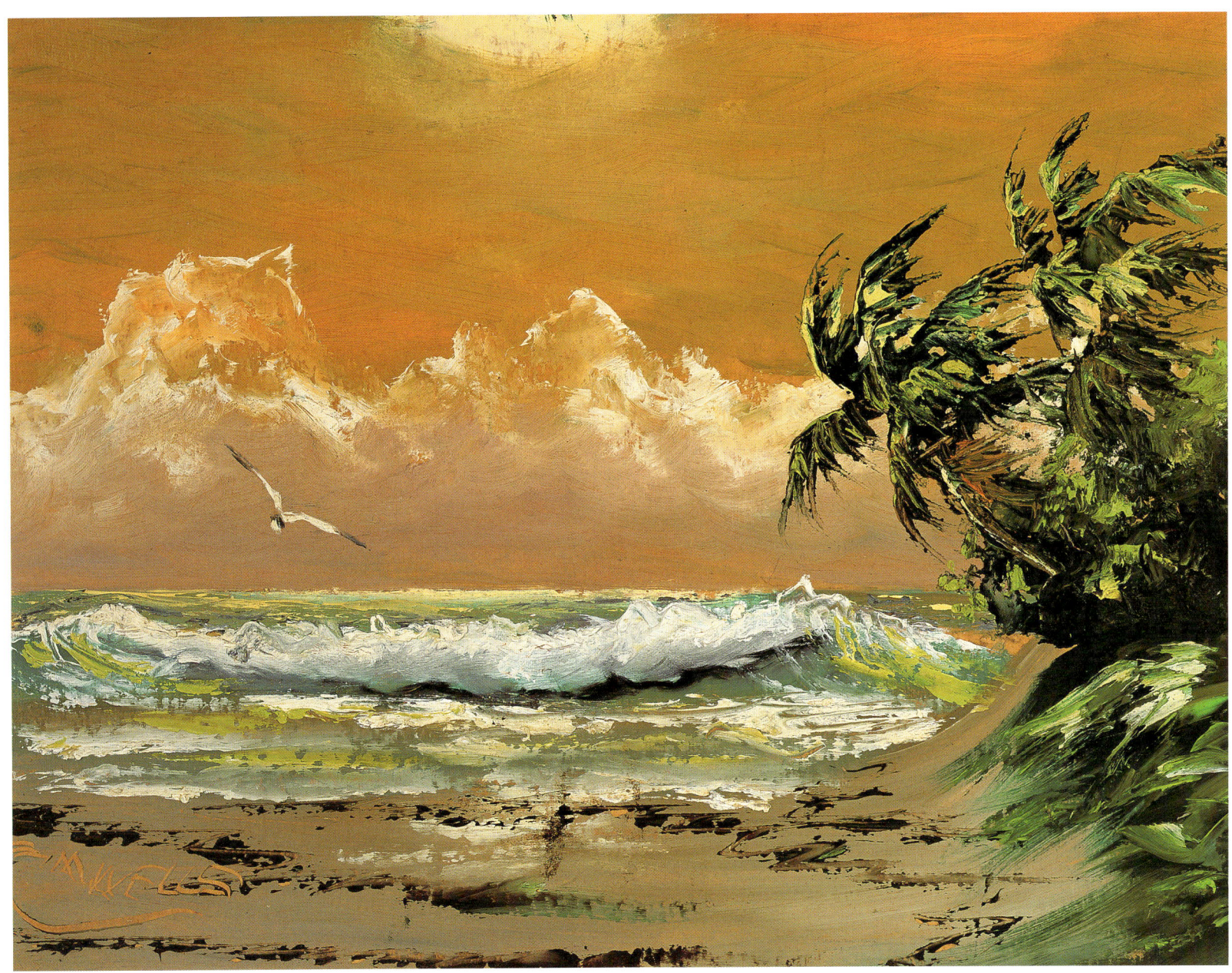

8. *Al Black*

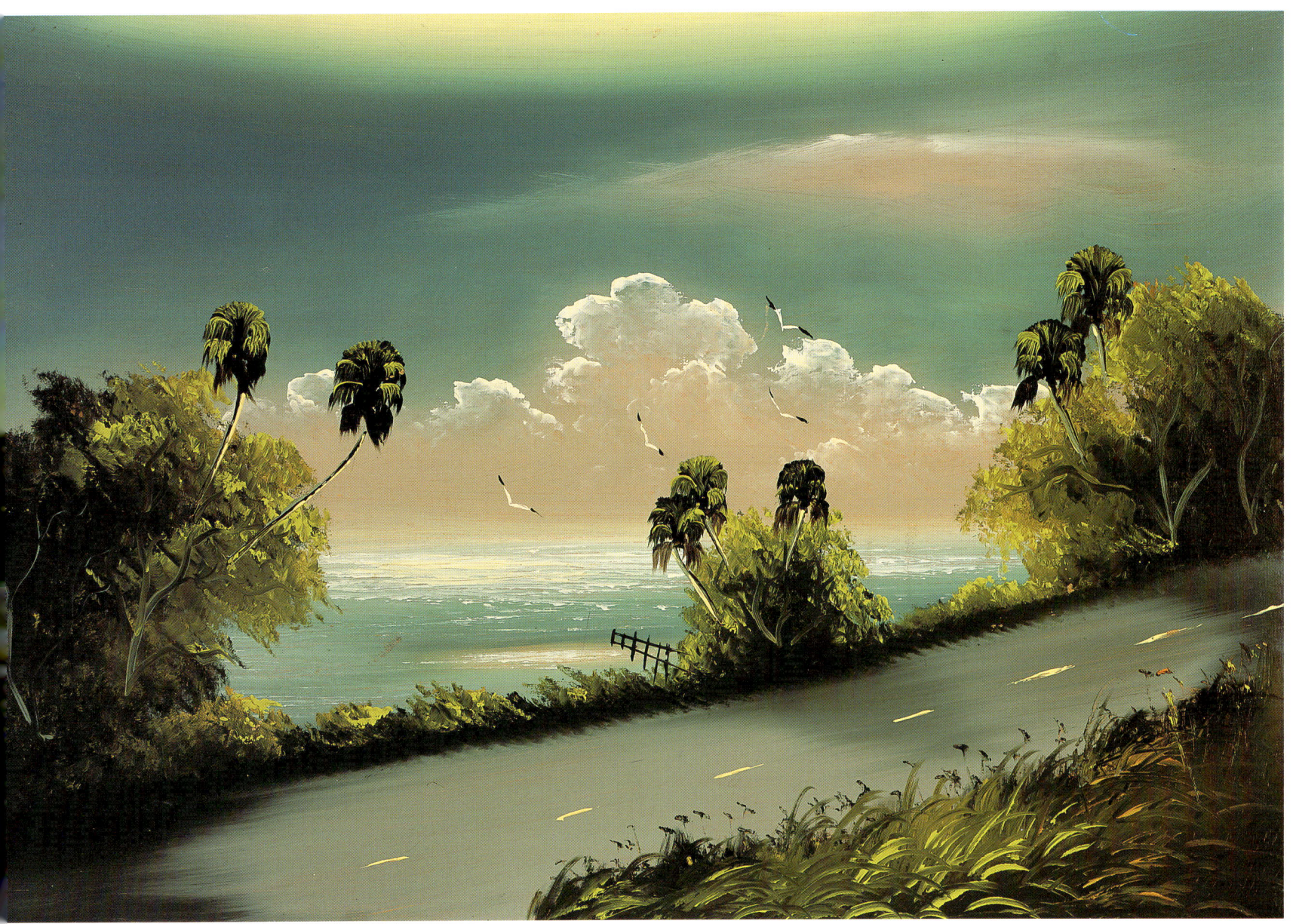

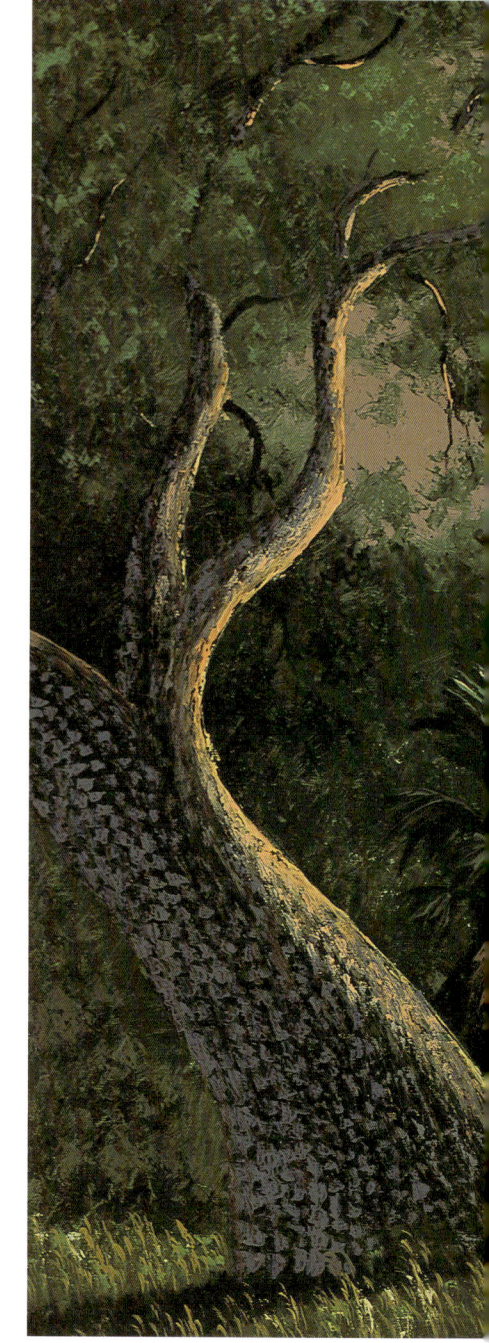

9. Livingston Roberts

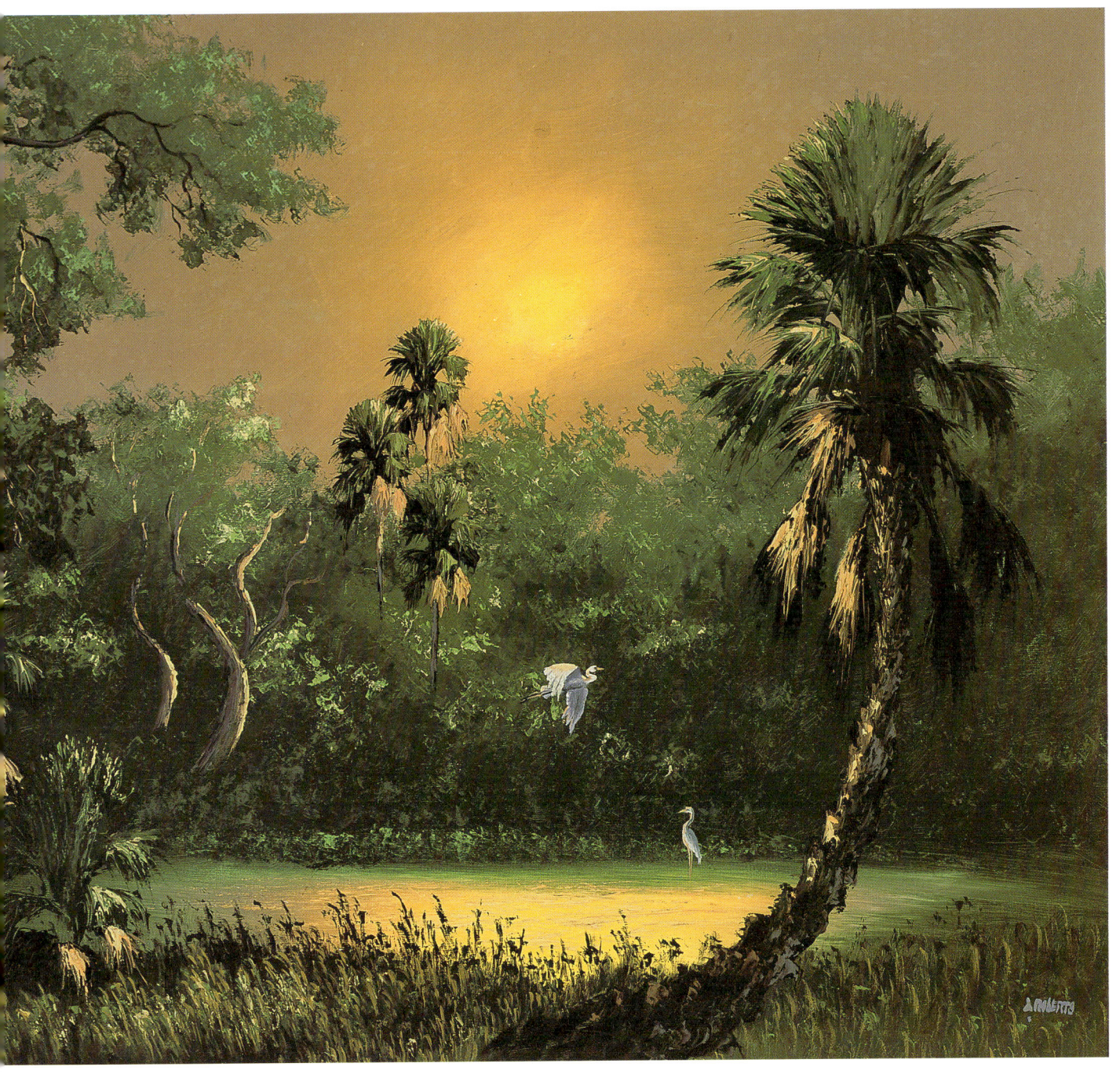

10. *Hezekiah Baker*

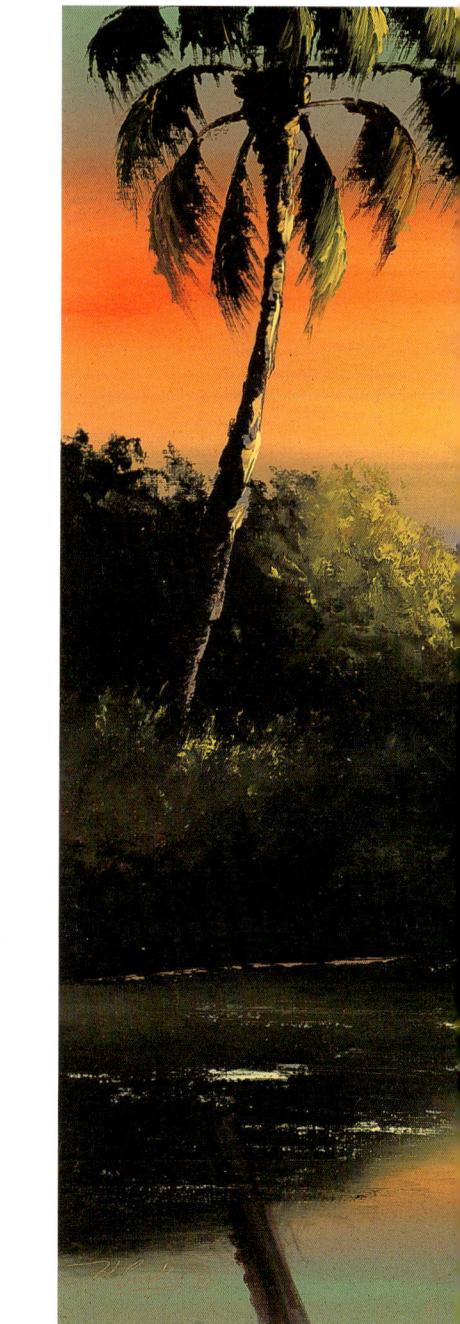

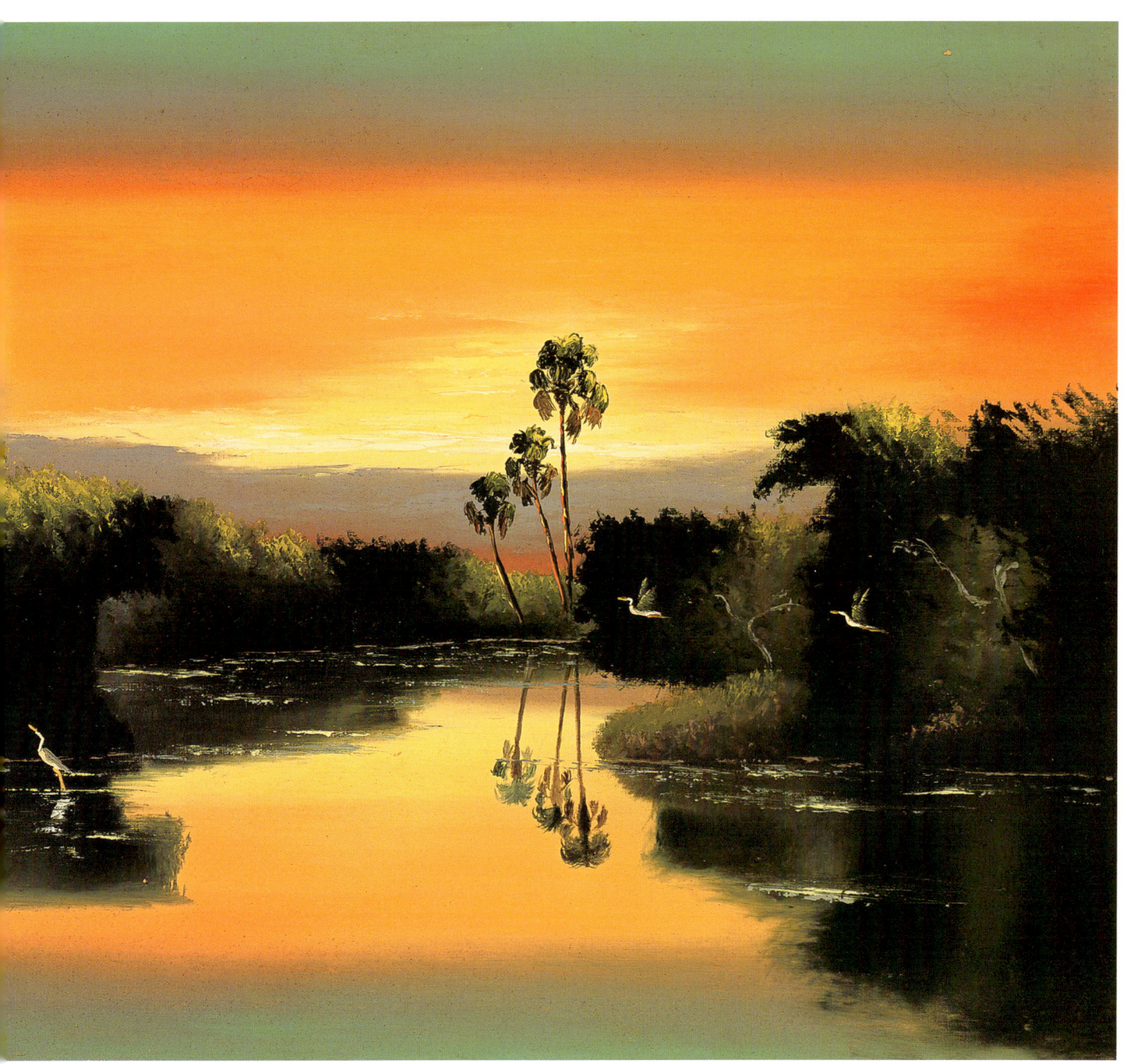

11. *Alfred Hair*

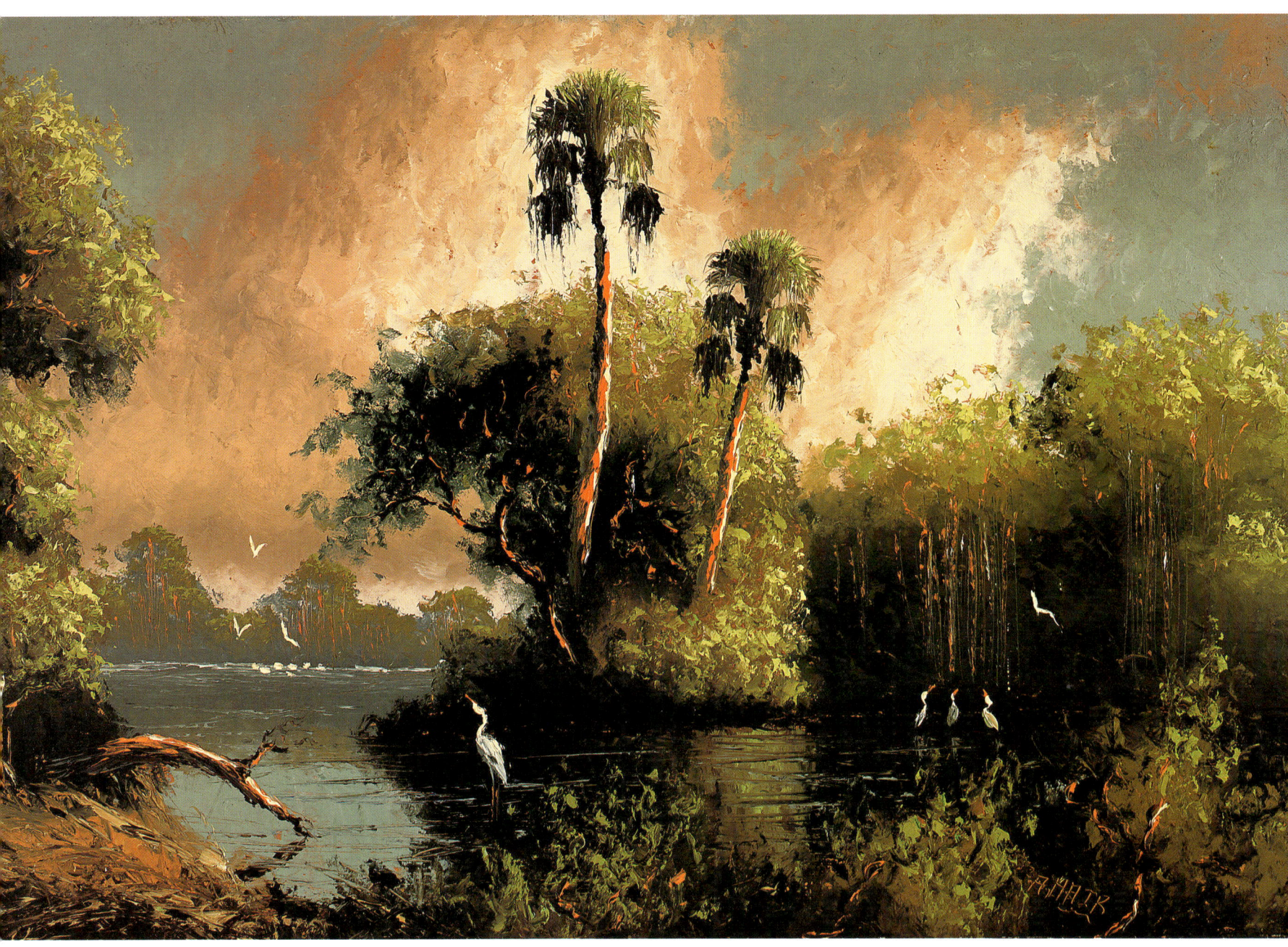

12. Ellis Buckner

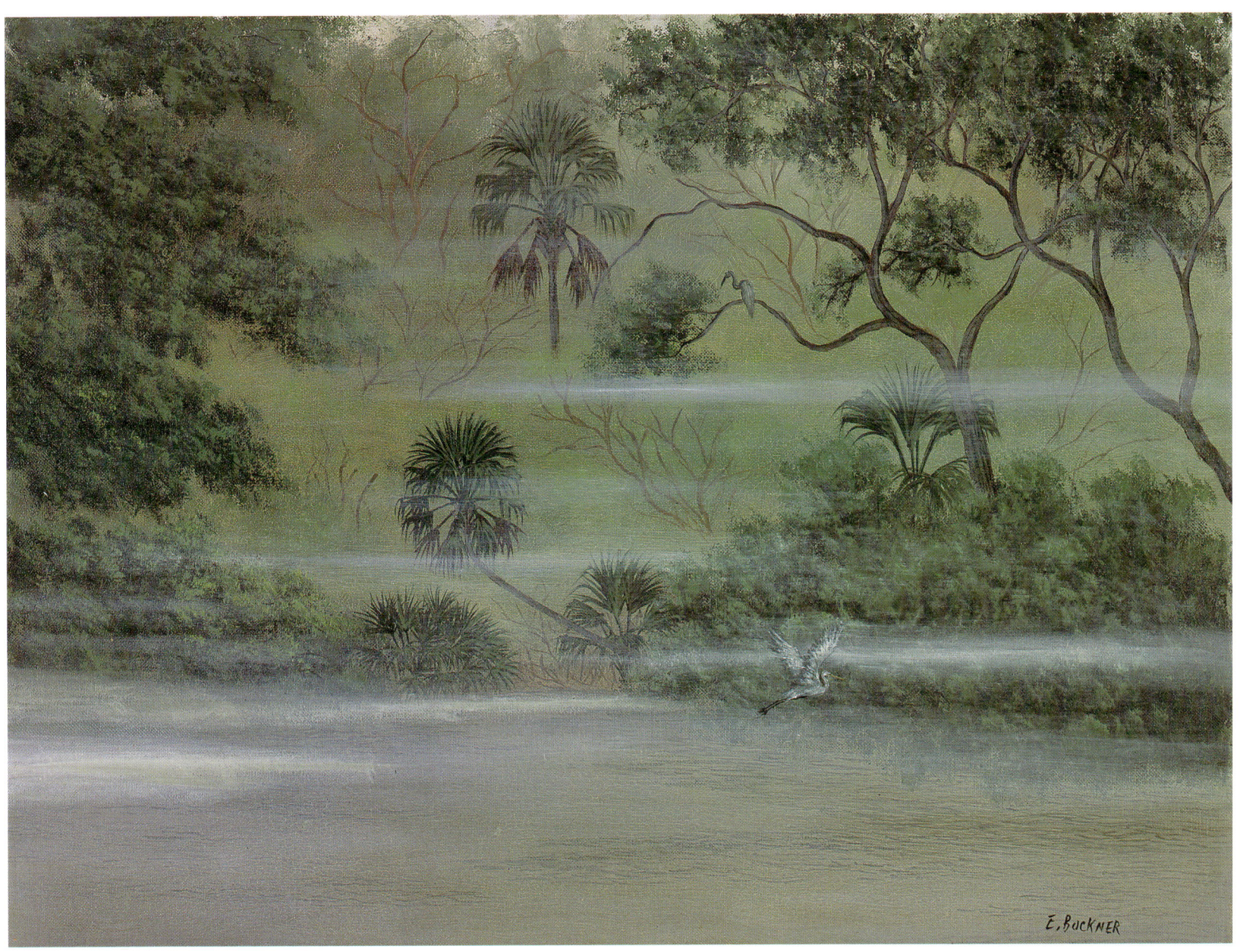

E. BUCKNER

13. Harold Newton

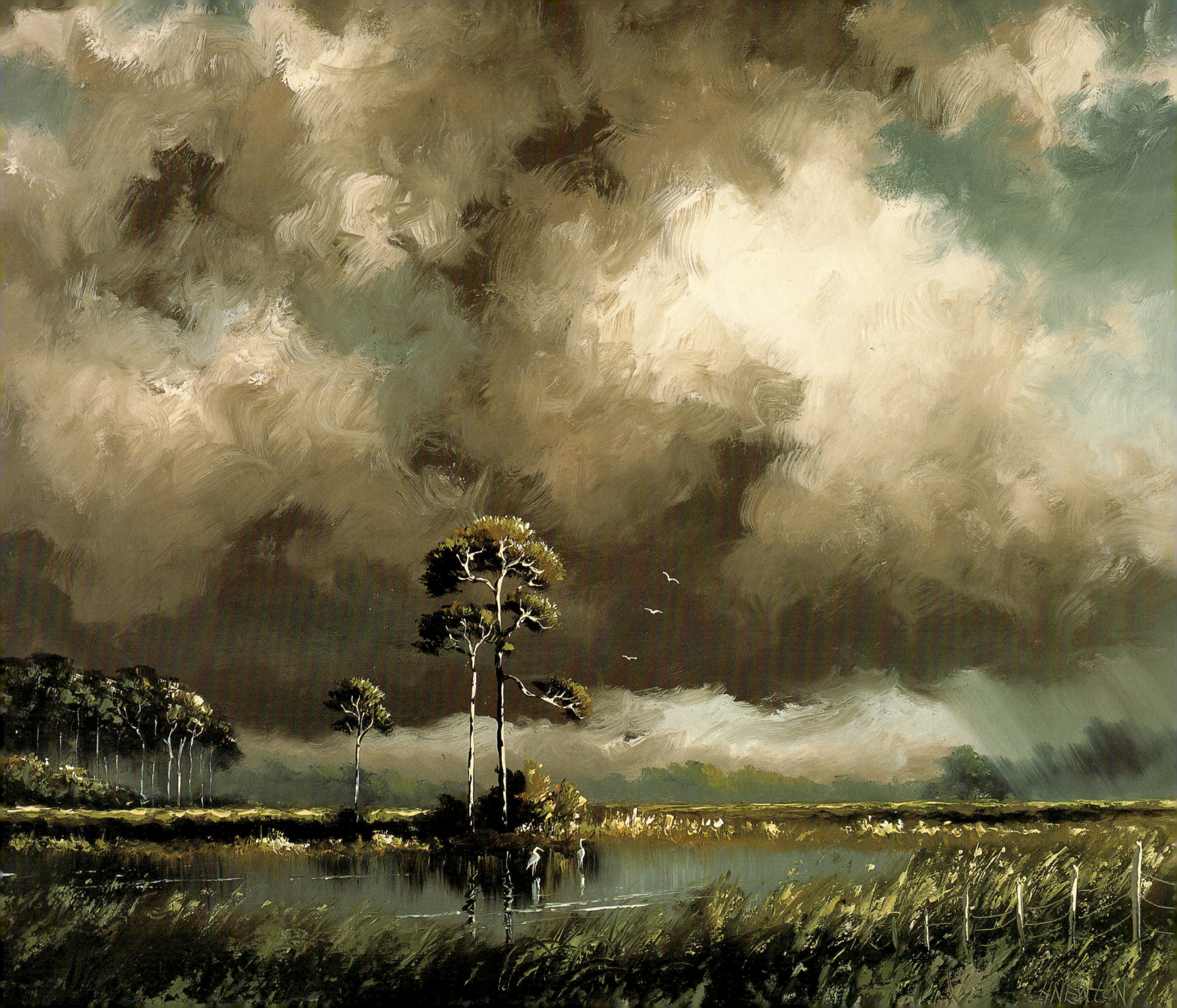

14. Johnny Daniels

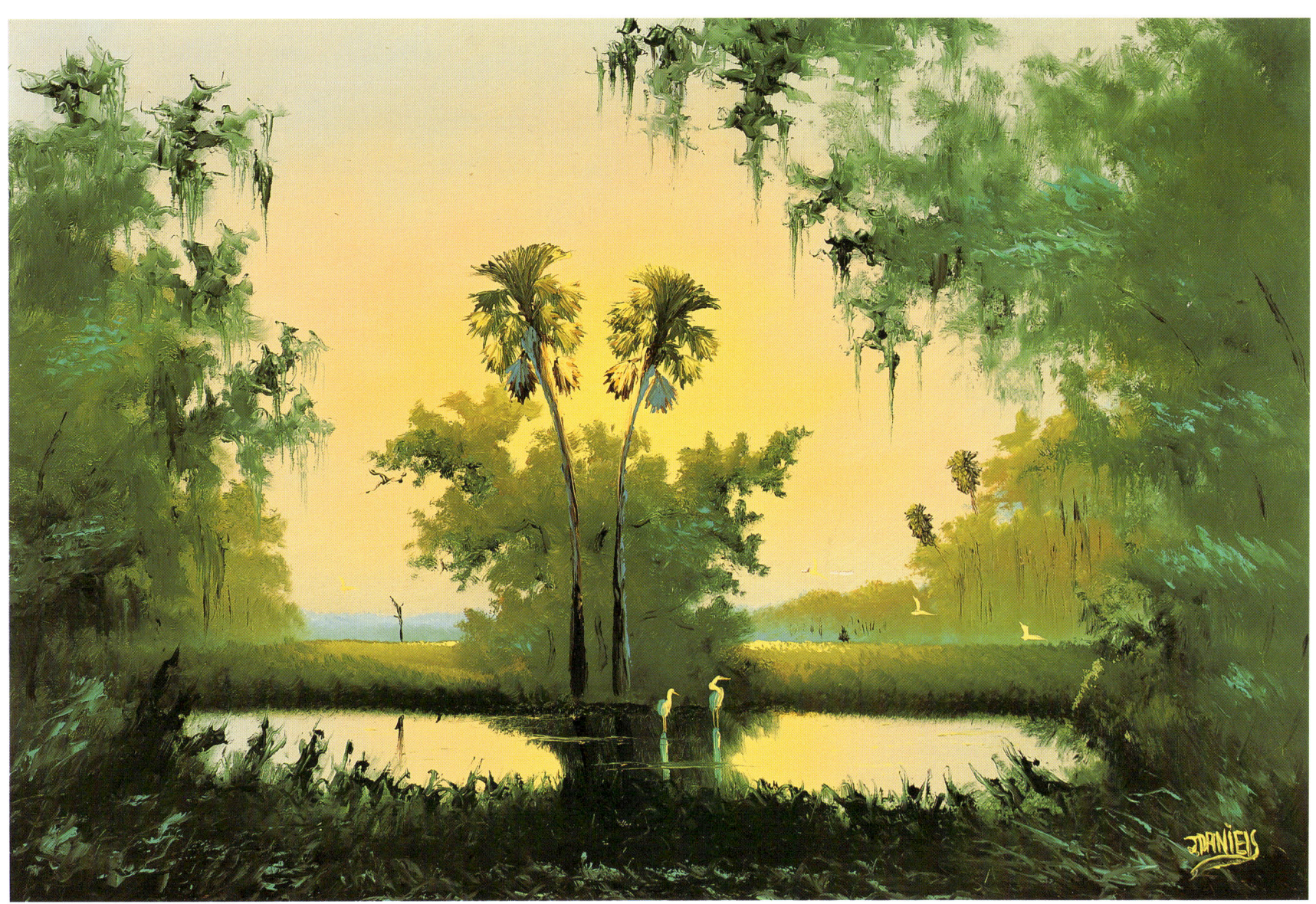

15. *Isaac Knight*

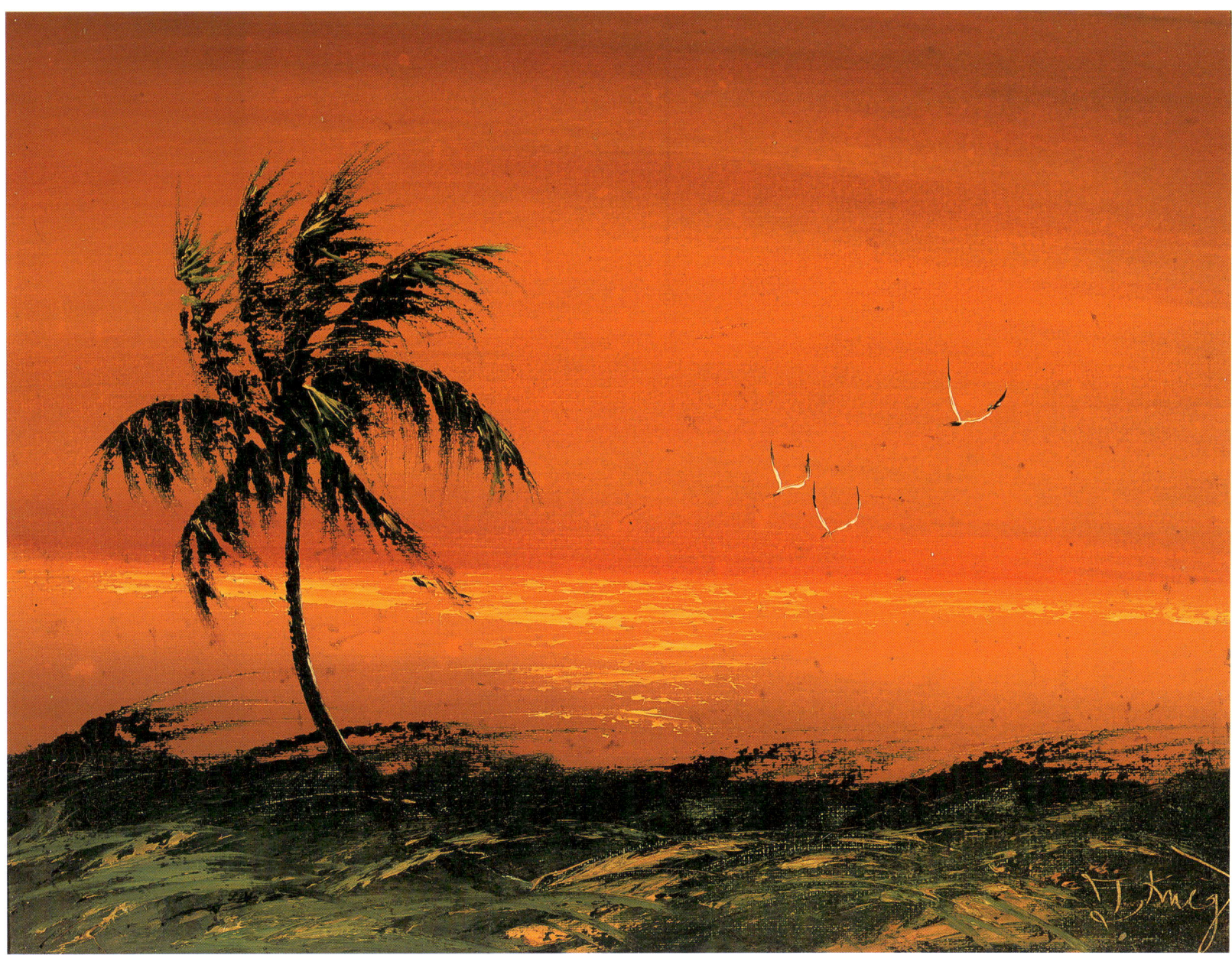

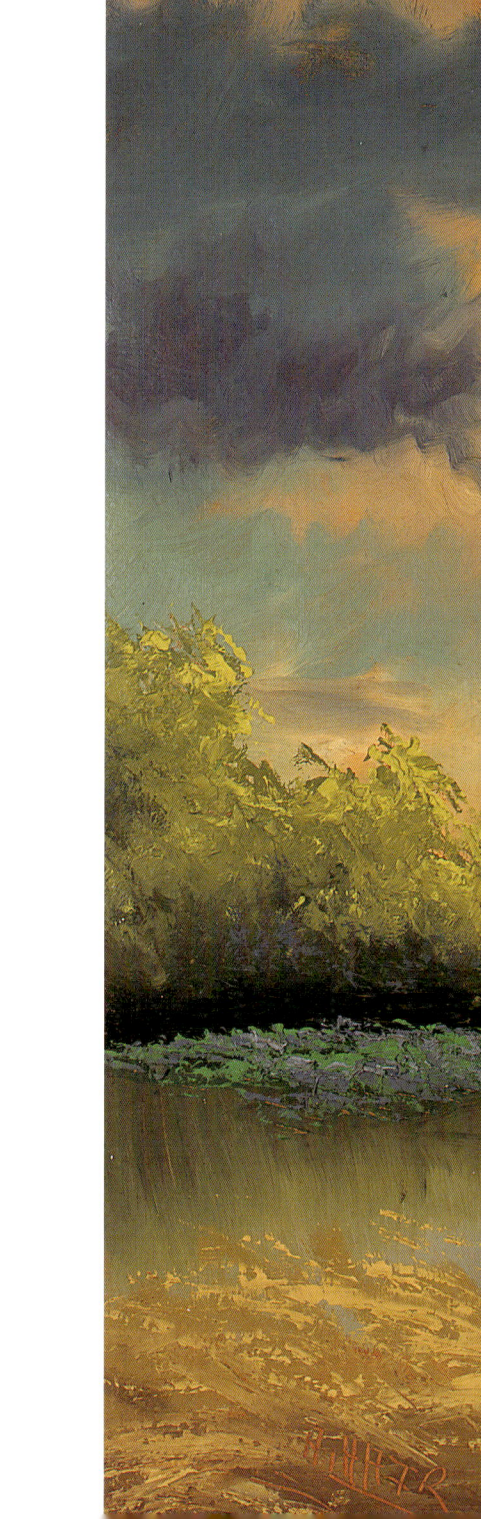

16. *Alfred Hair*

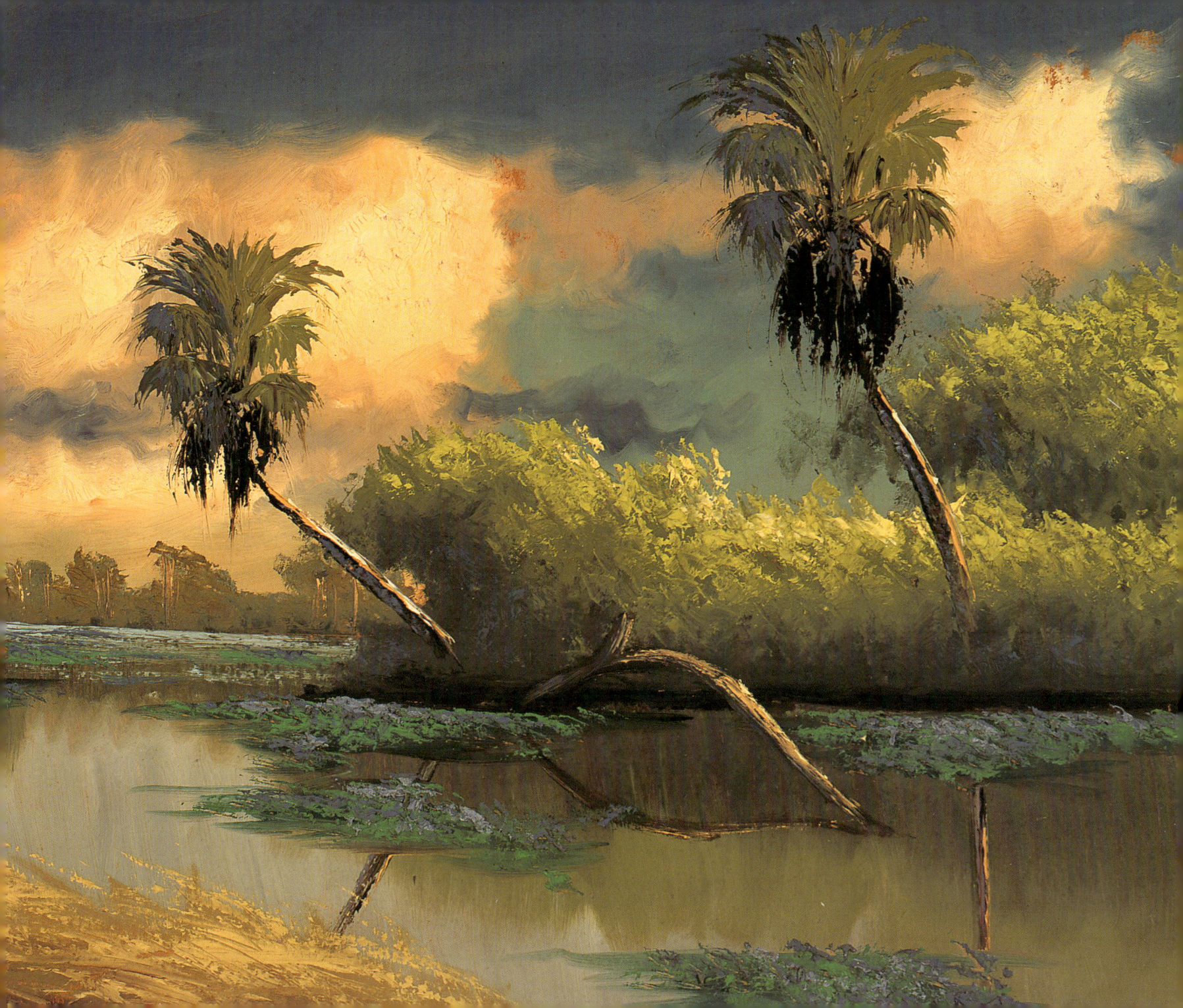

17. Unsigned, attributed to Willie Daniels

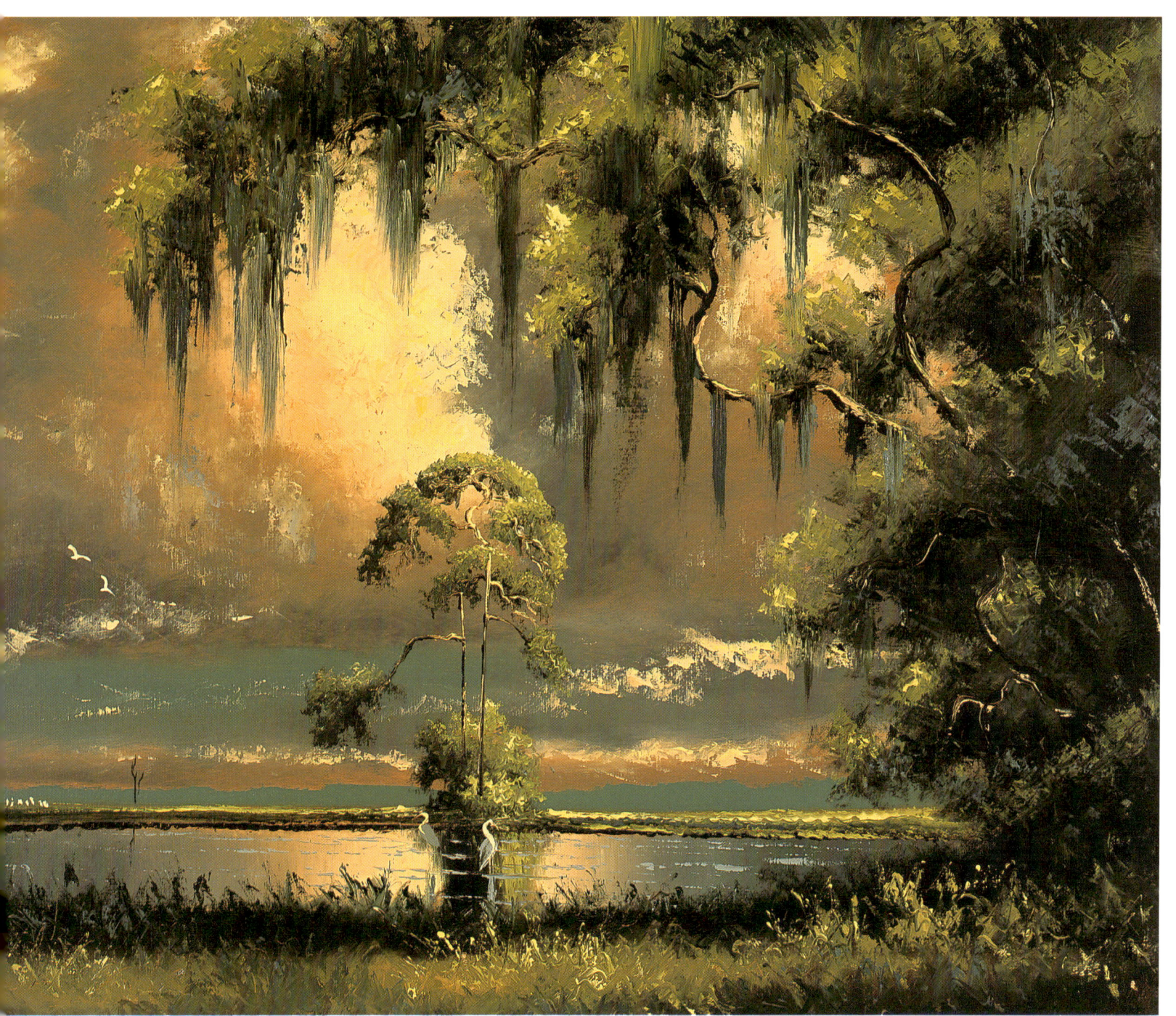

18. Sam Newton

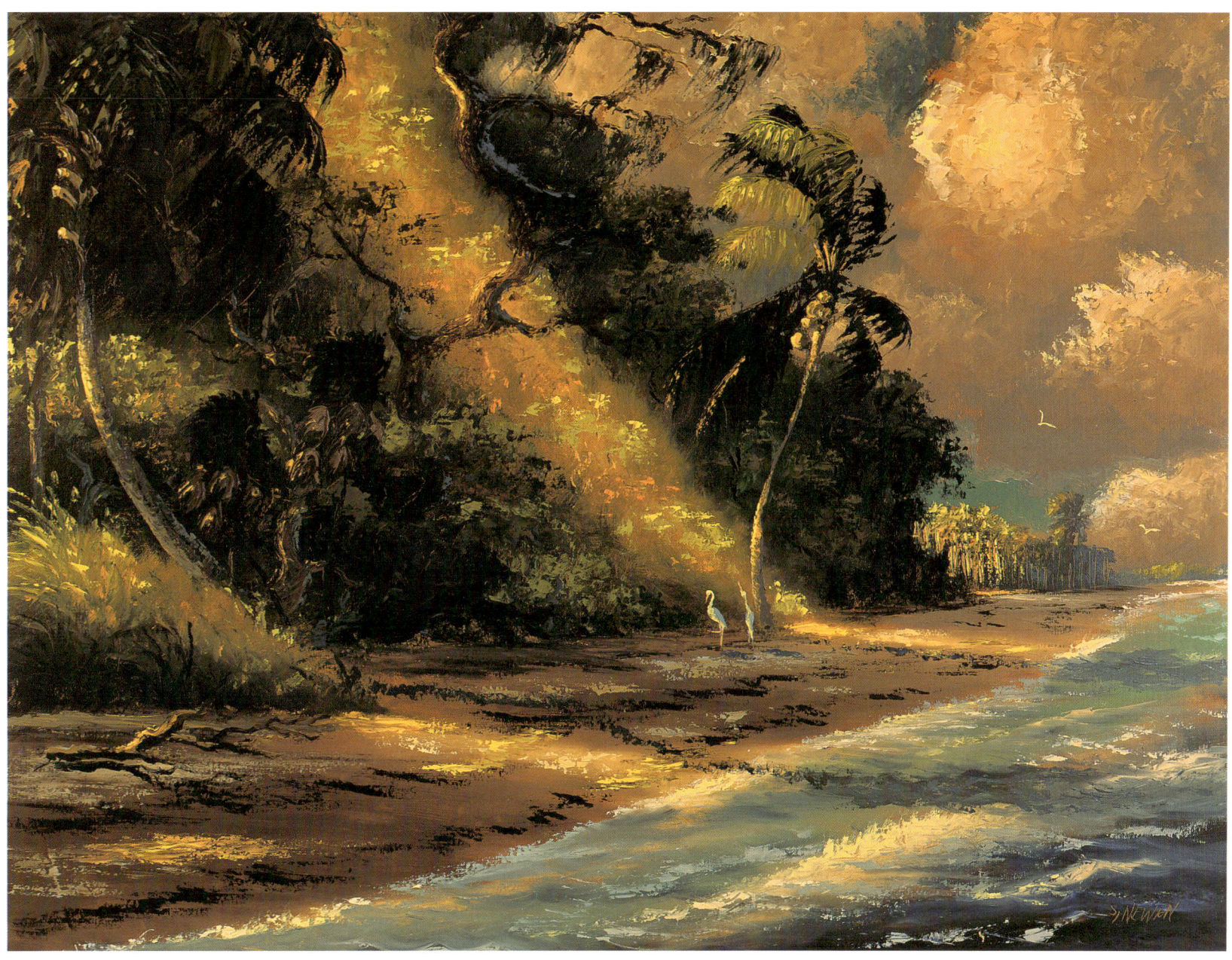

19. Lemuel Newton

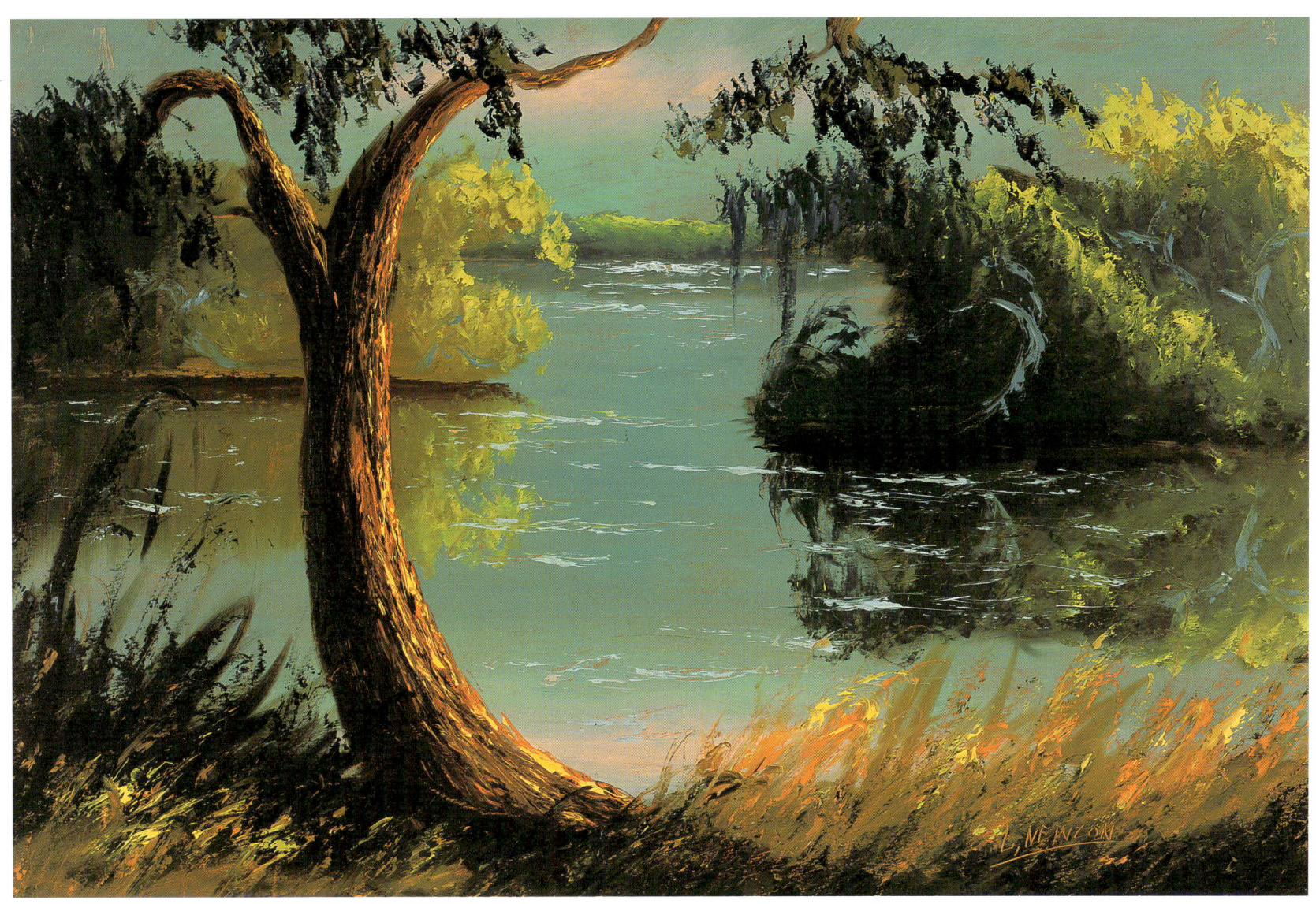

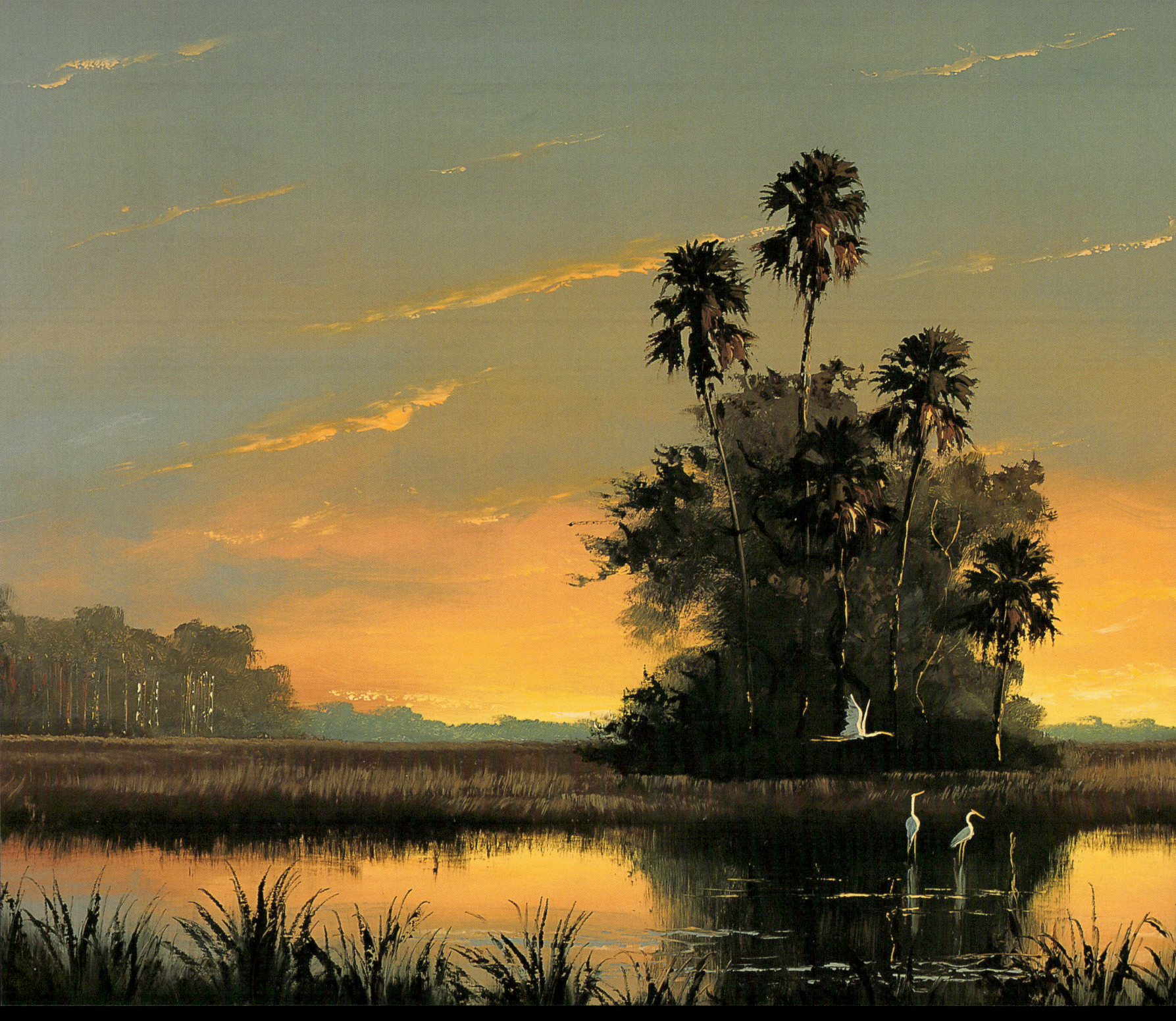

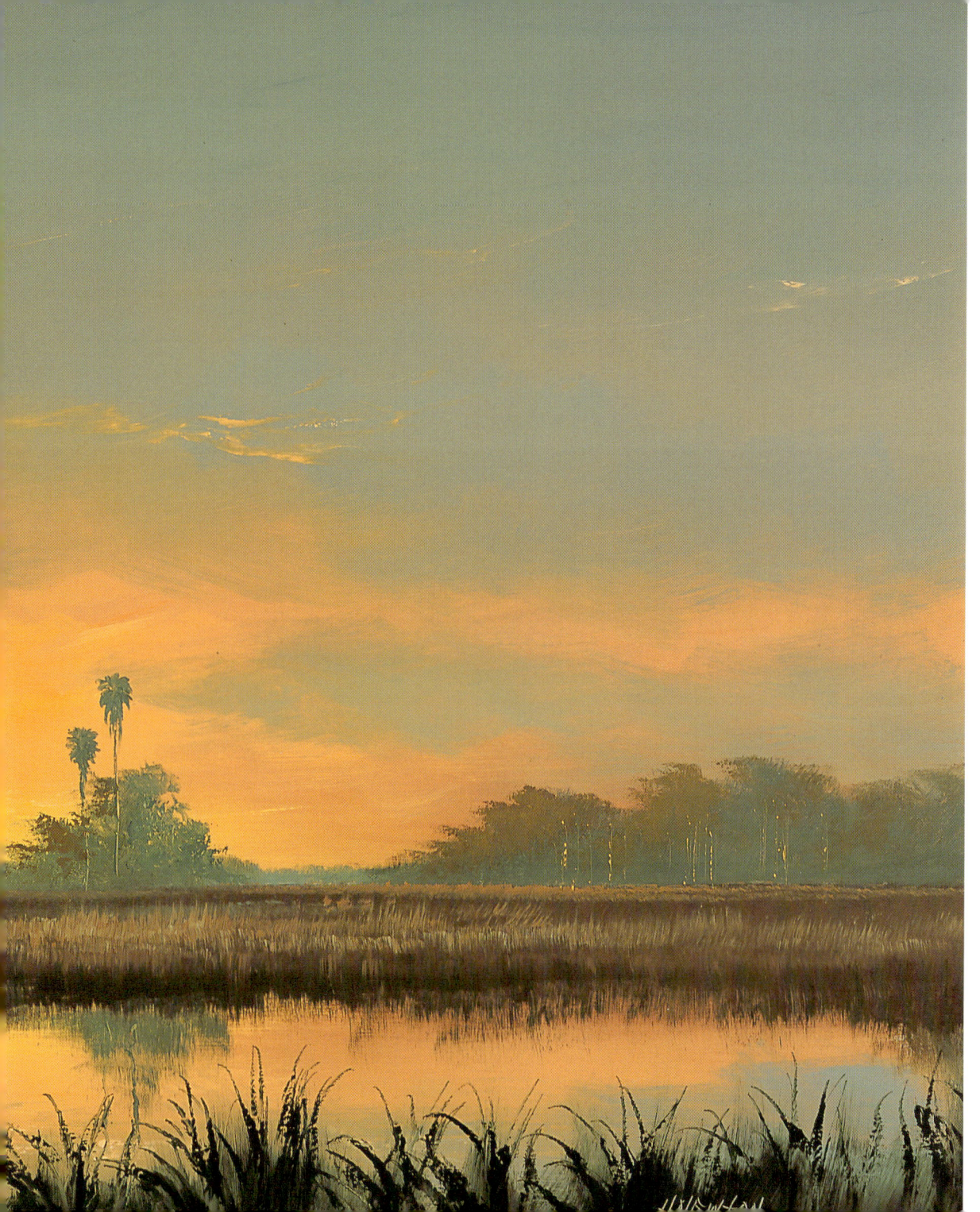

20. *Harold Newton*

21. Unsigned, attributed to *Alfred Hair*

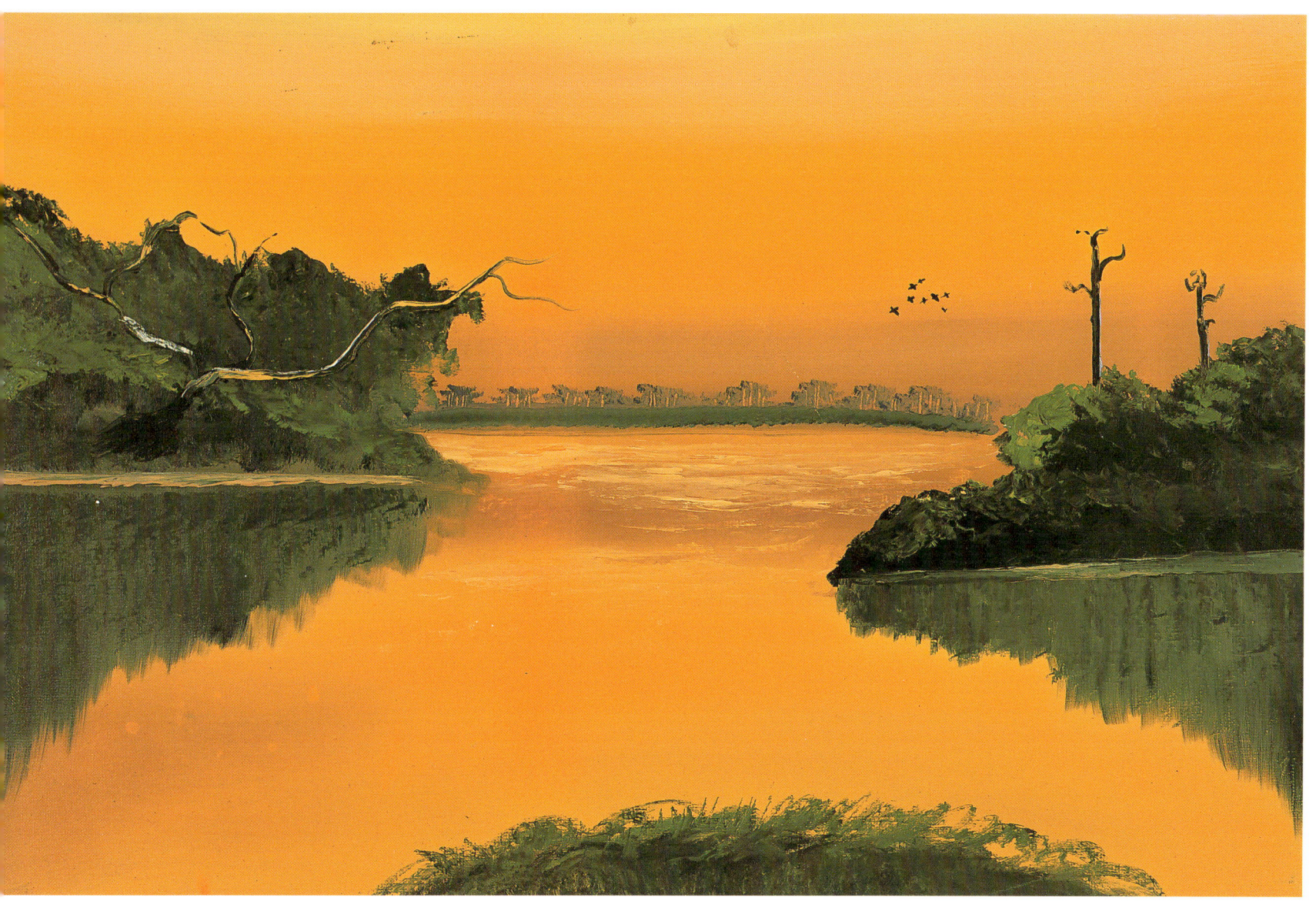

22. *Alfred Hair*

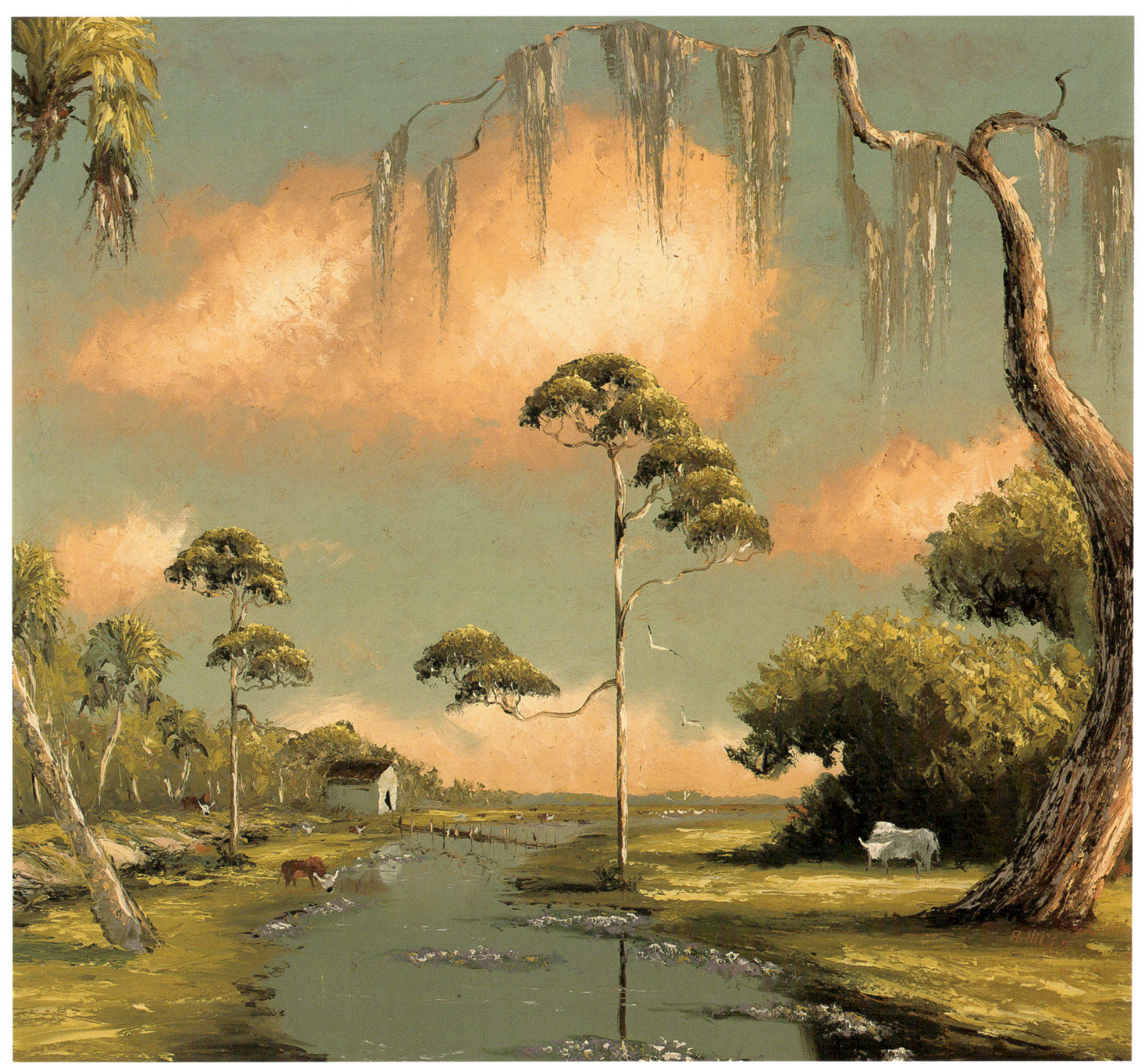

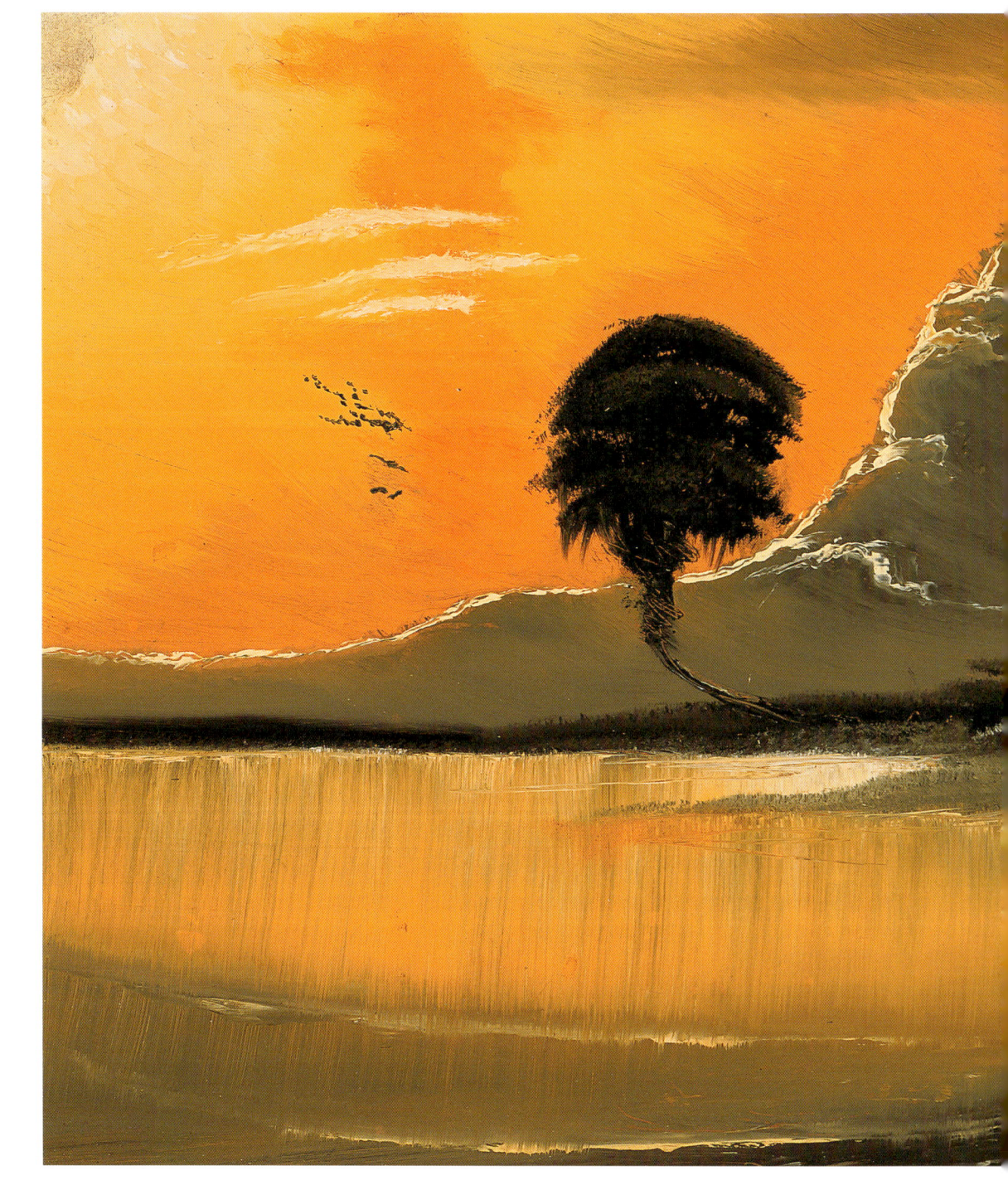

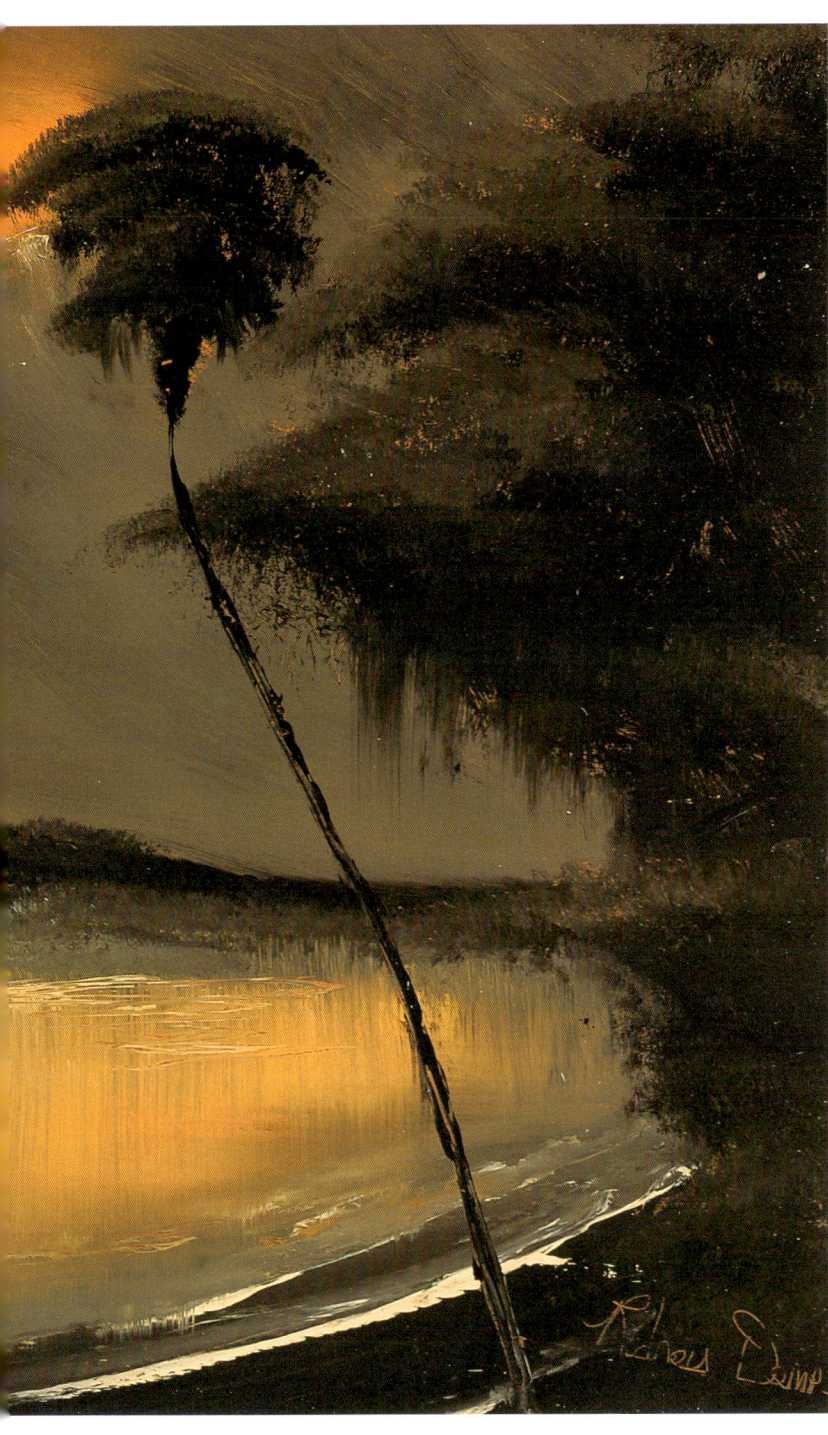

23. *Rodney Demps*

24. *Al Black*

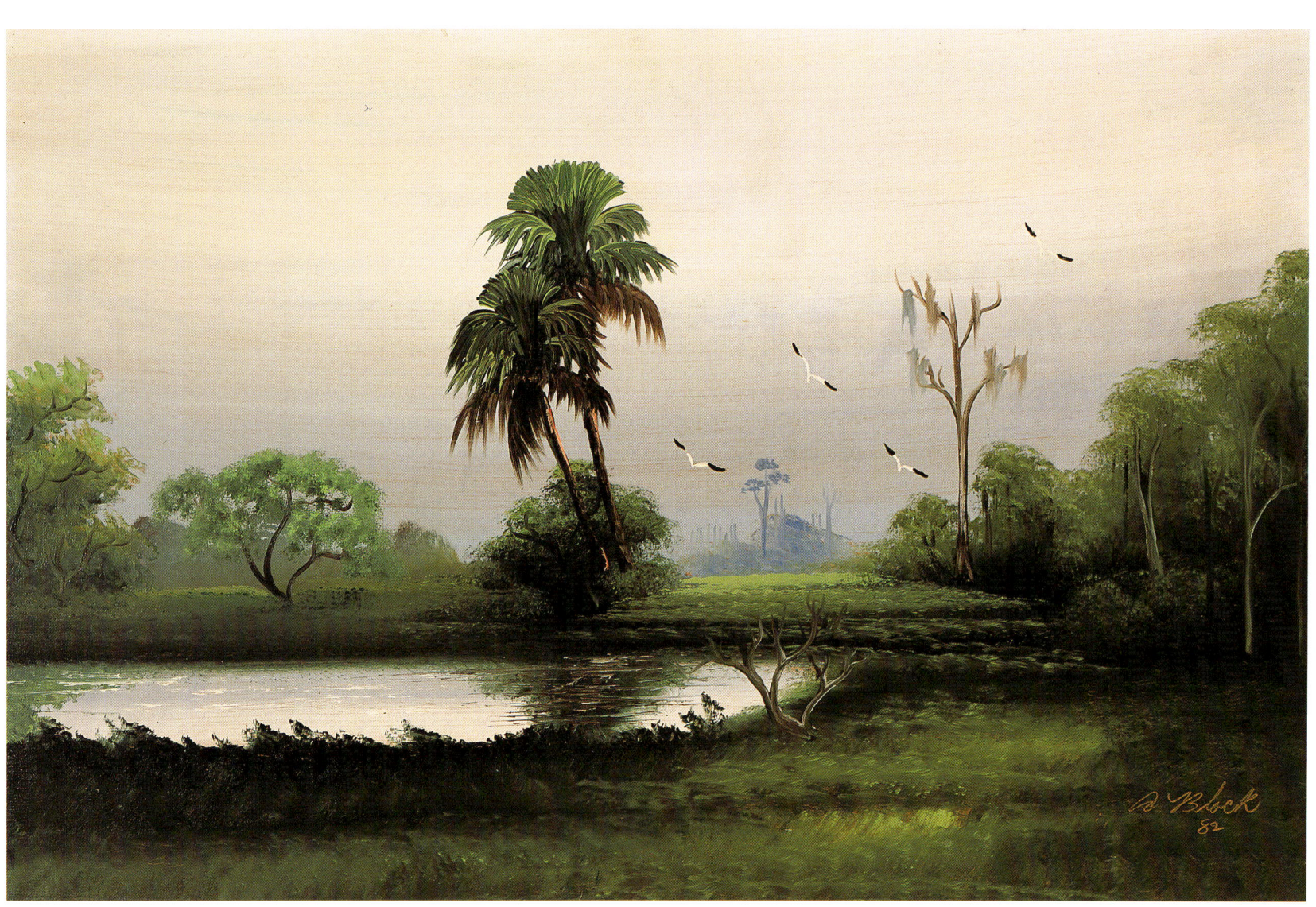

25. *Alfred Hair*

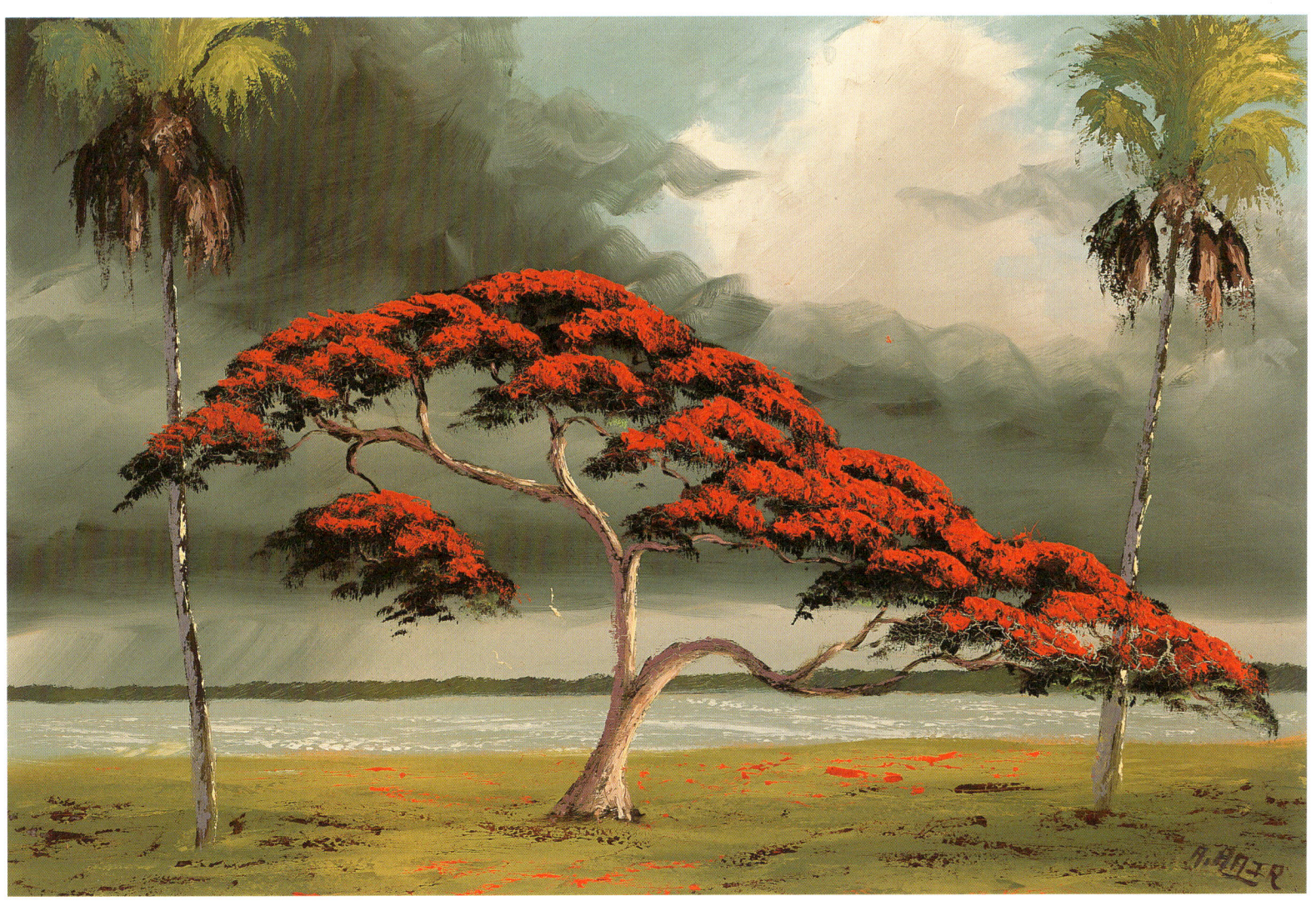

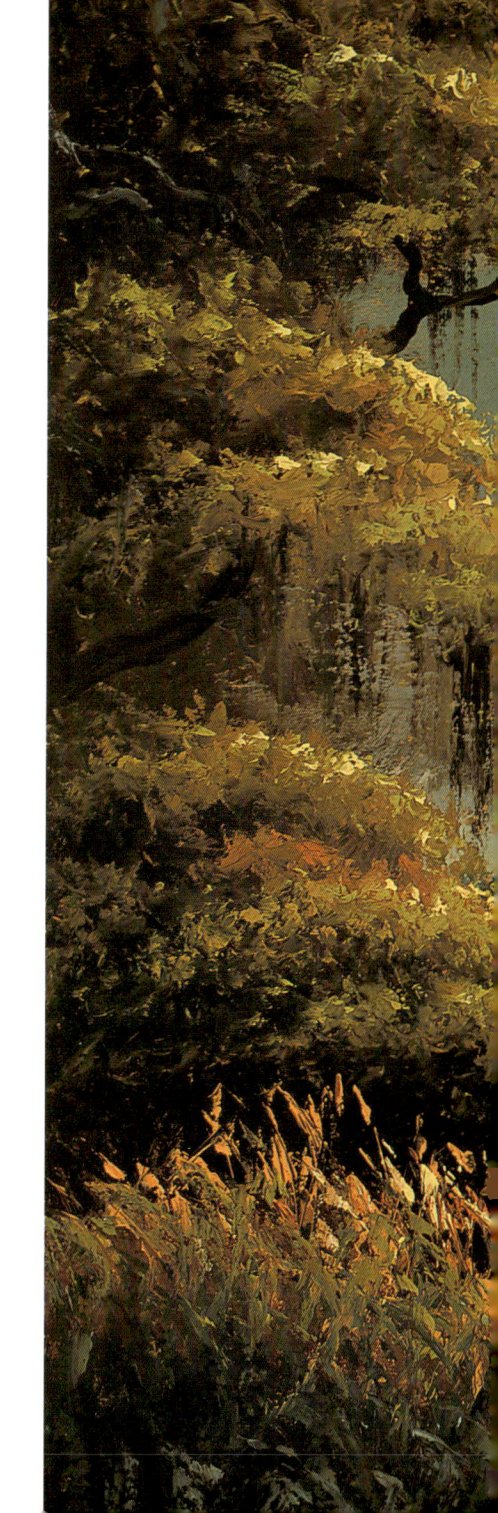

26. *Harold Newton*

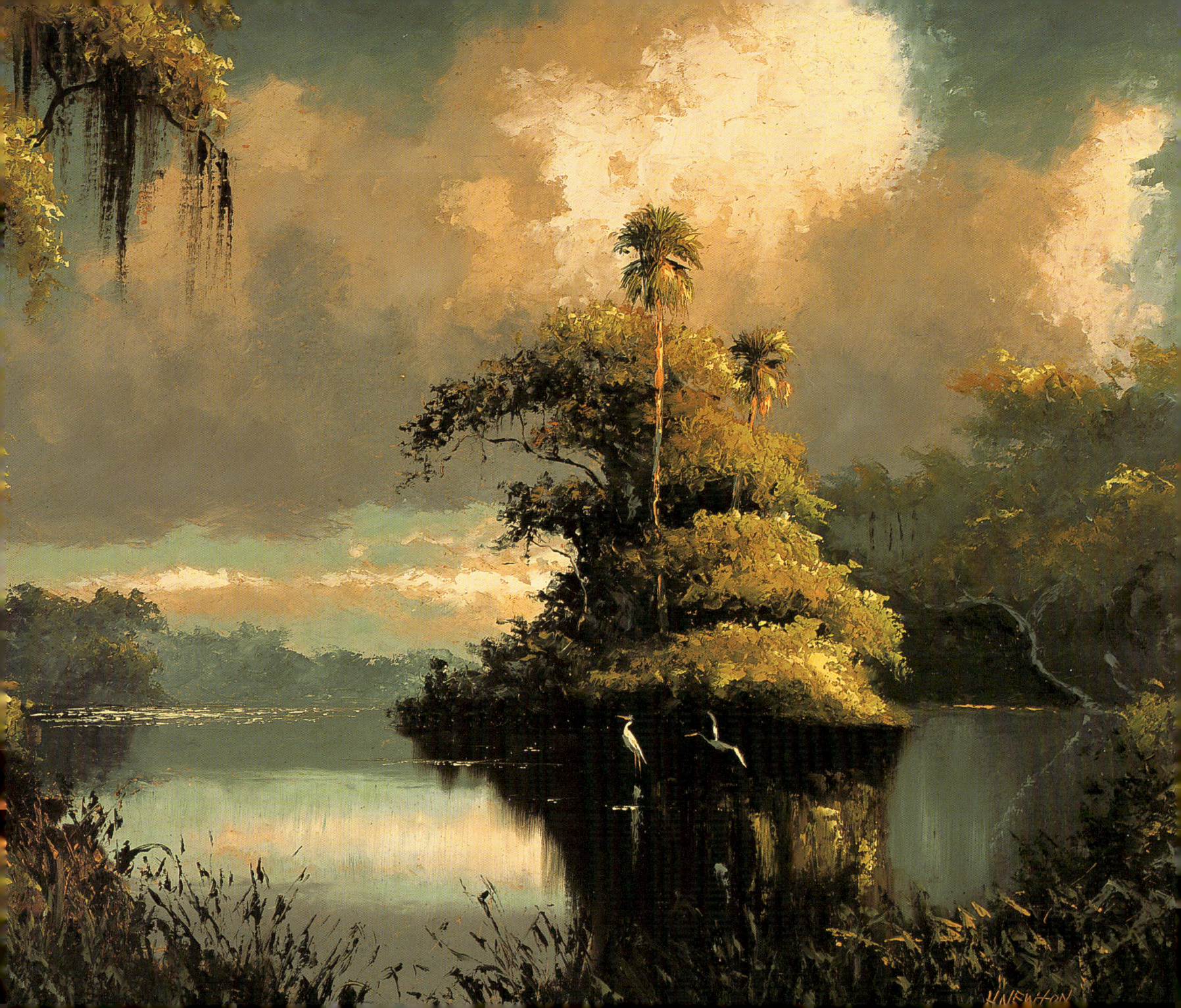

27. *Al Black*

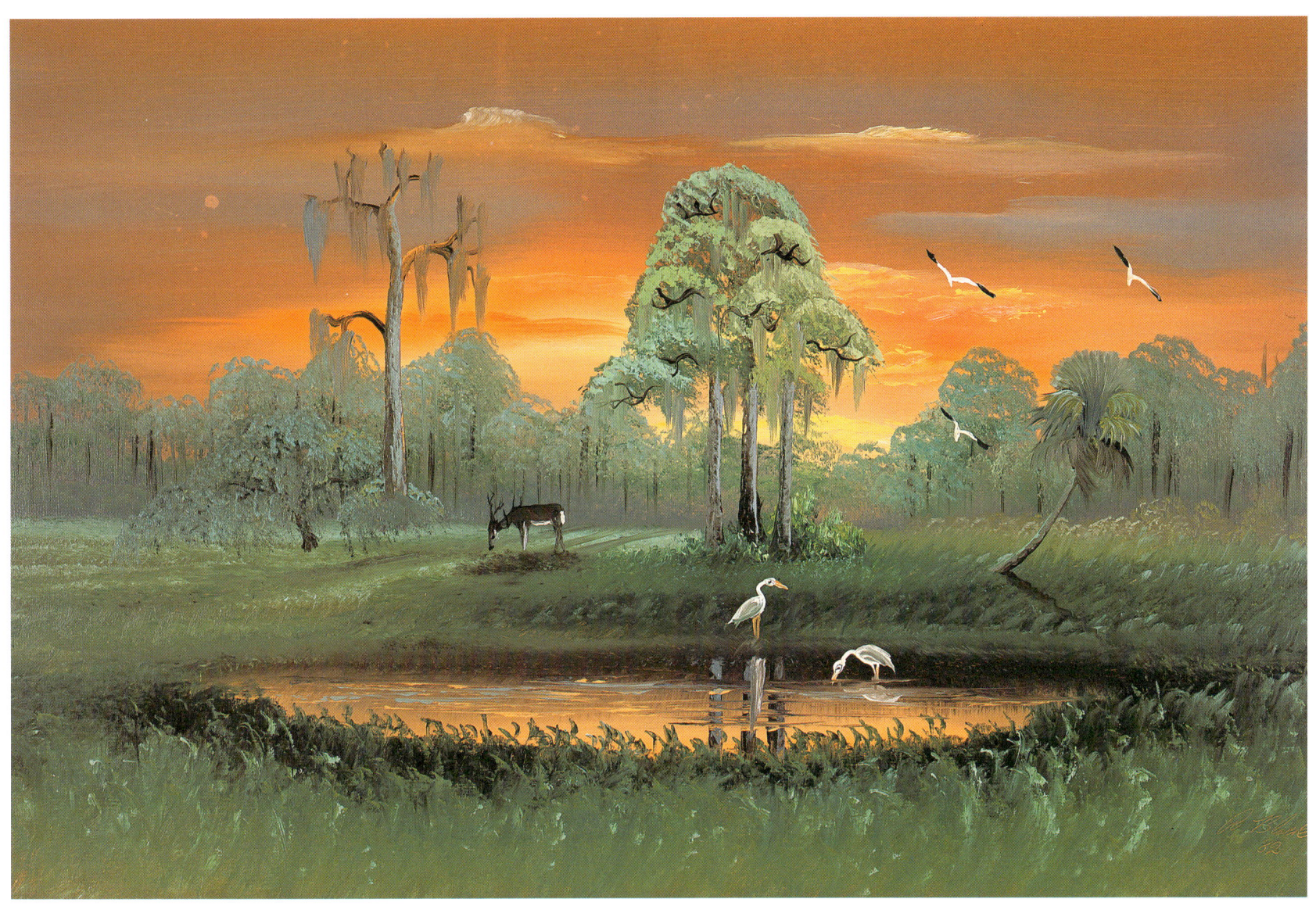

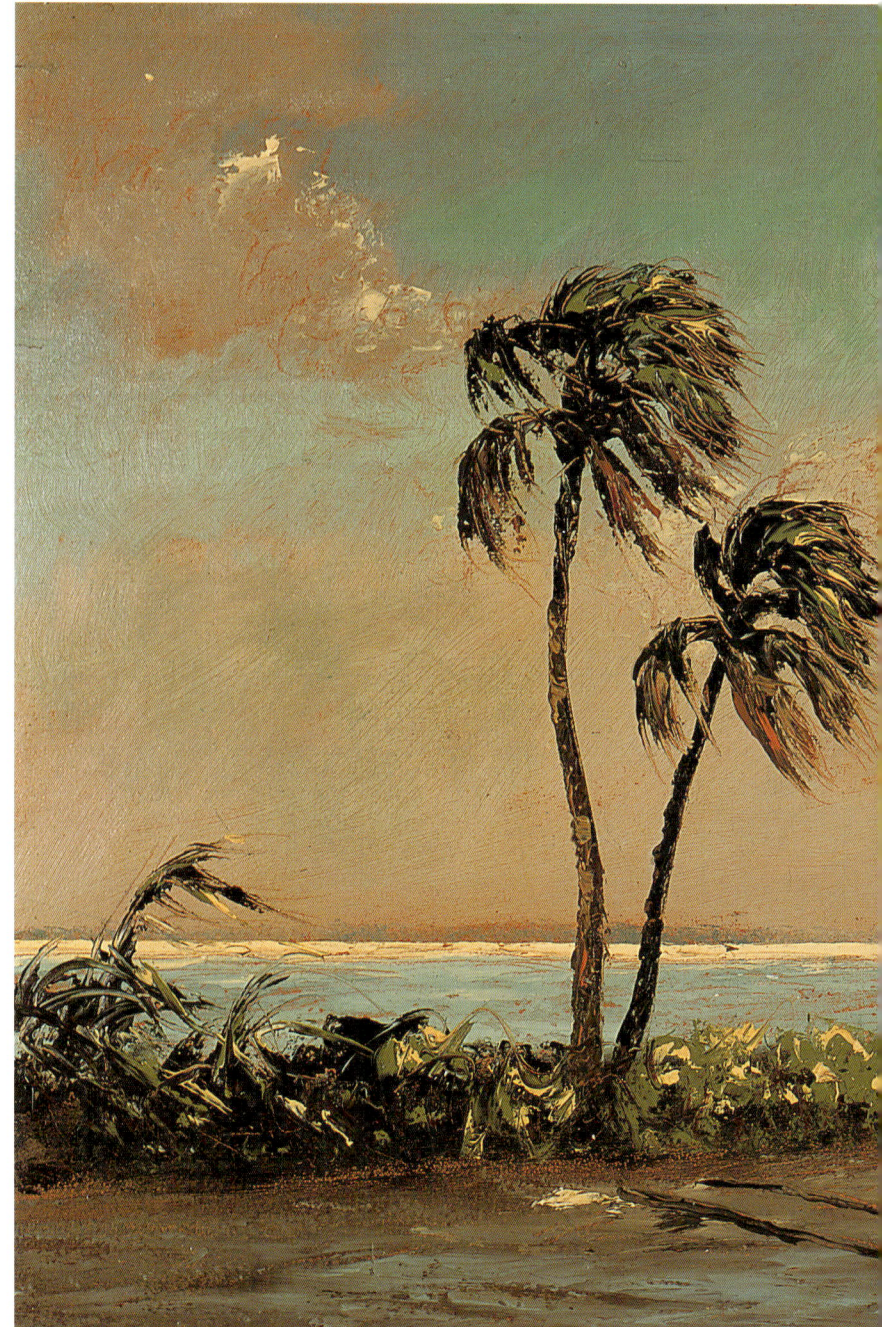

28. Harold Newton

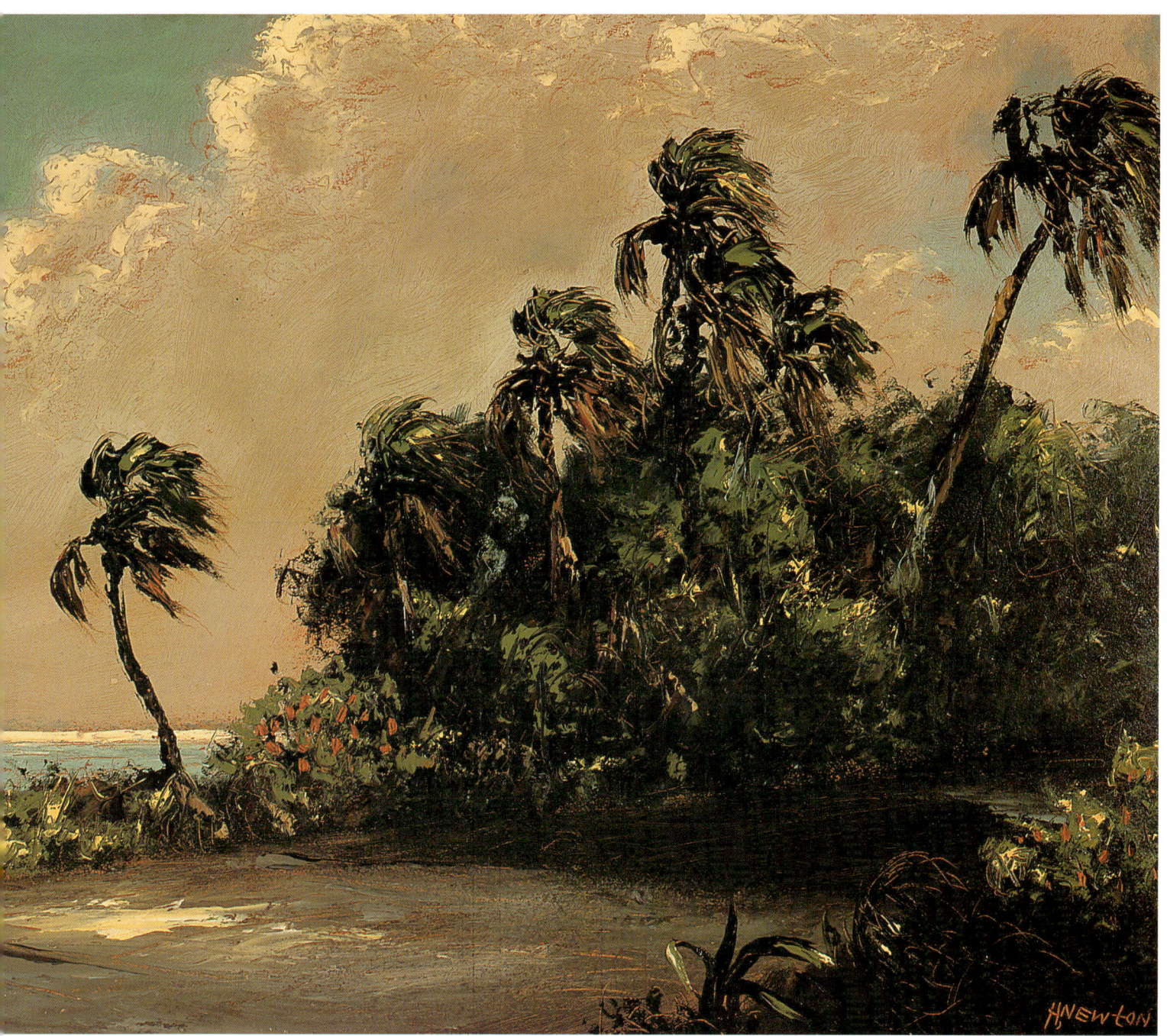

29. *Alfonso Moran*

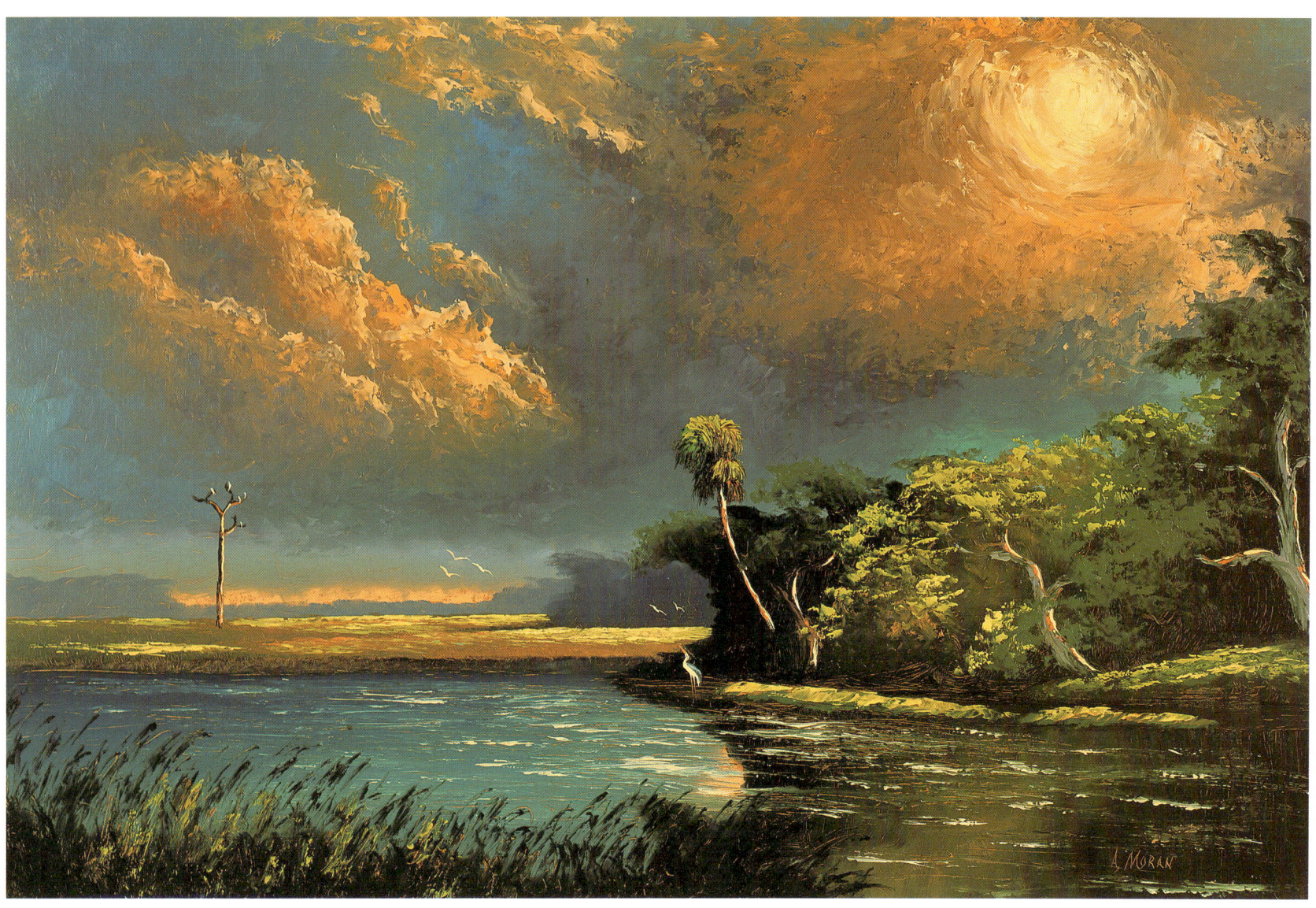

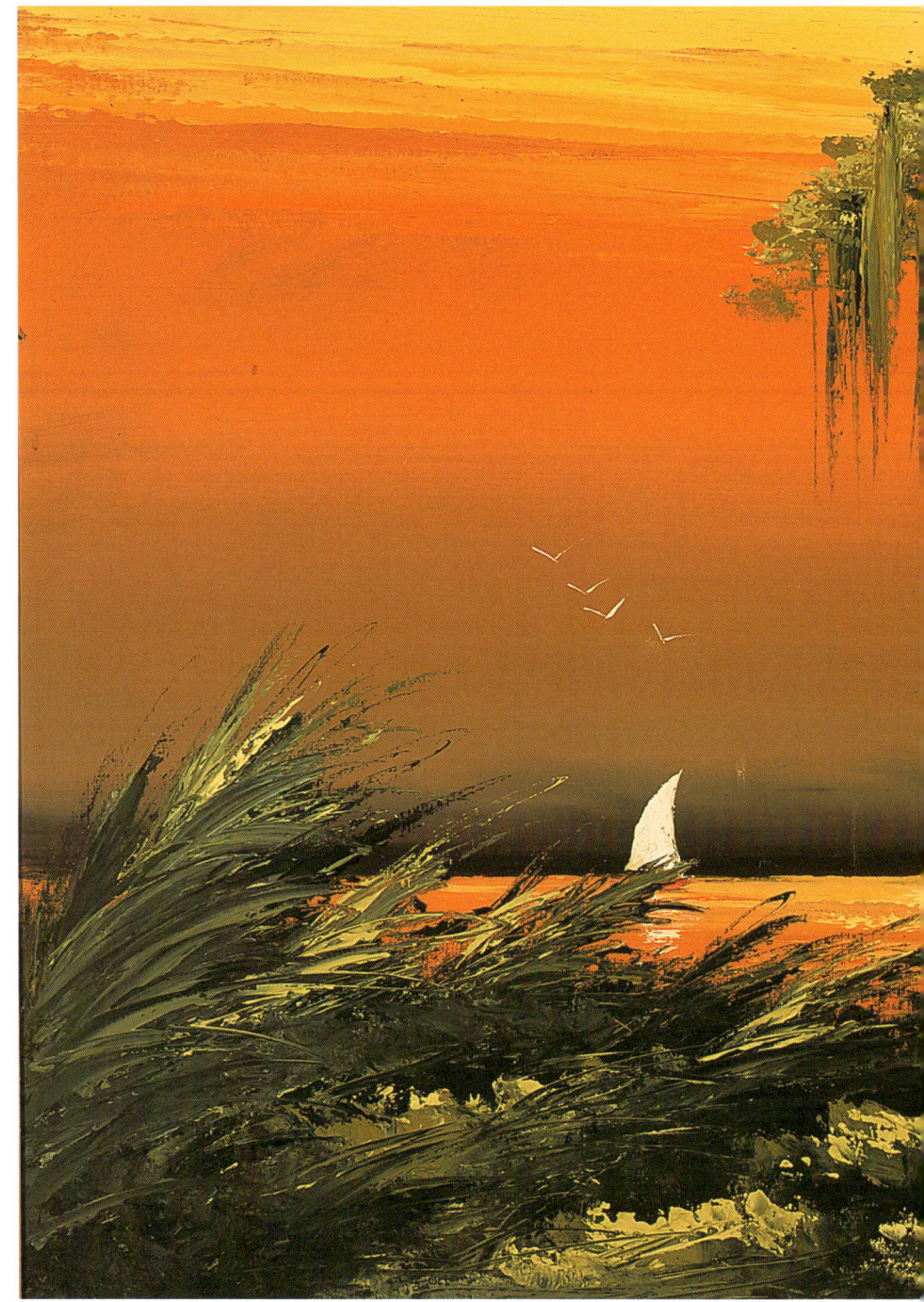

30. James Gibson

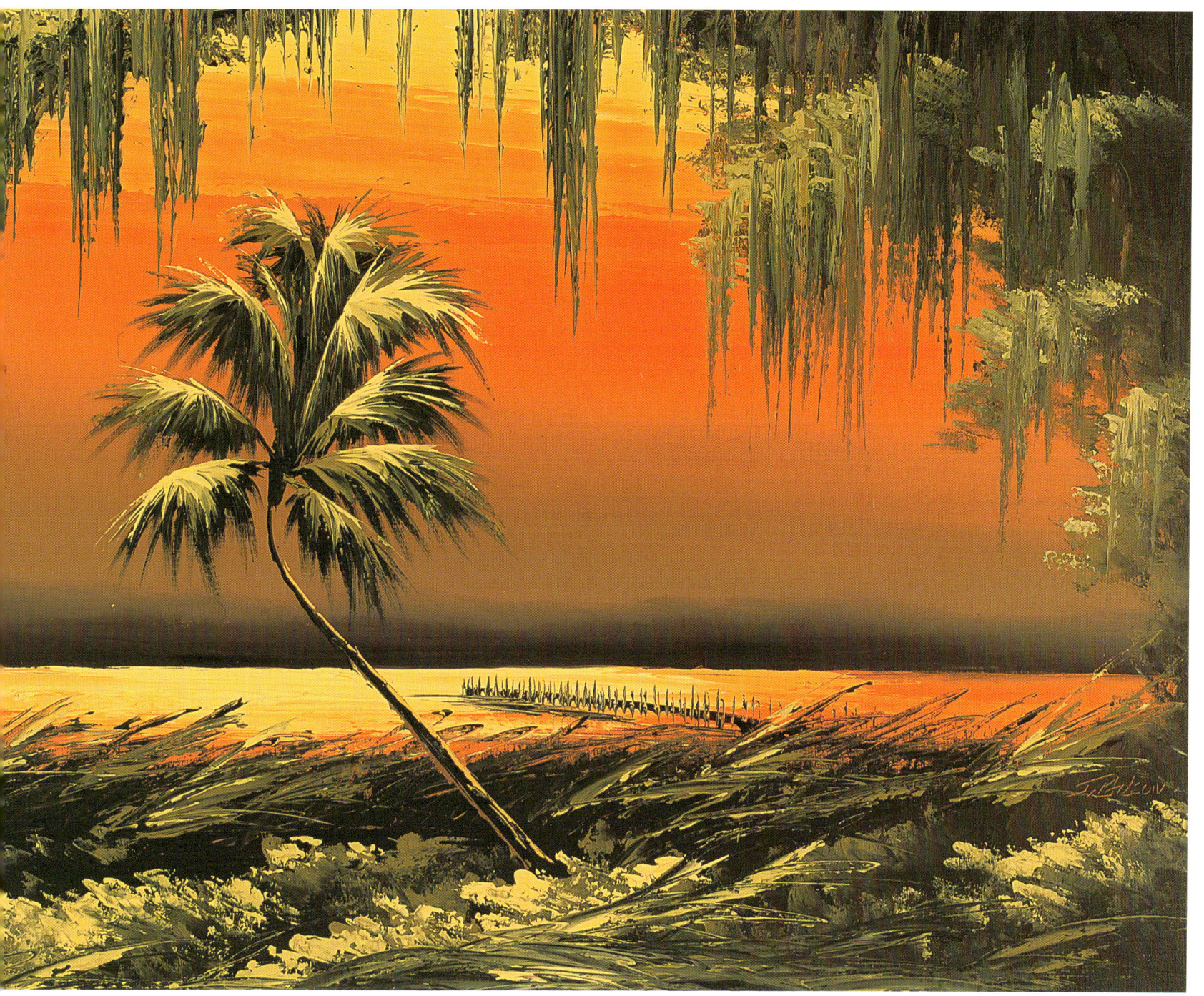

31. George Buckner

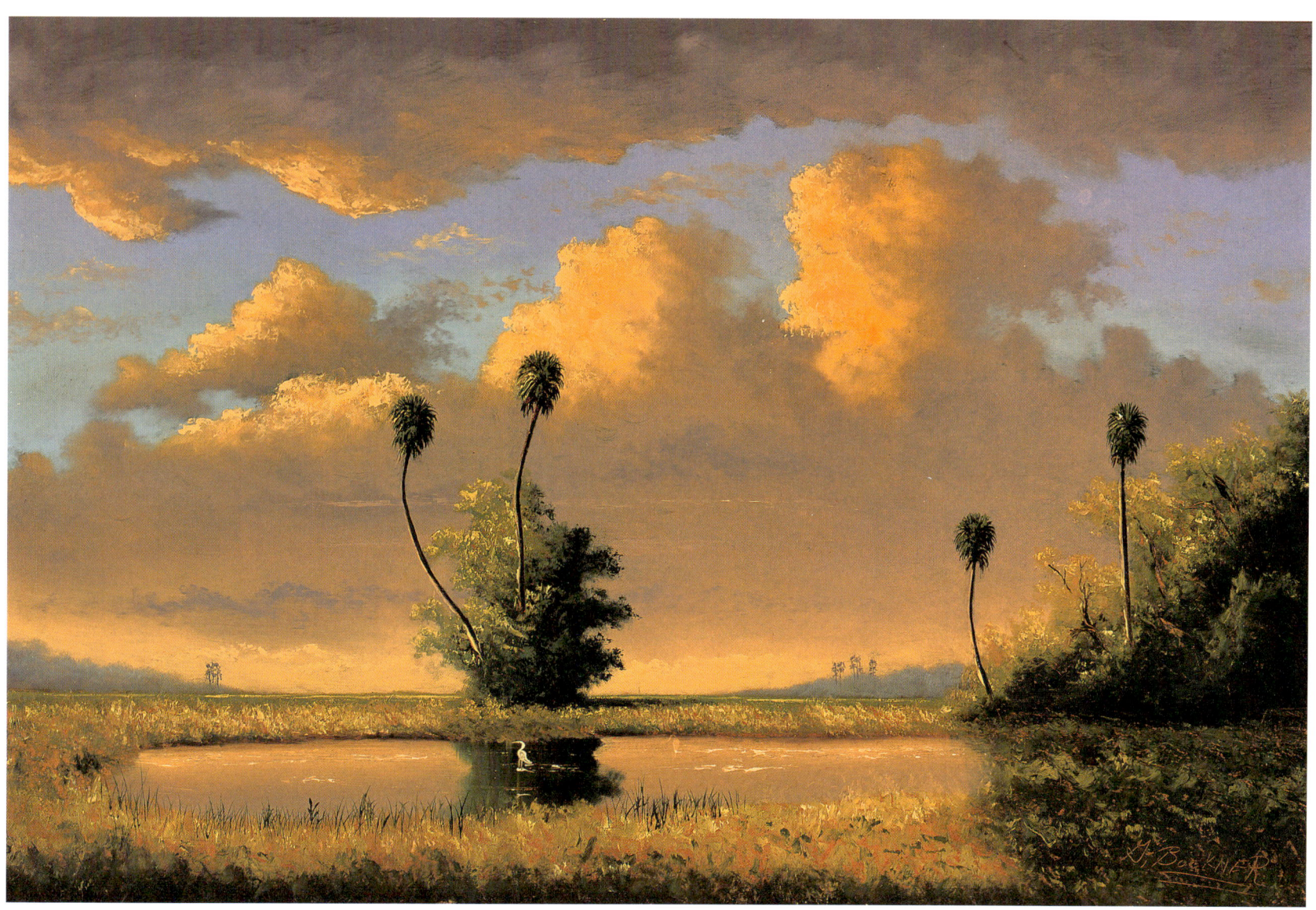

32. Roy McLendon

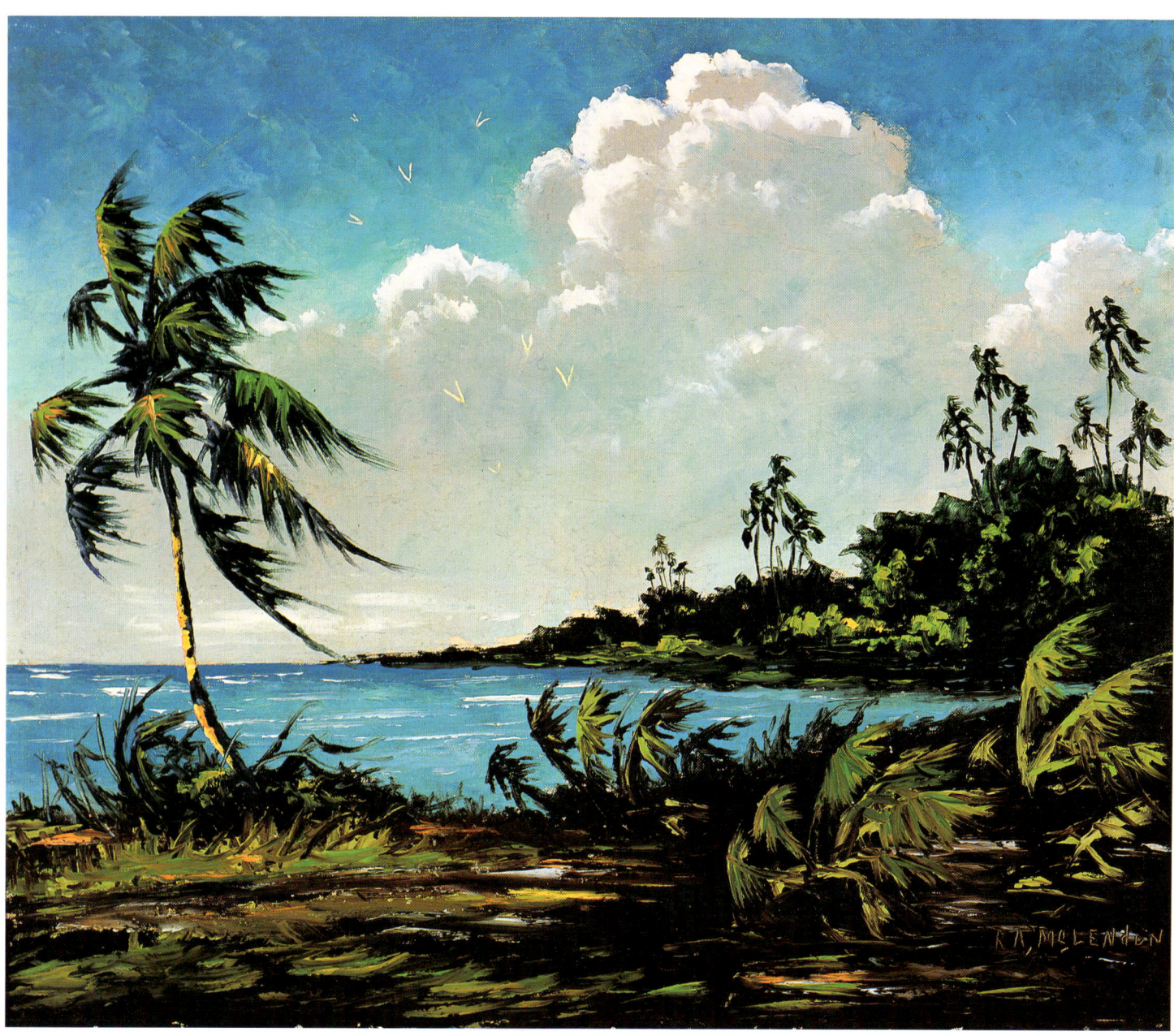

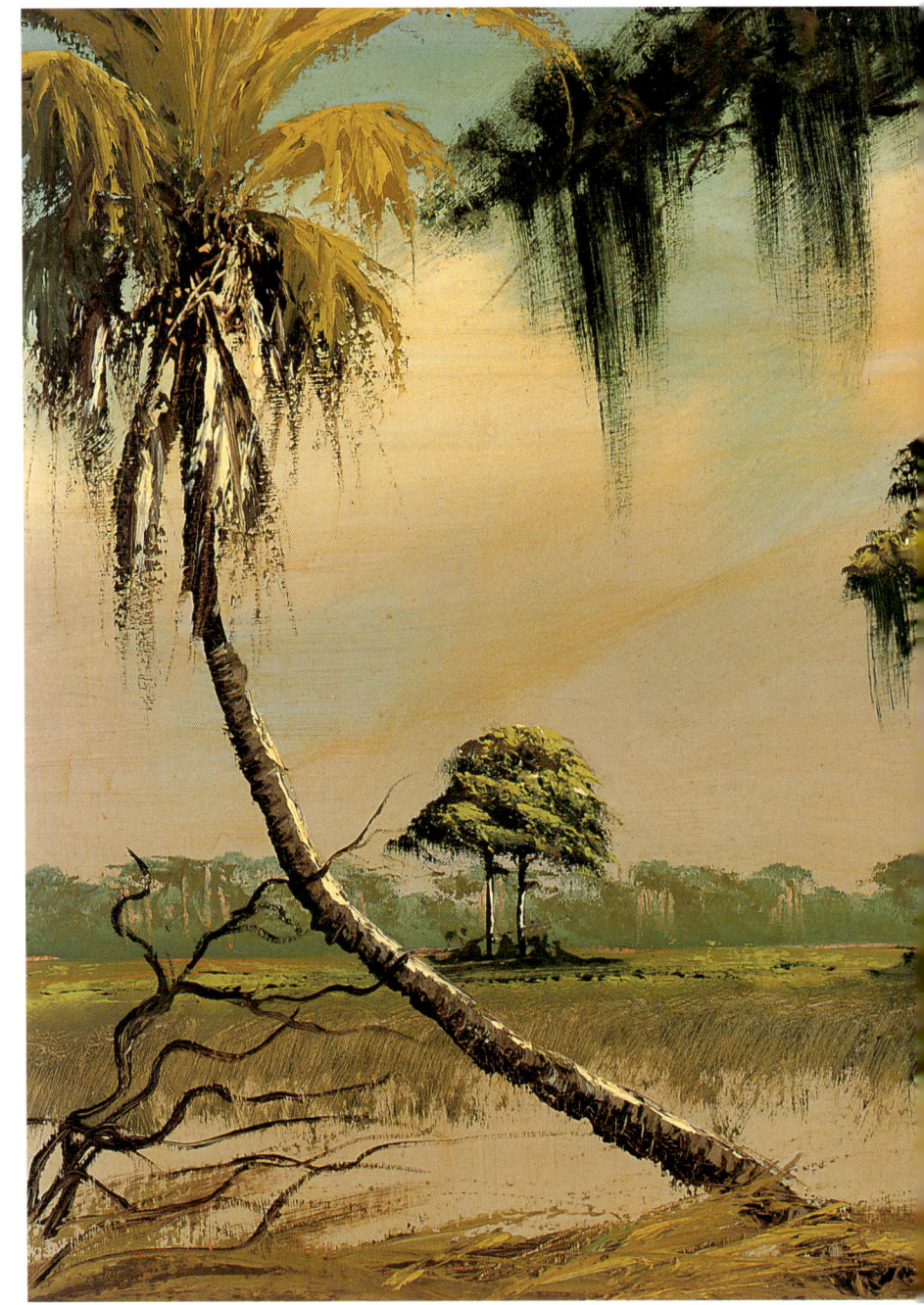

33. *Alfred Hair*

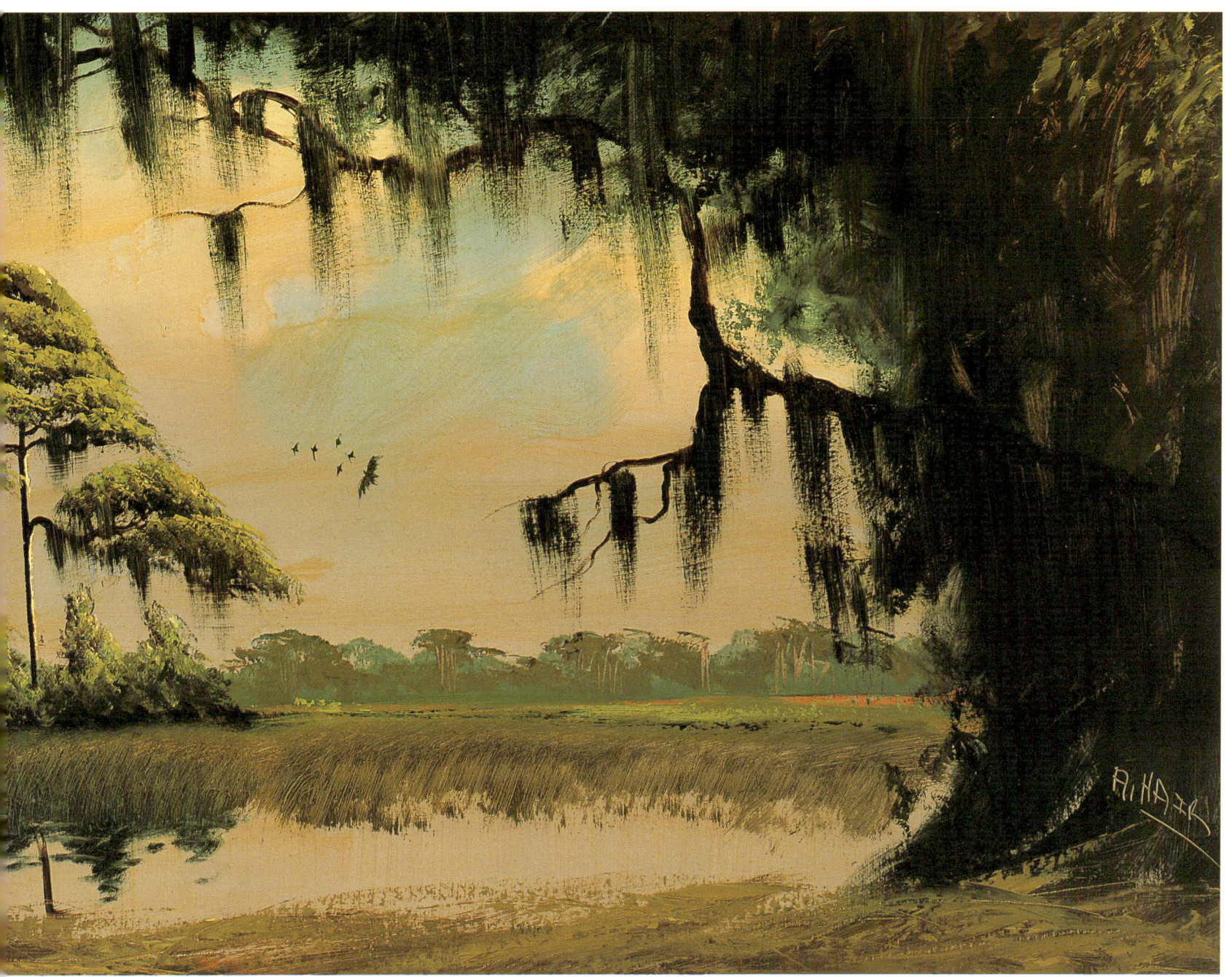

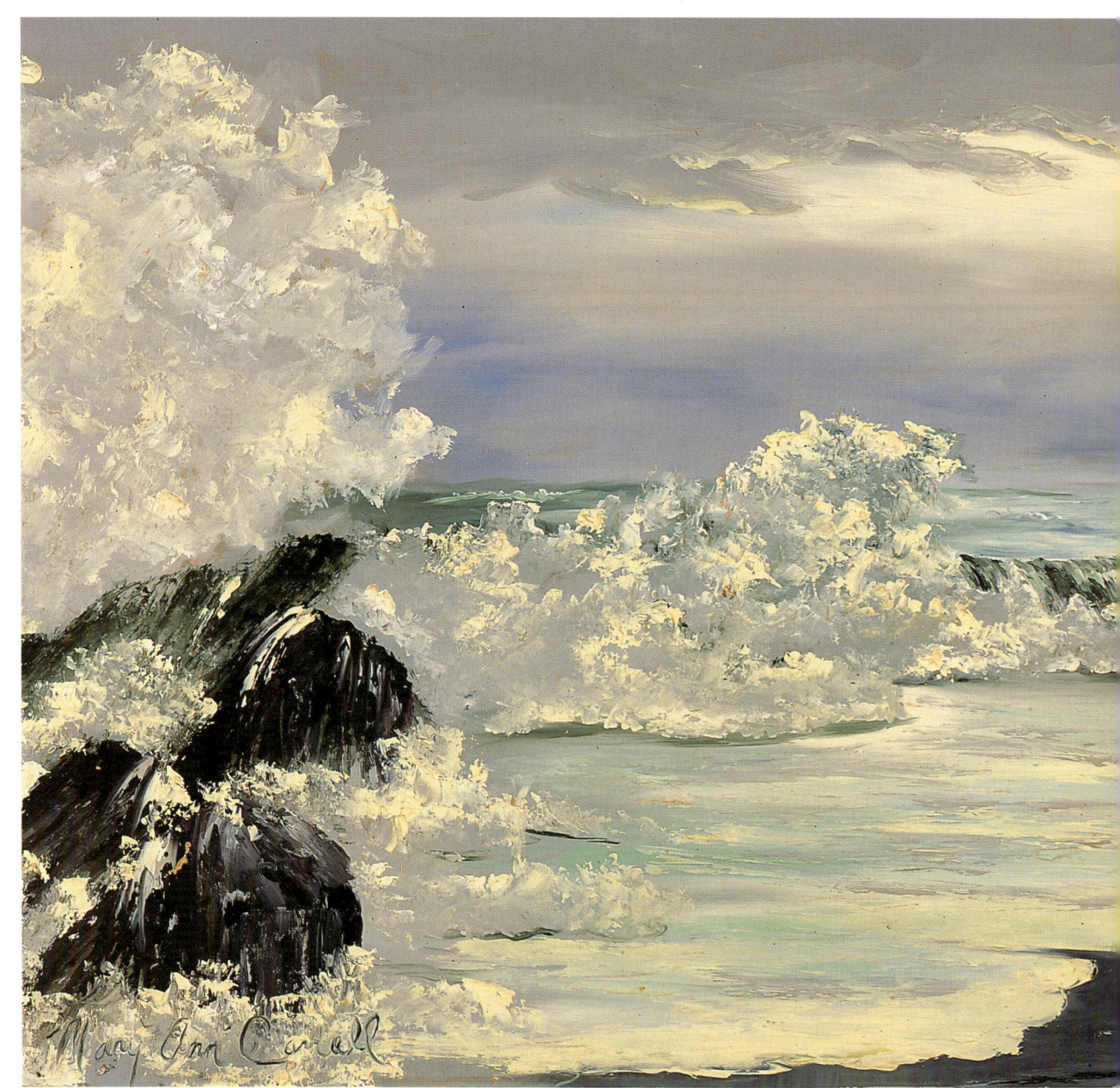

34. Mary Ann Carroll

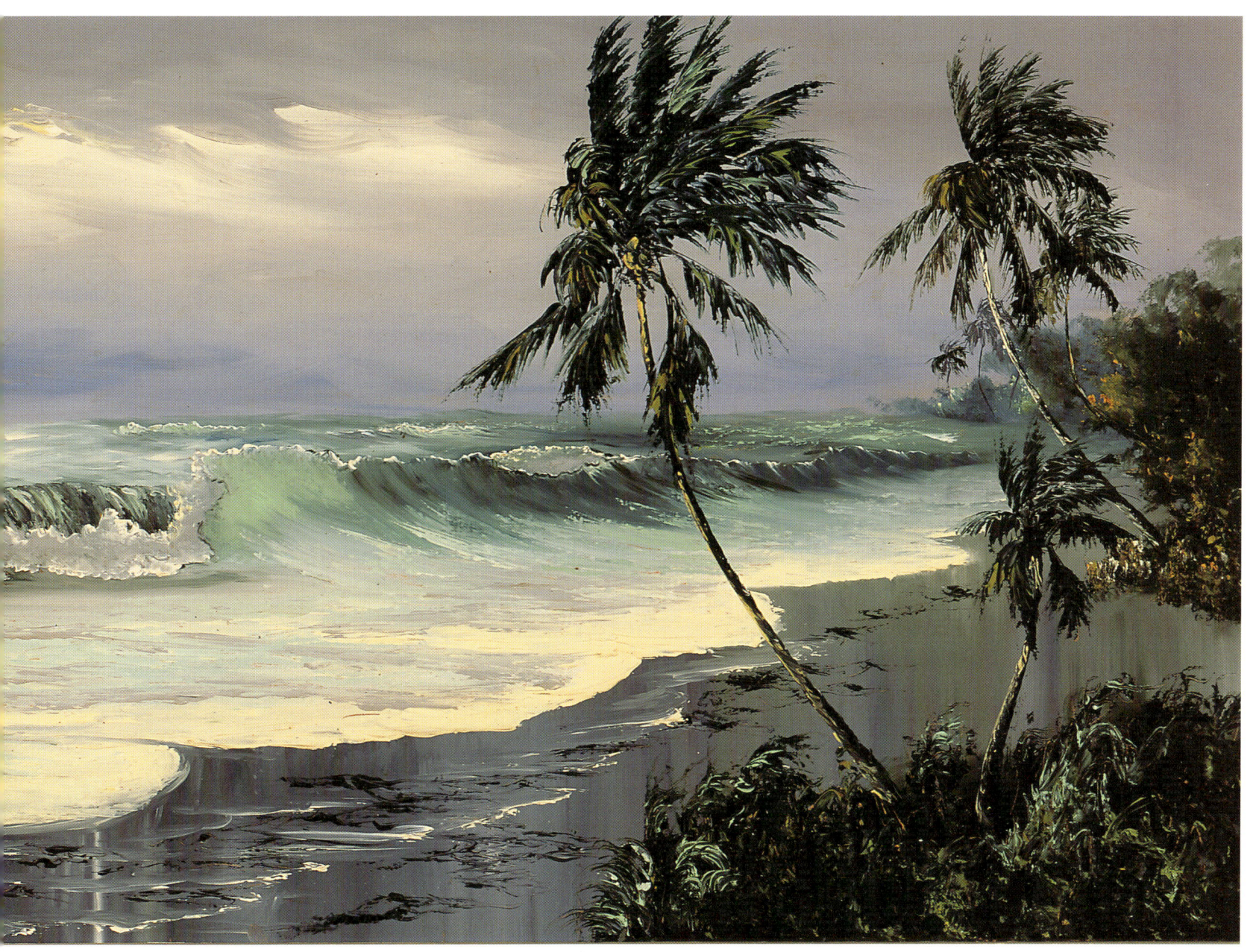

35. James Gibson

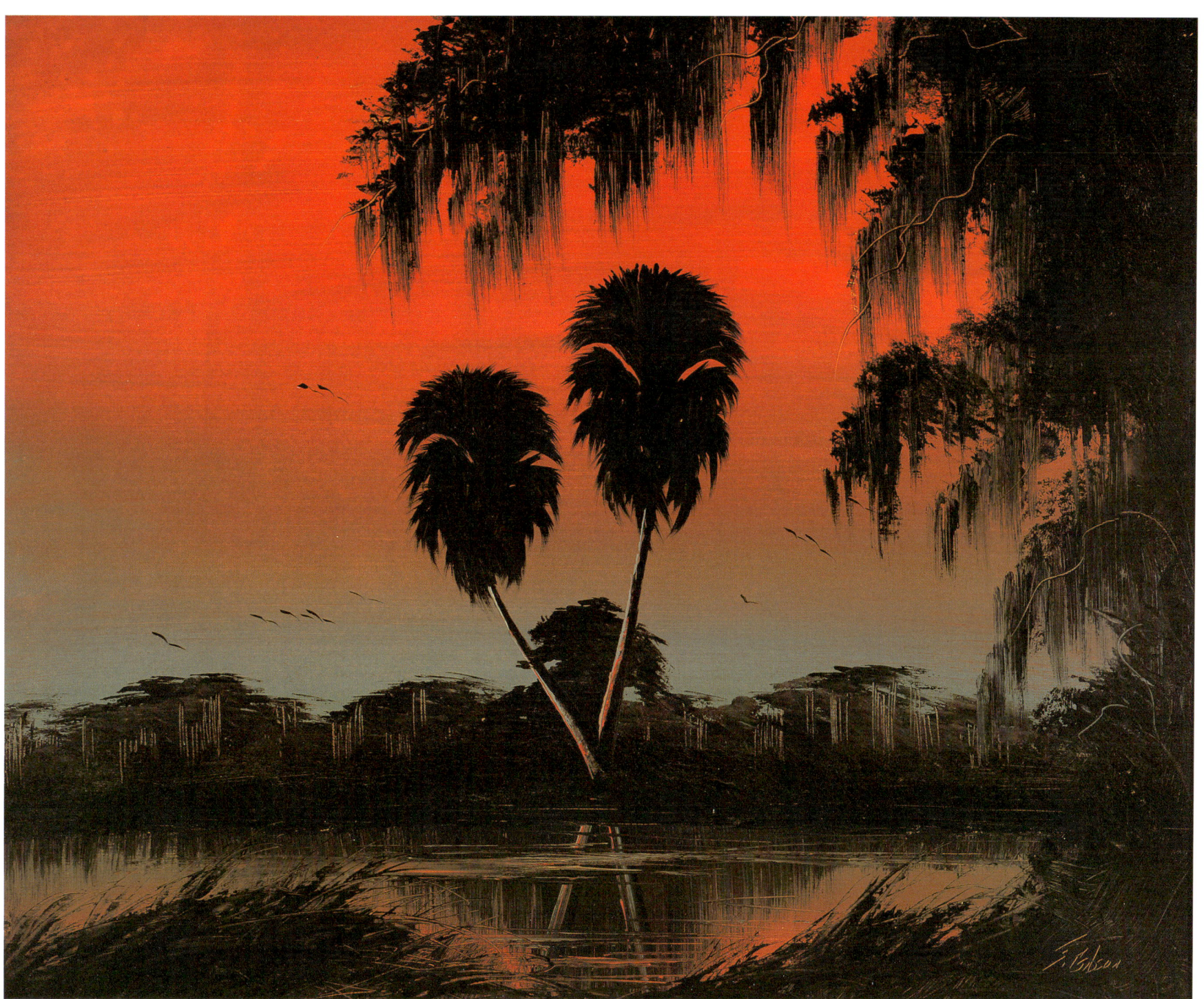

36. Mary Ann Carroll

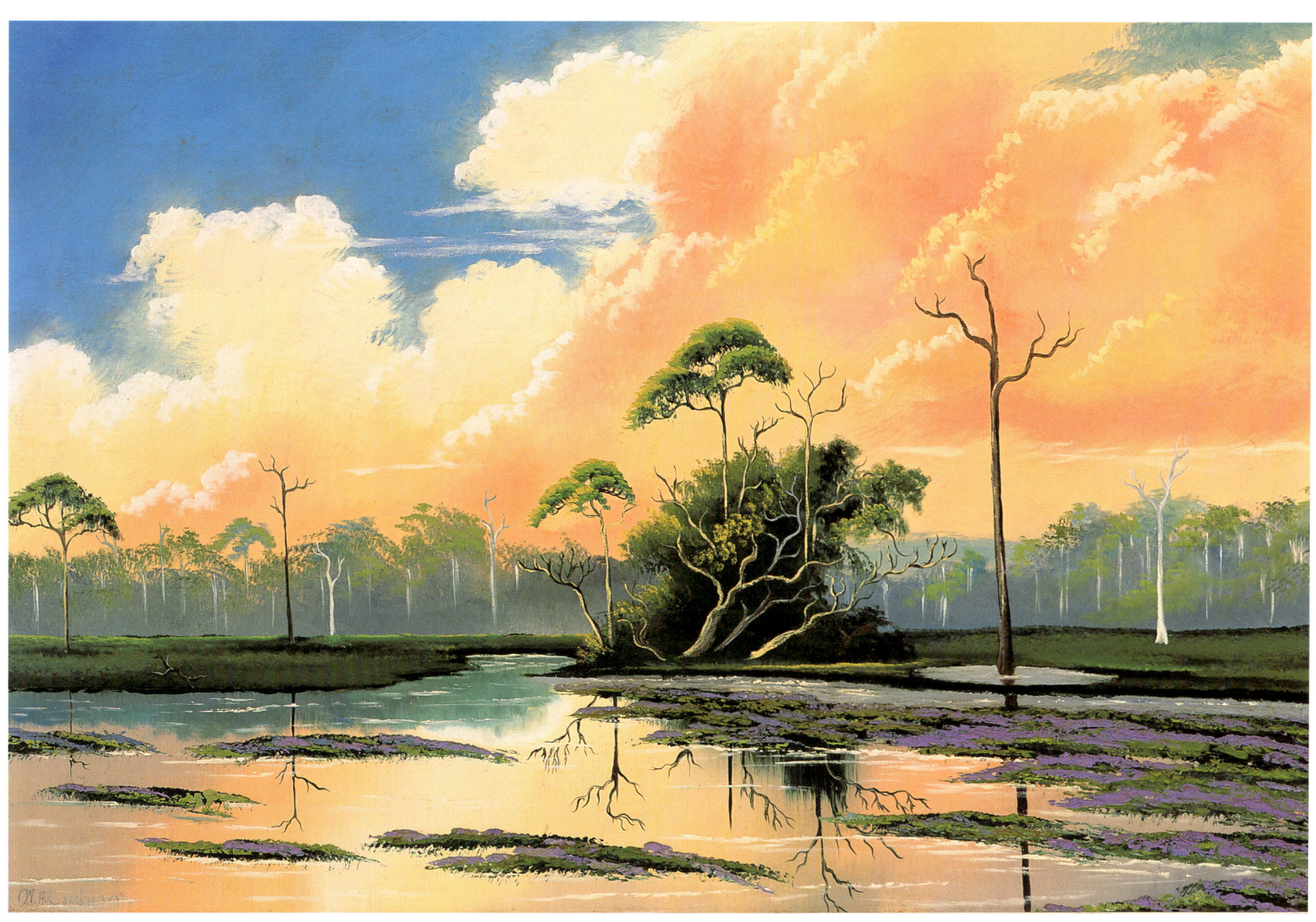

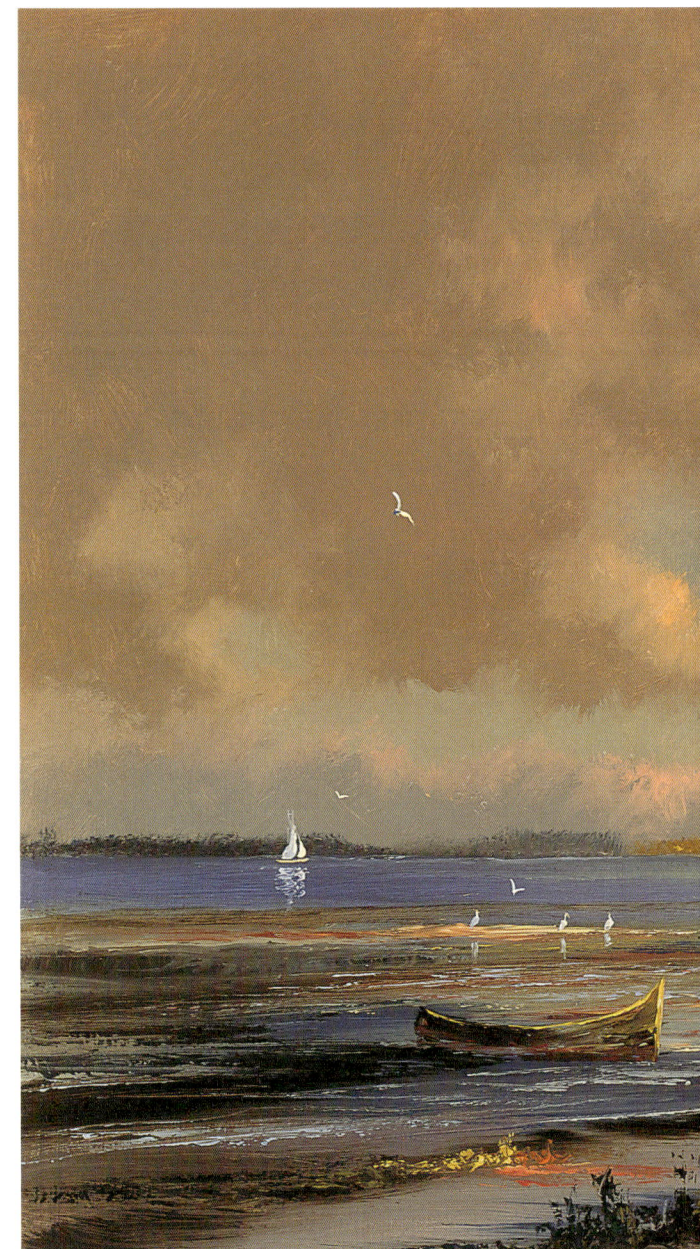

37. Harold Newton

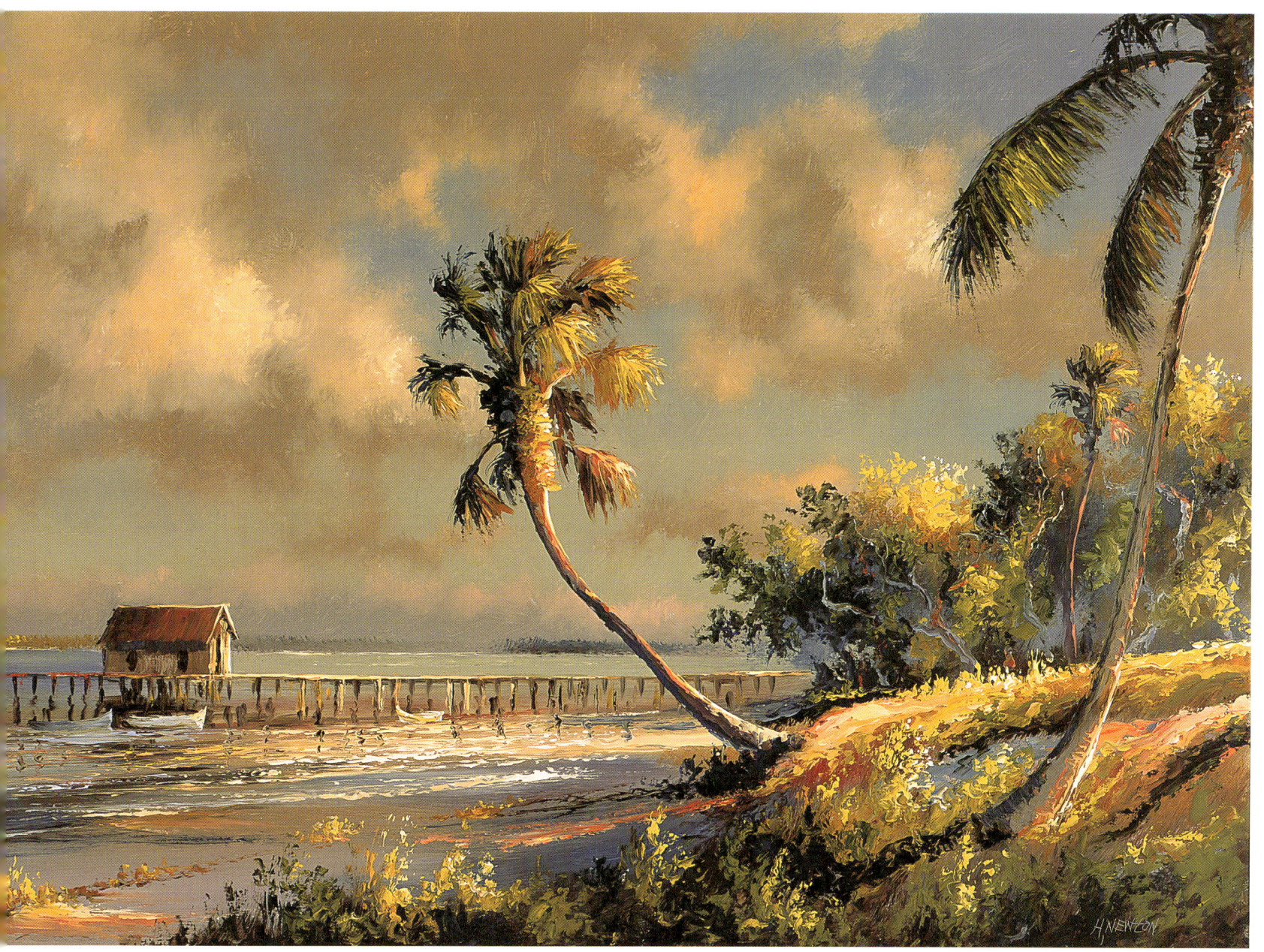

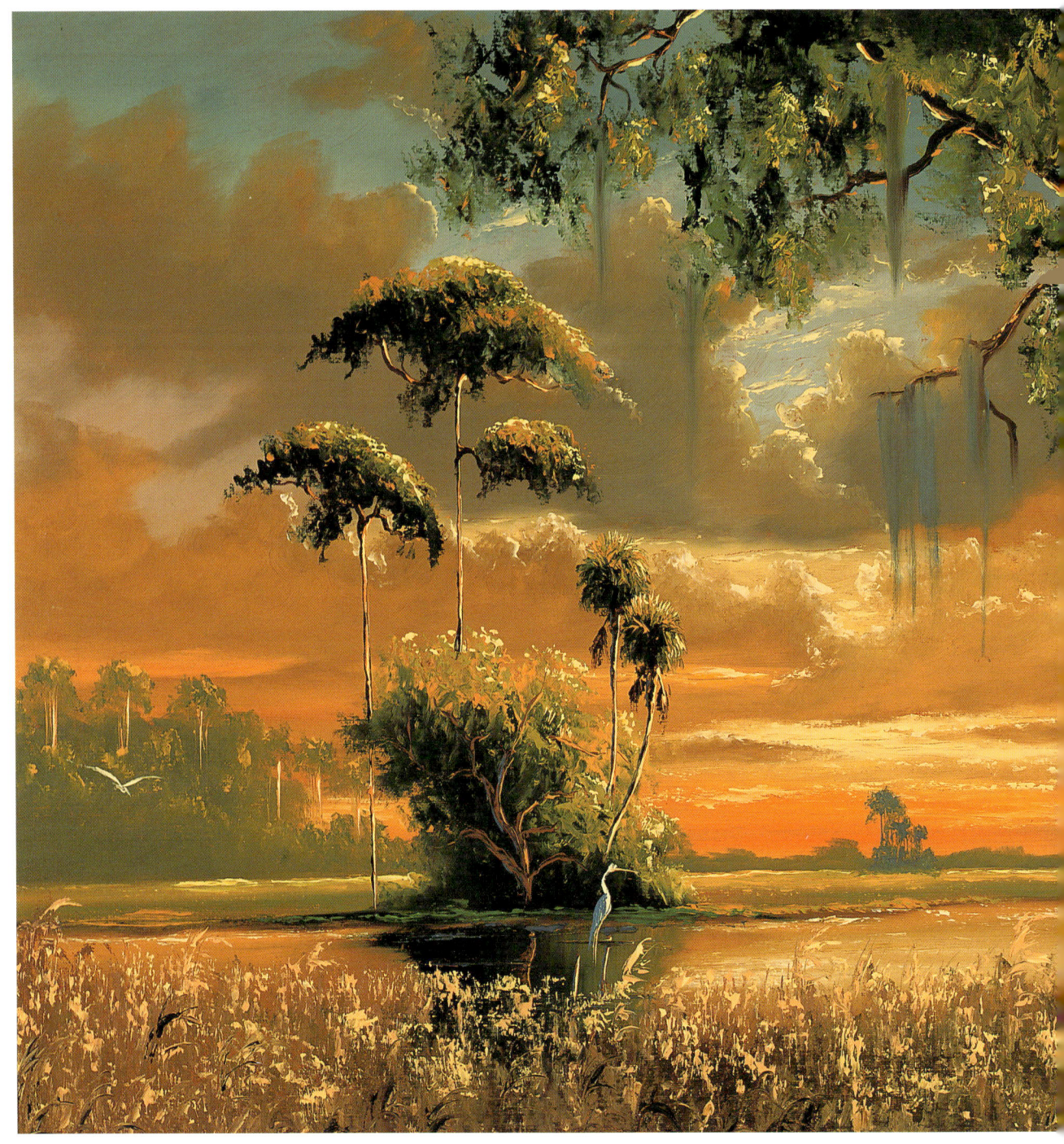

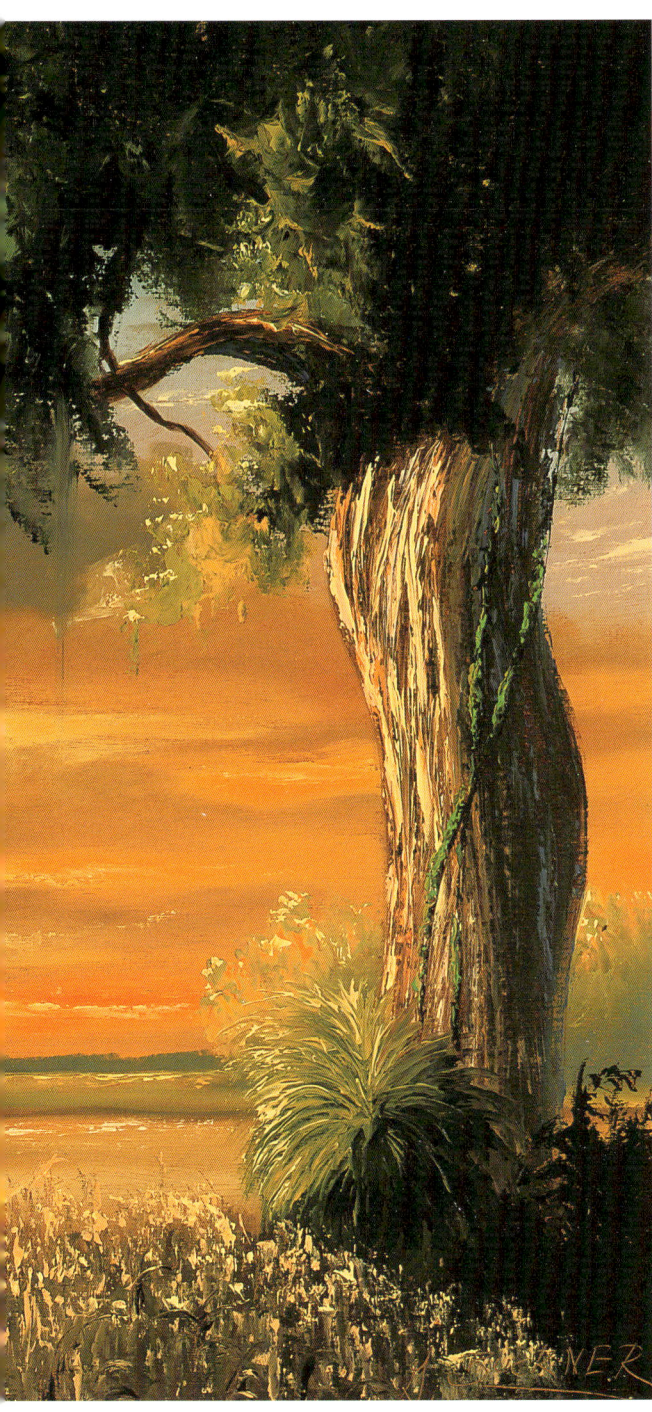

38. George Buckner

39. *Willie Daniels*

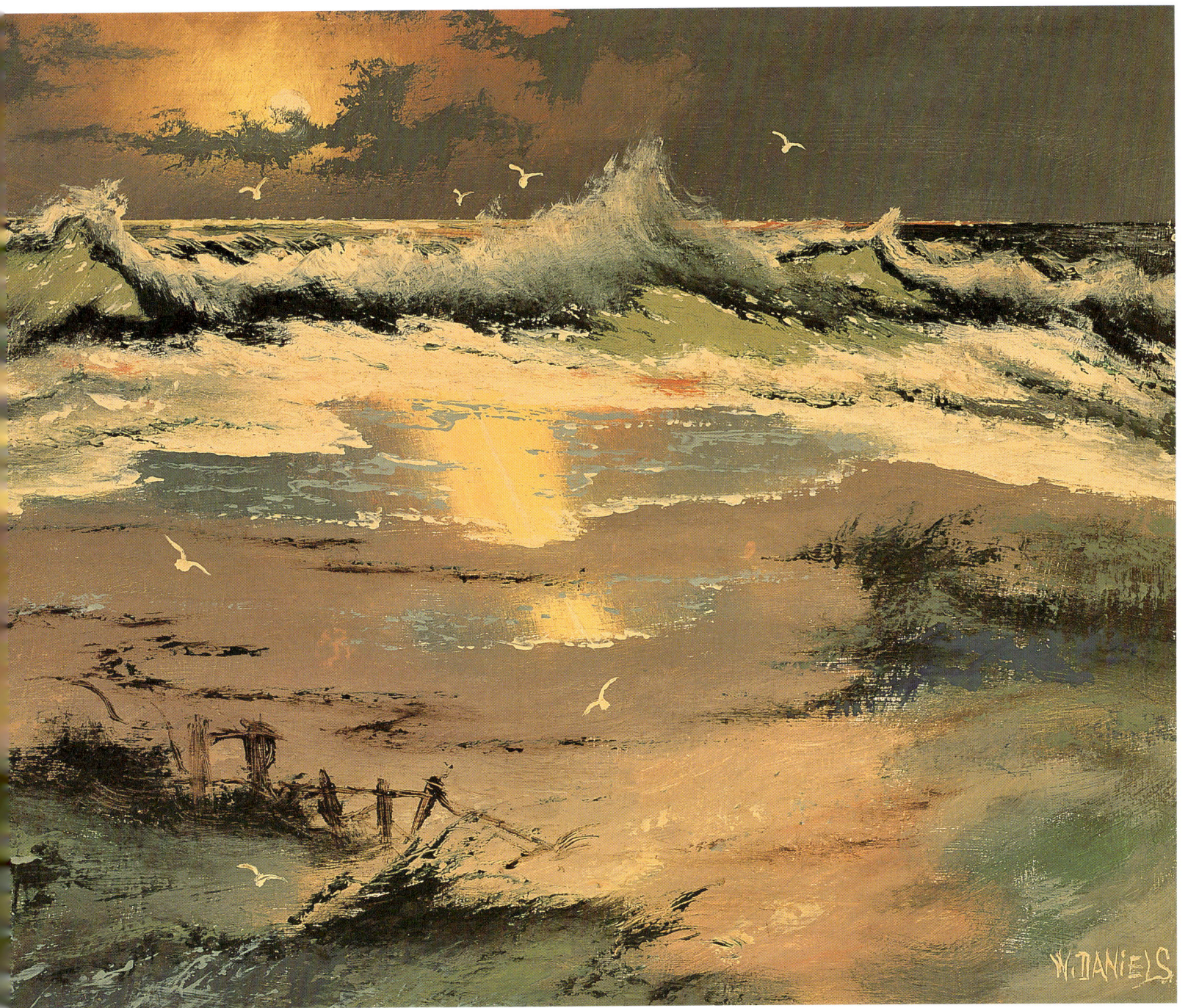

40. Mary Ann Carroll

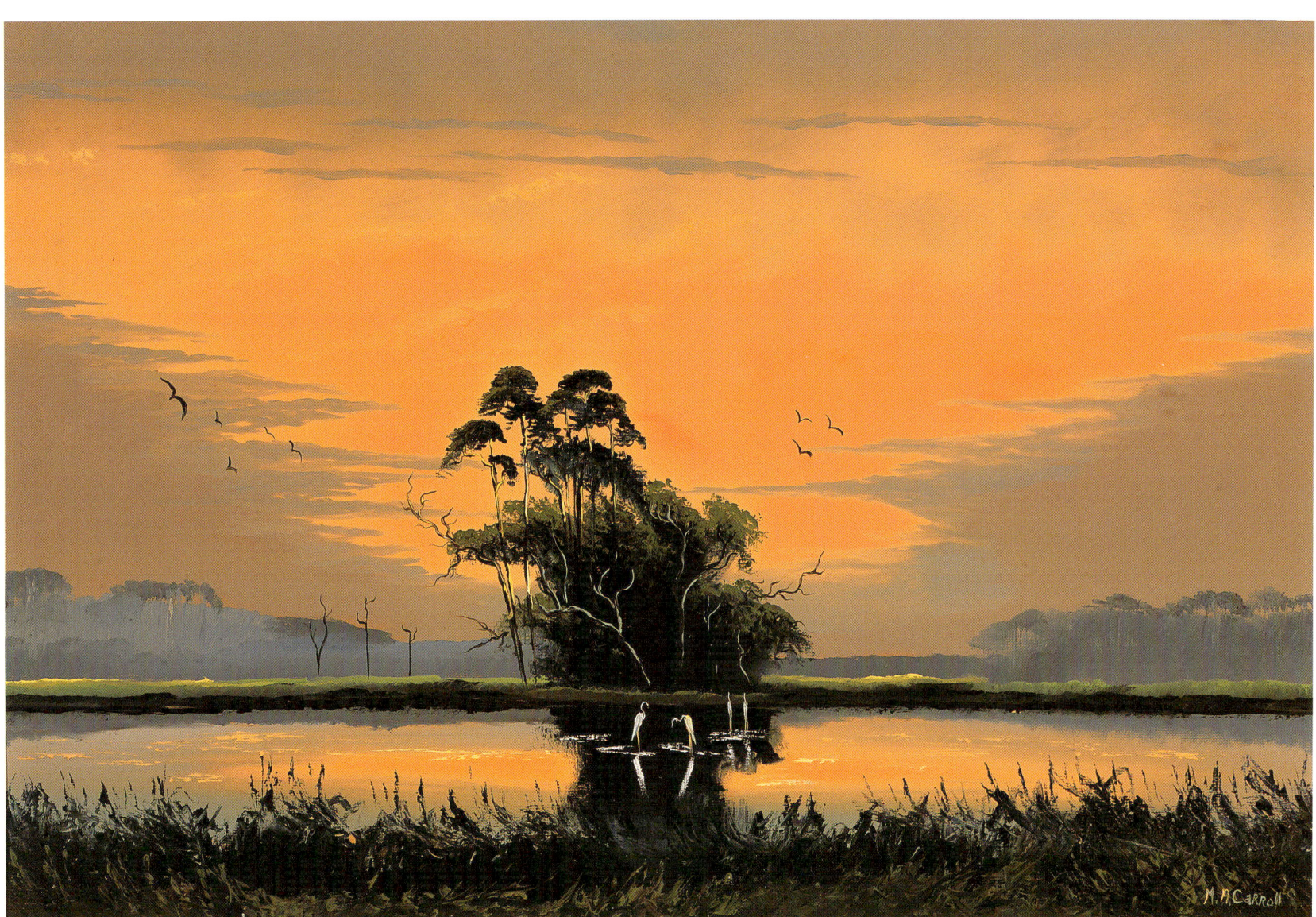

41. *Alfred Hair*

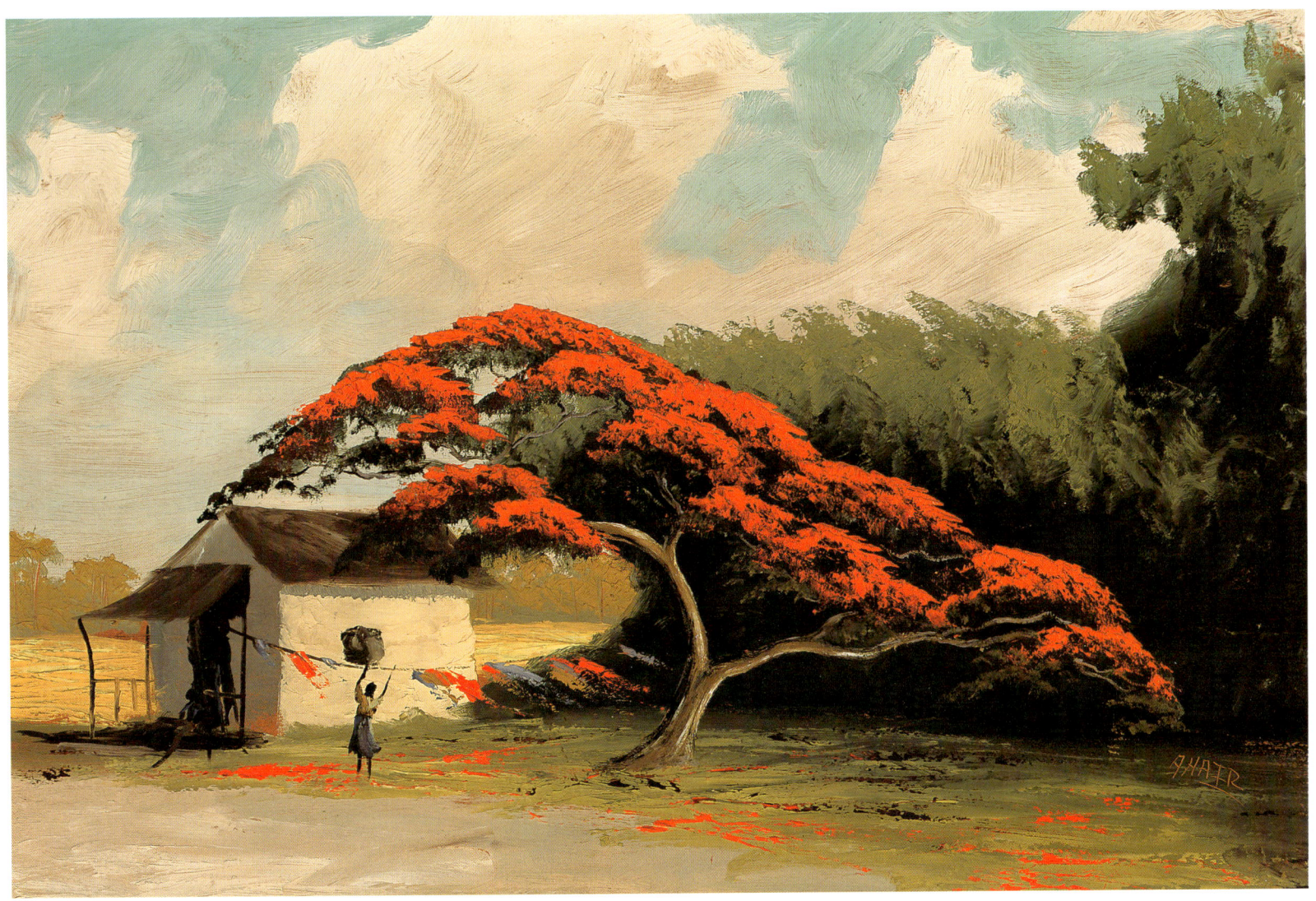

42.Willie Reagan

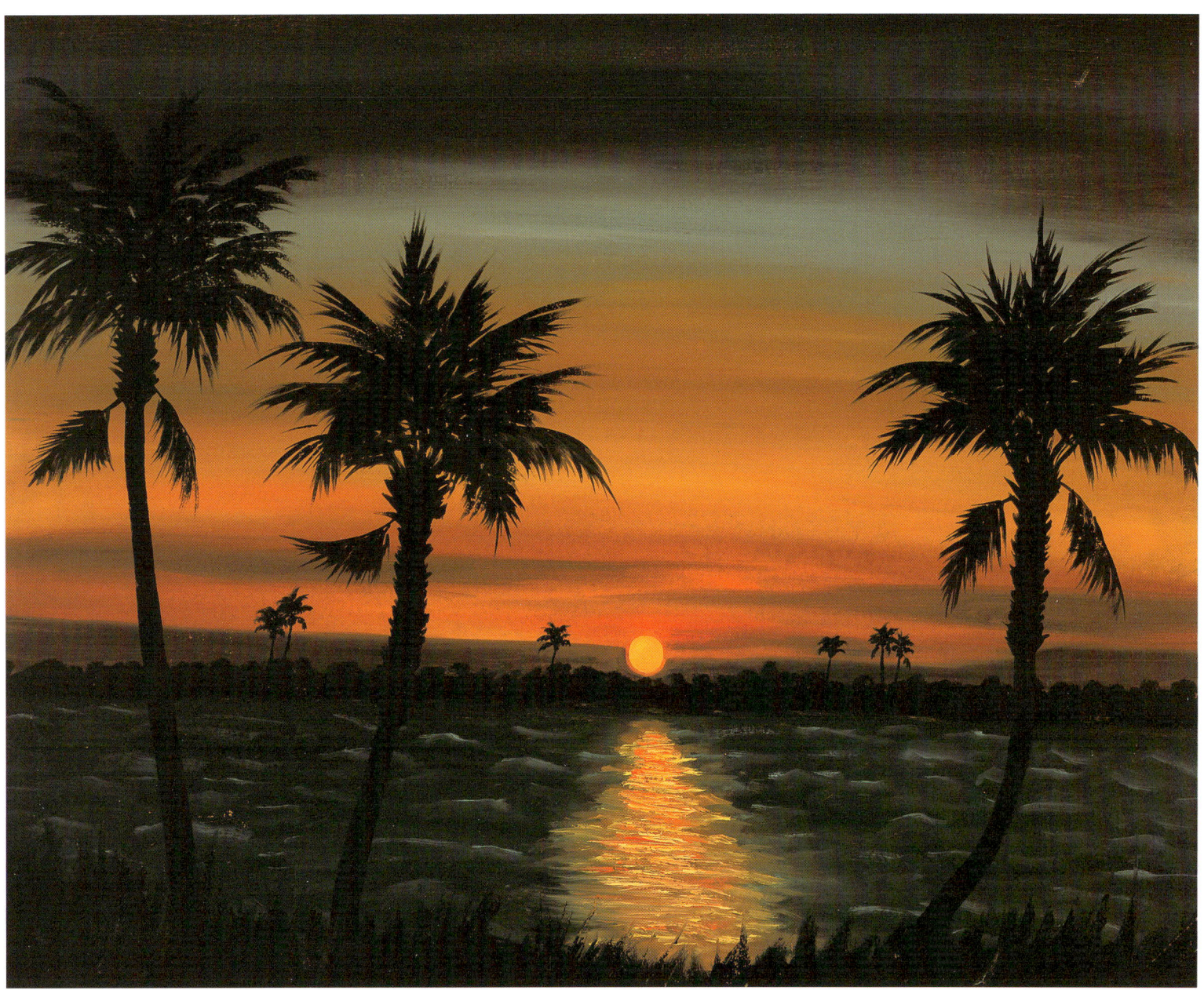

43. Harold Newton

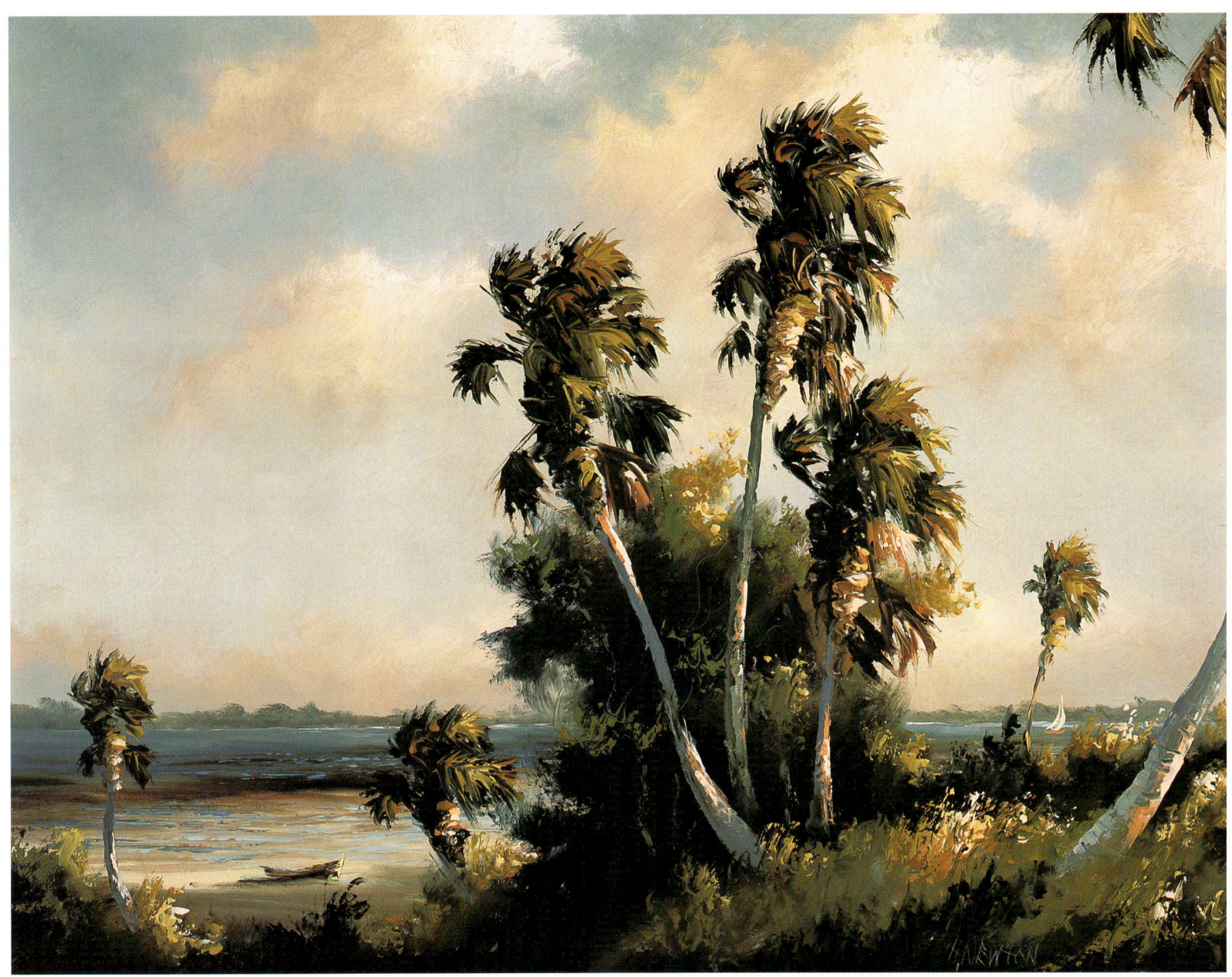

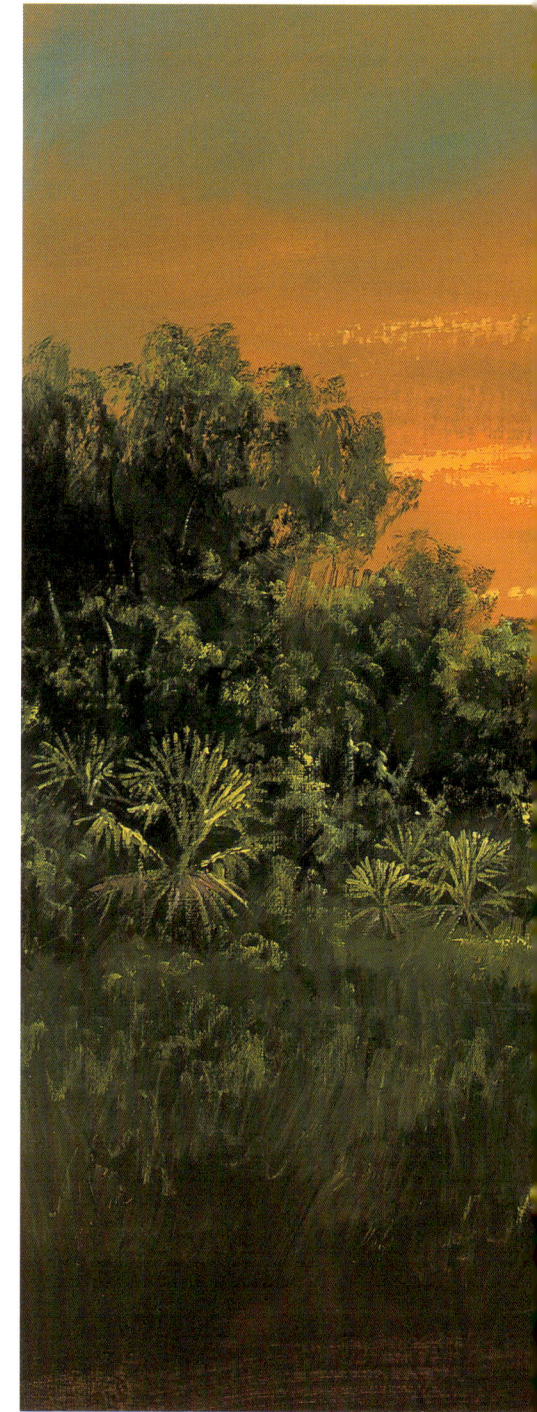

44. Roy McLendon

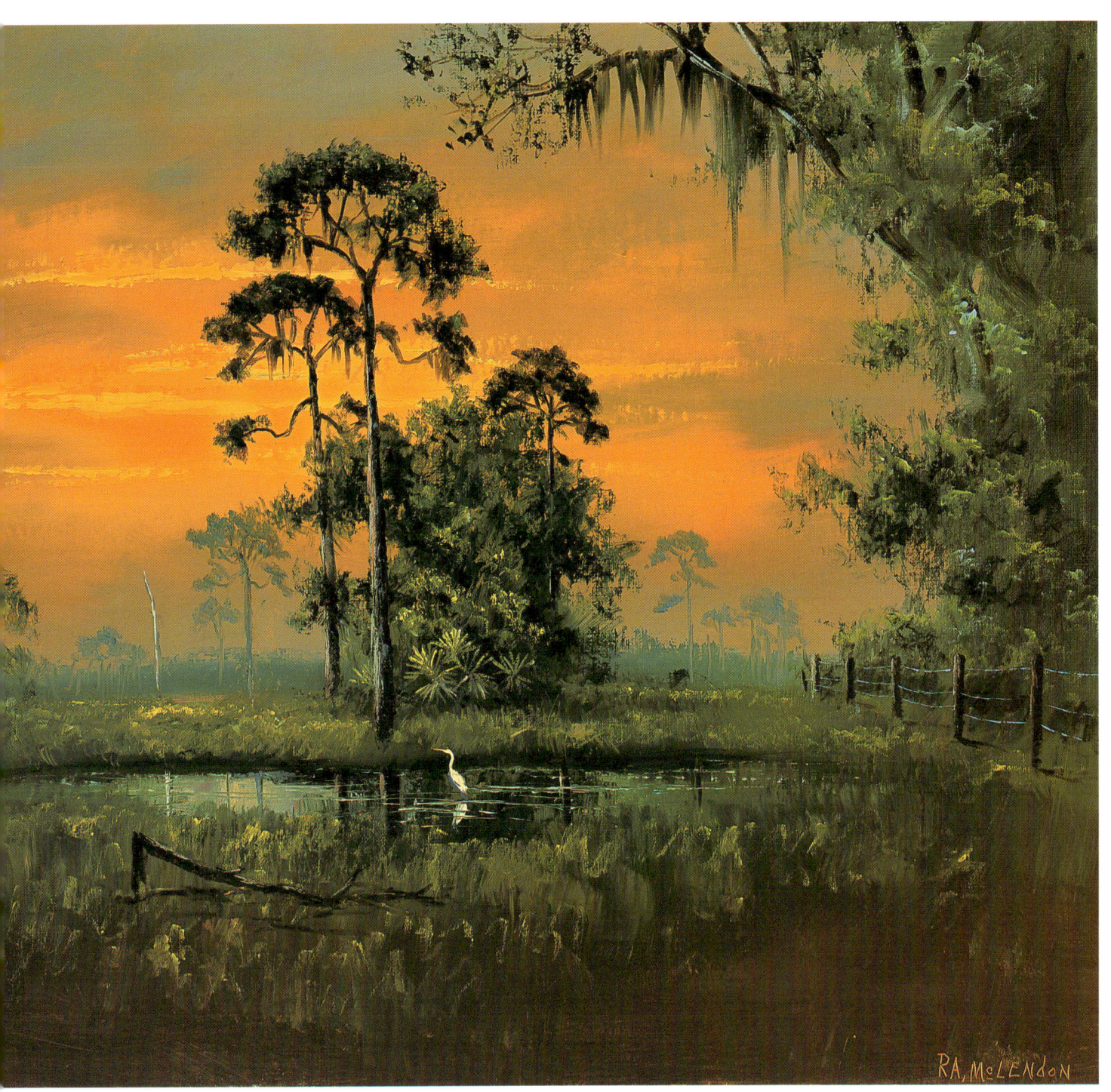

45. Hezekiah Baker

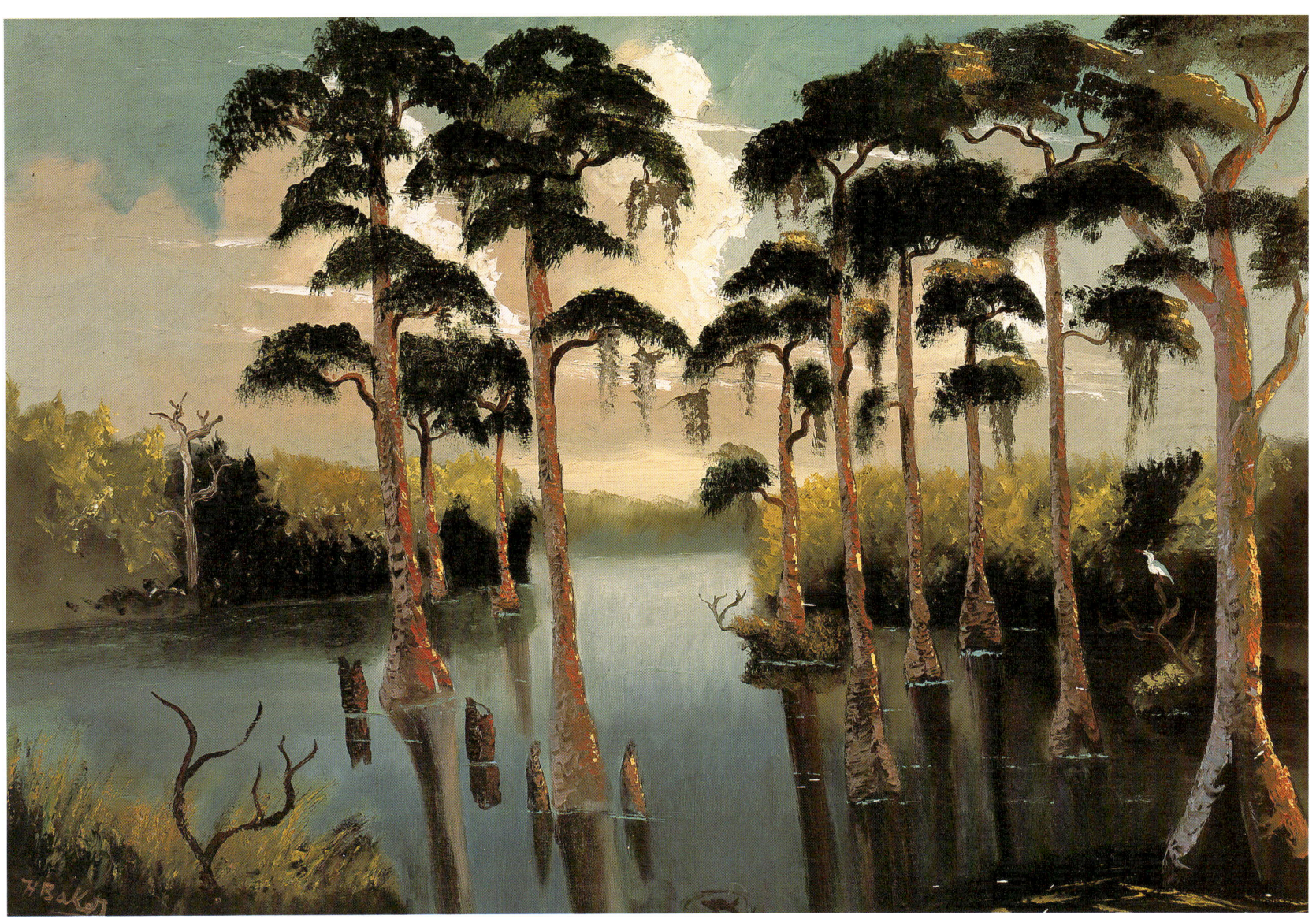

46. Sam Newton

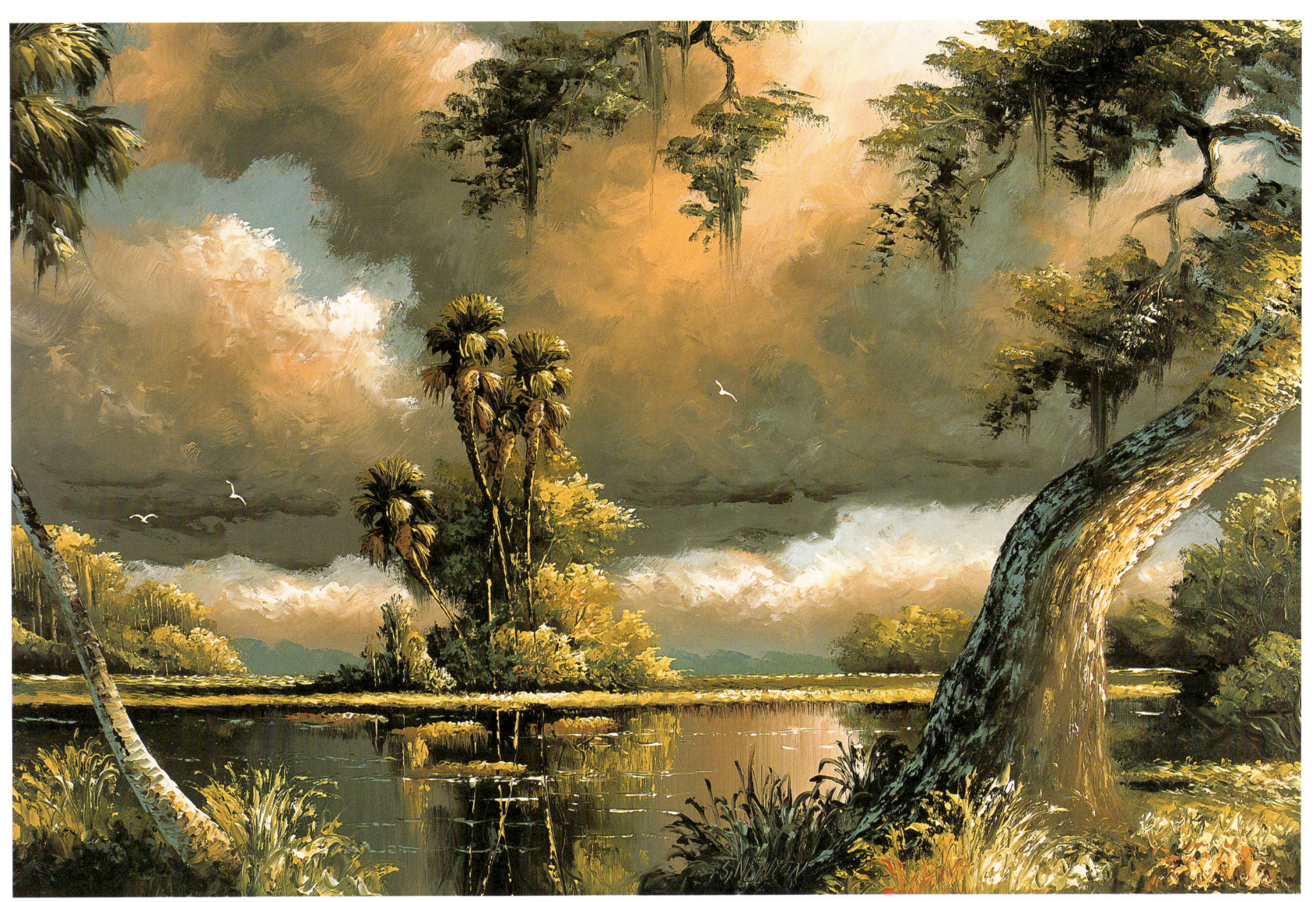

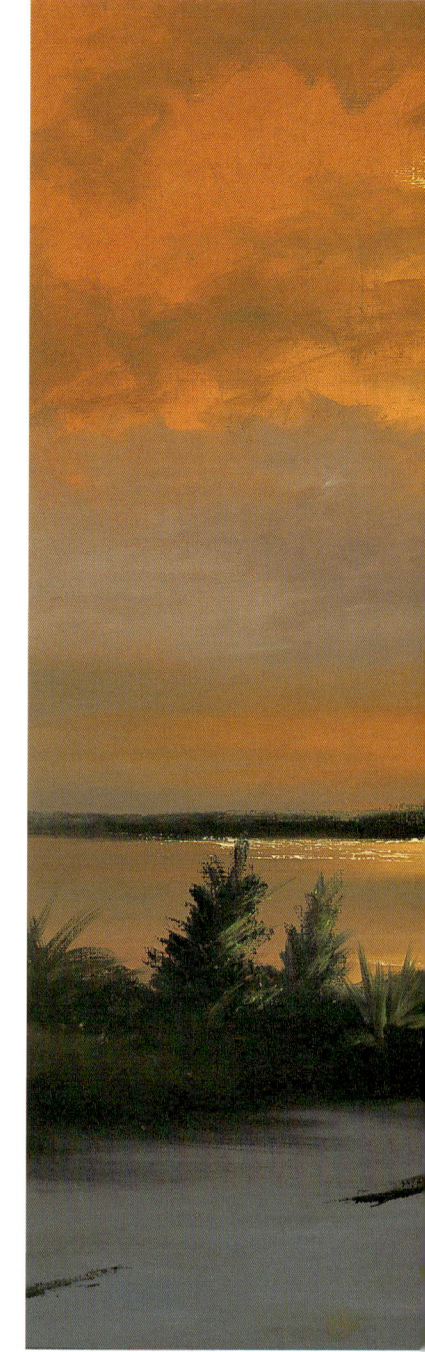

47. Livingston Roberts

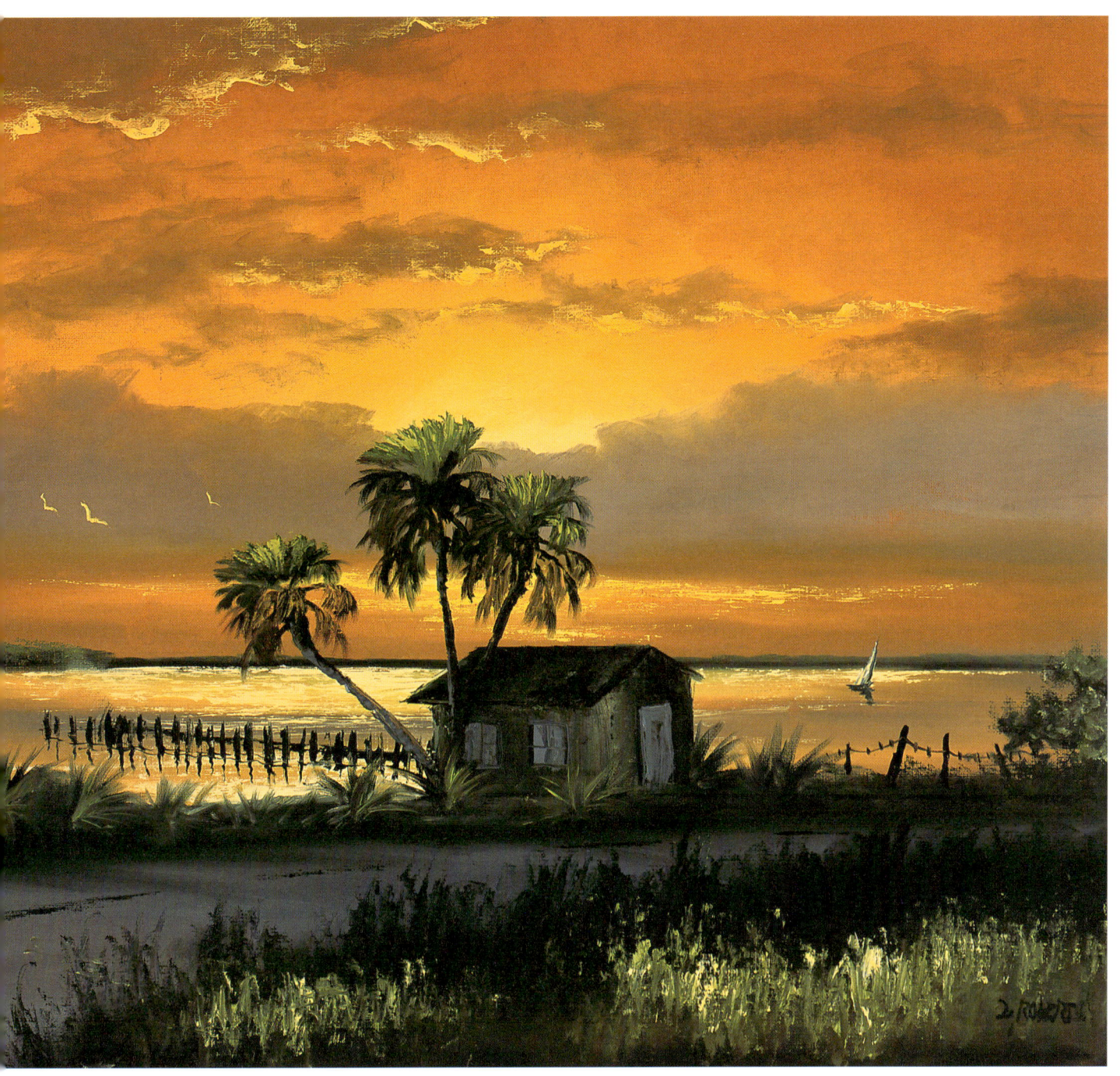

48. Harold Newton

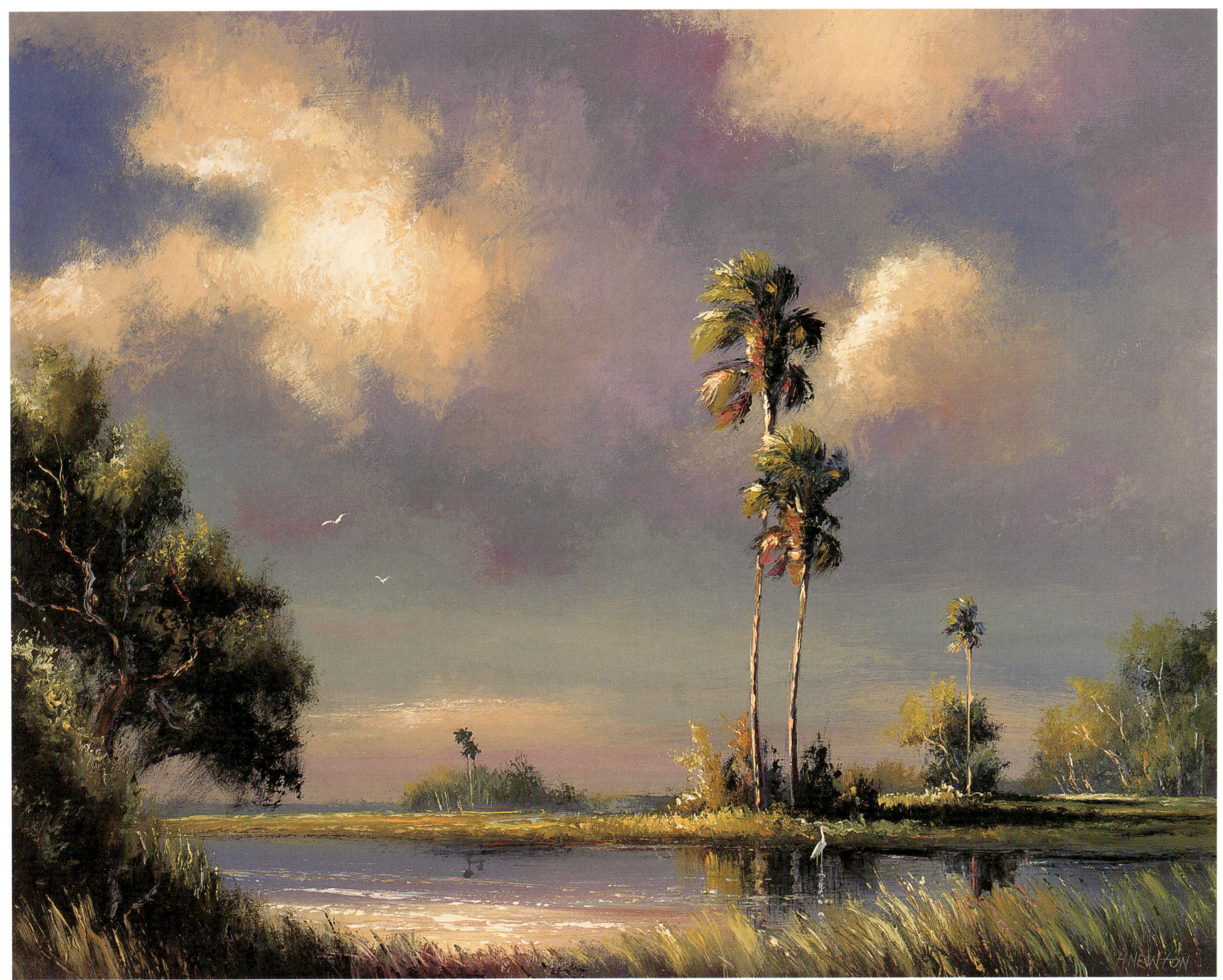

49. *Alfred Hair*

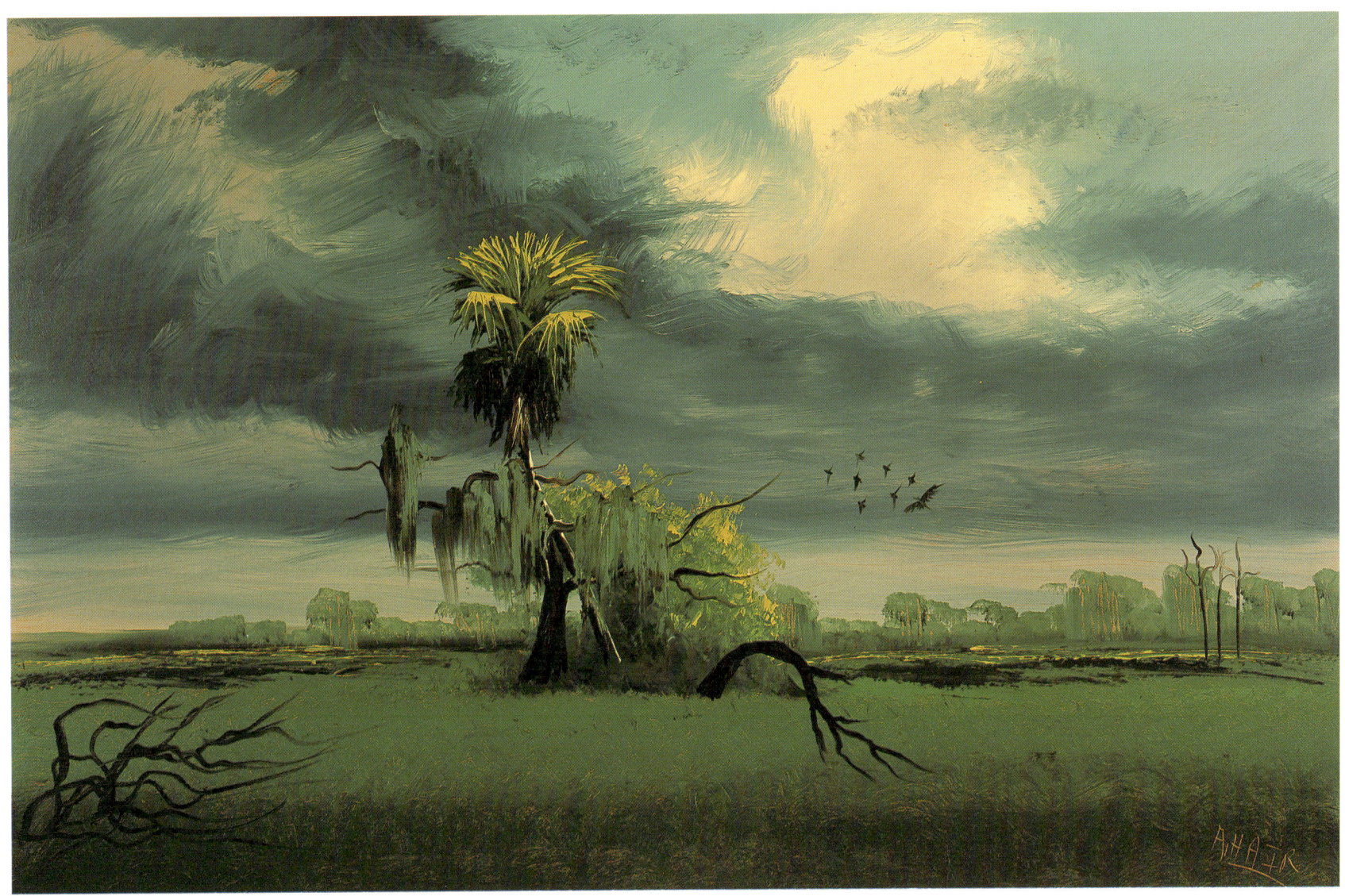

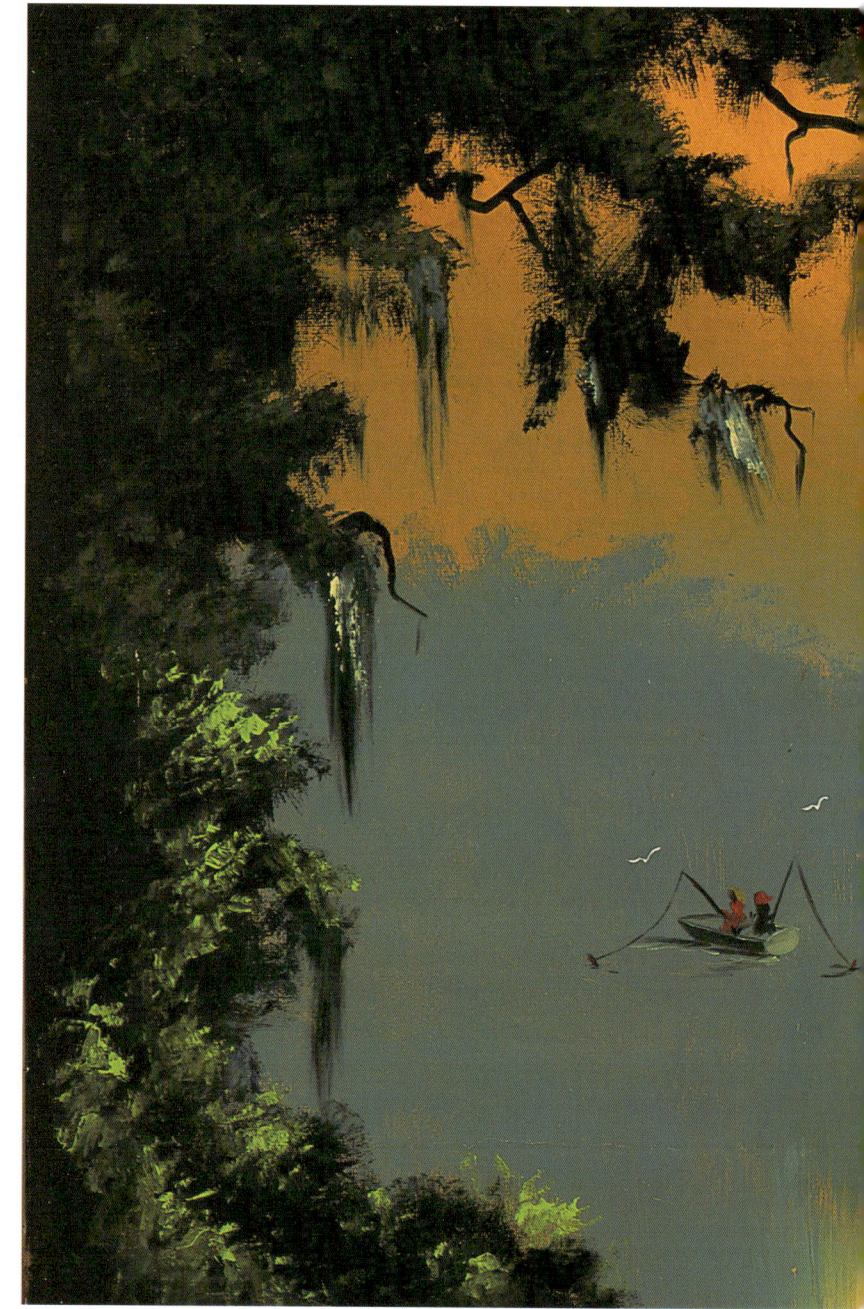

50. John Maynor

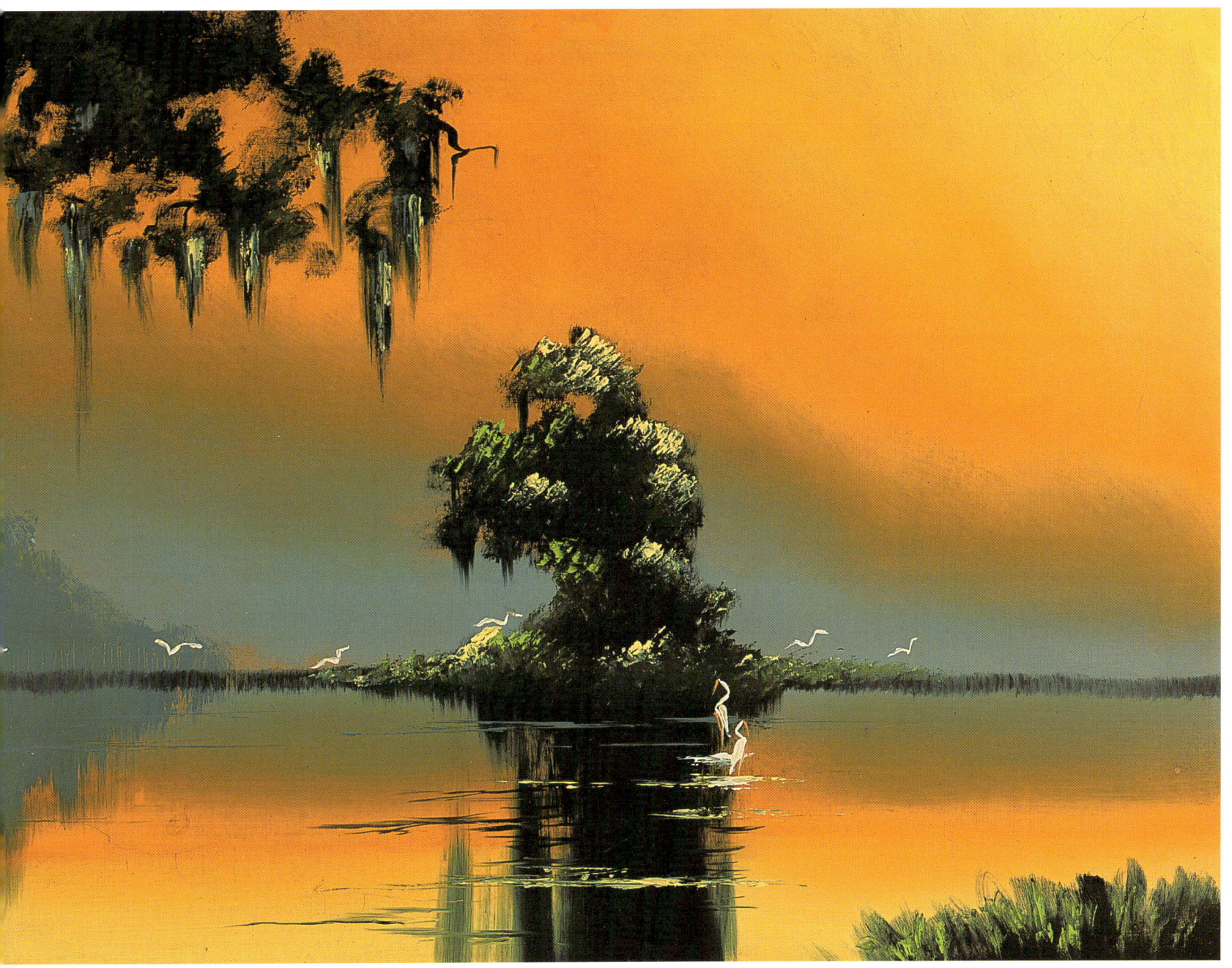

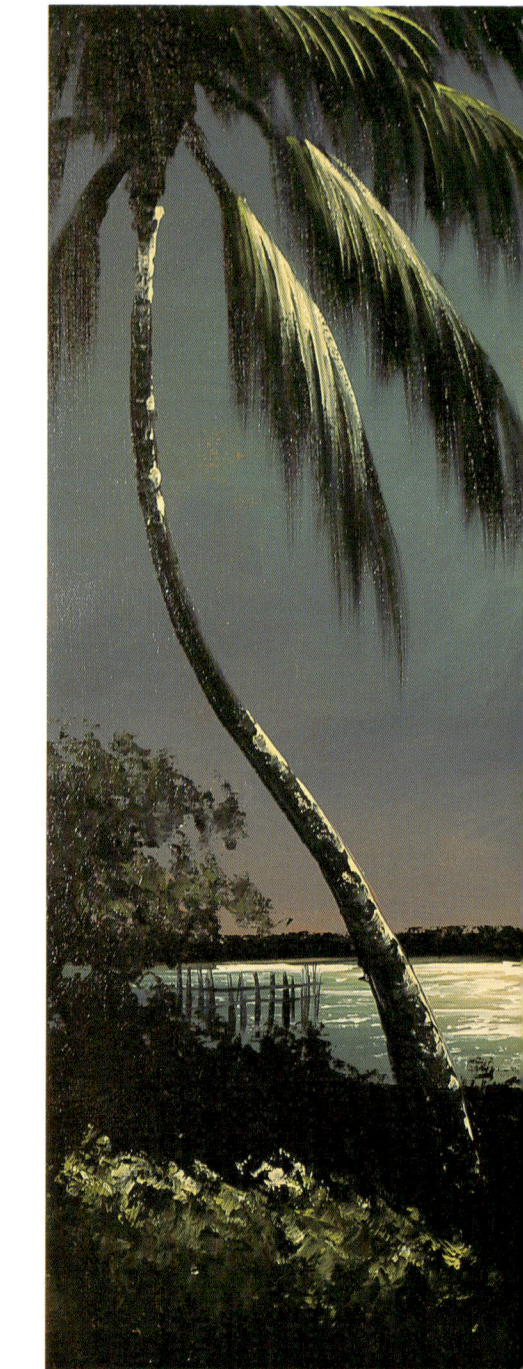

51. Livingston Roberts

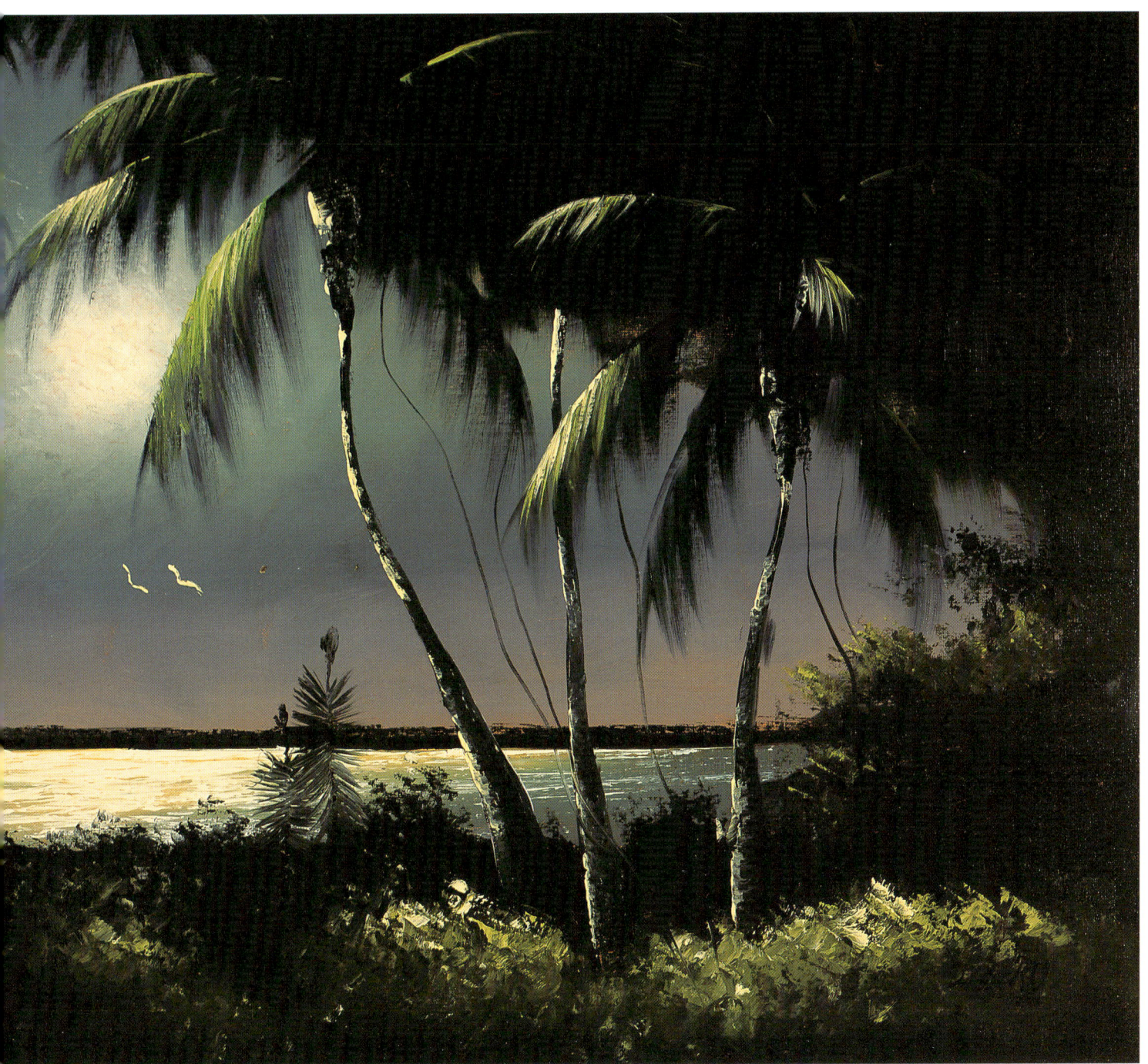

52. Johnny Daniels

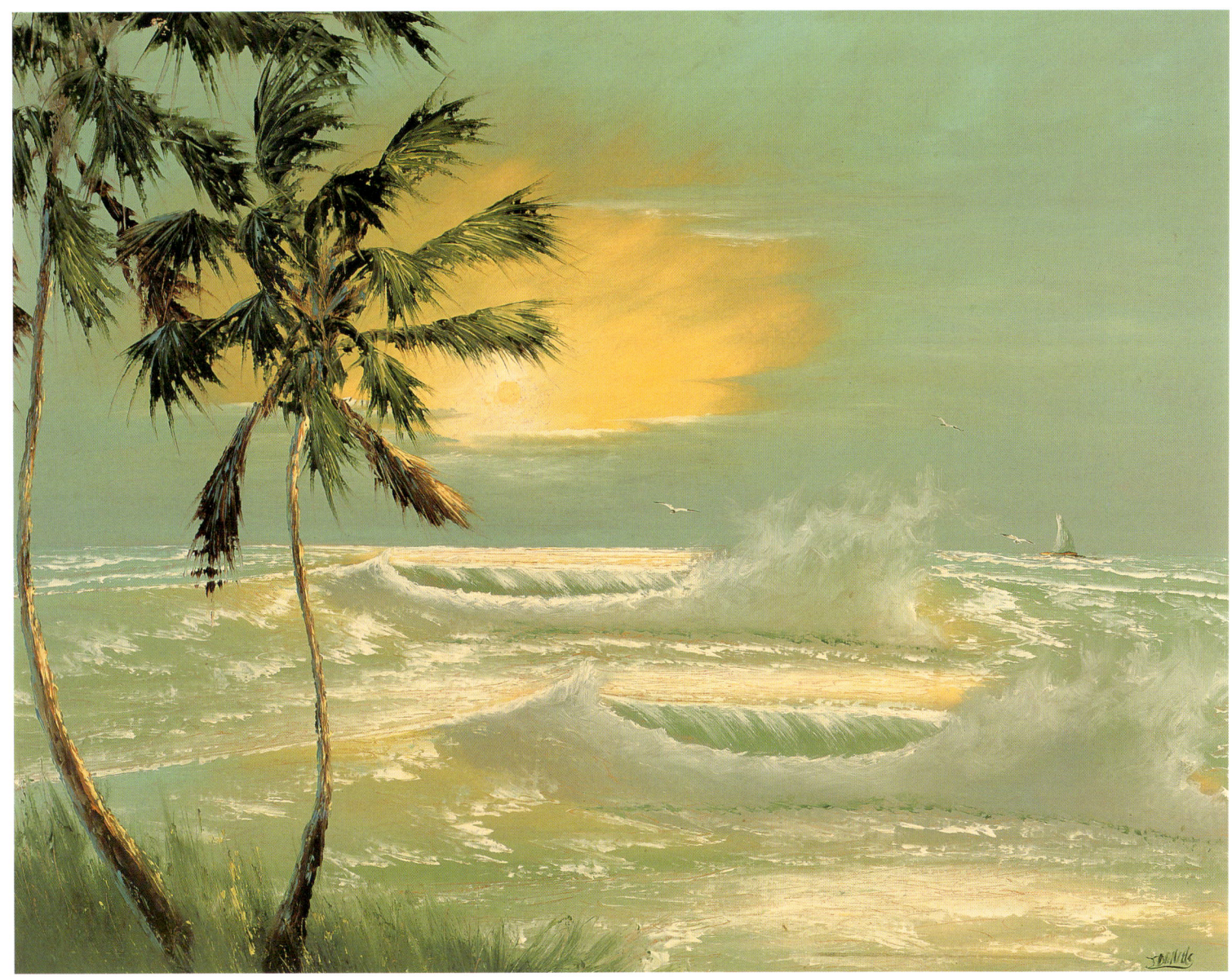

53. Livingston Roberts

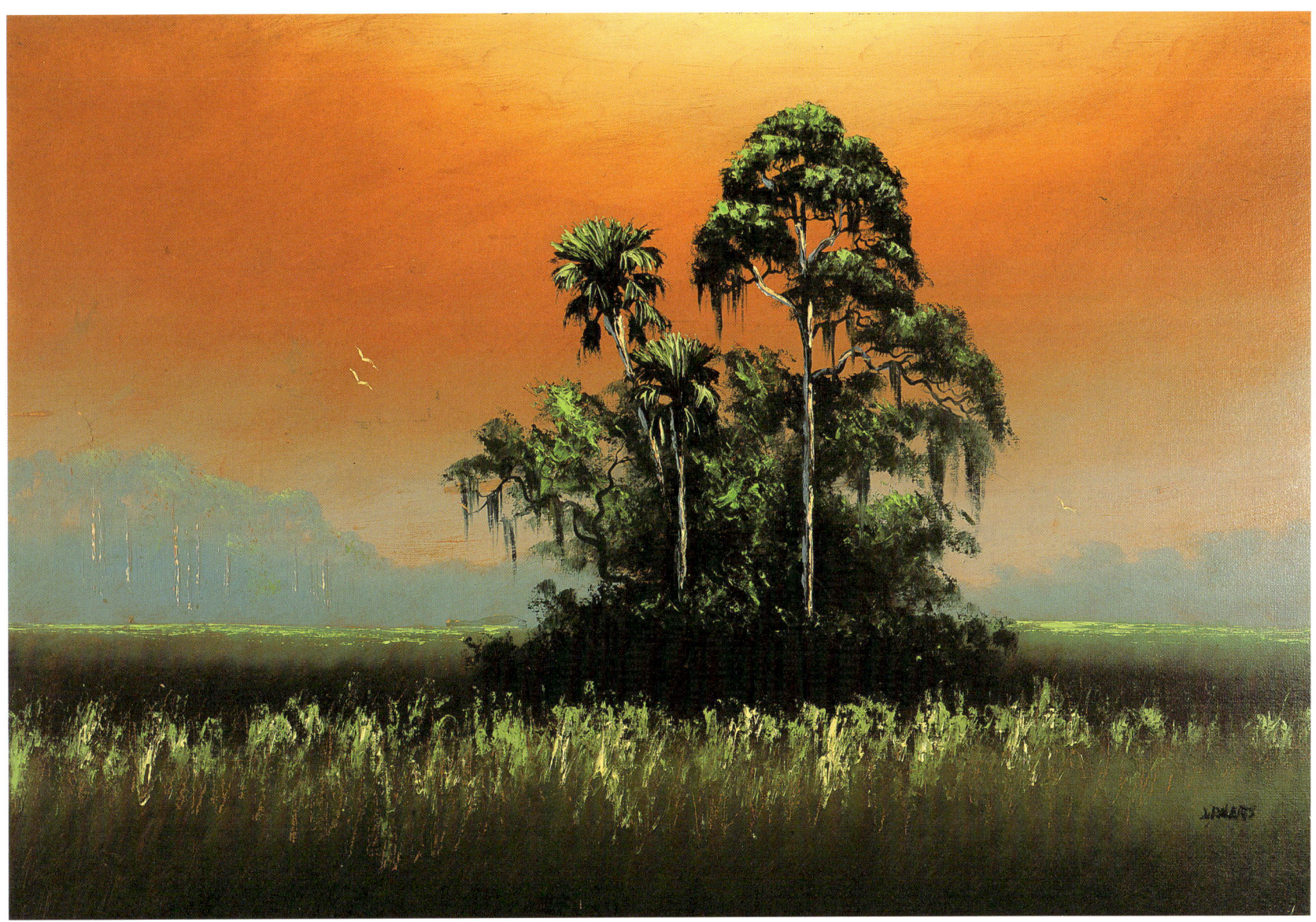

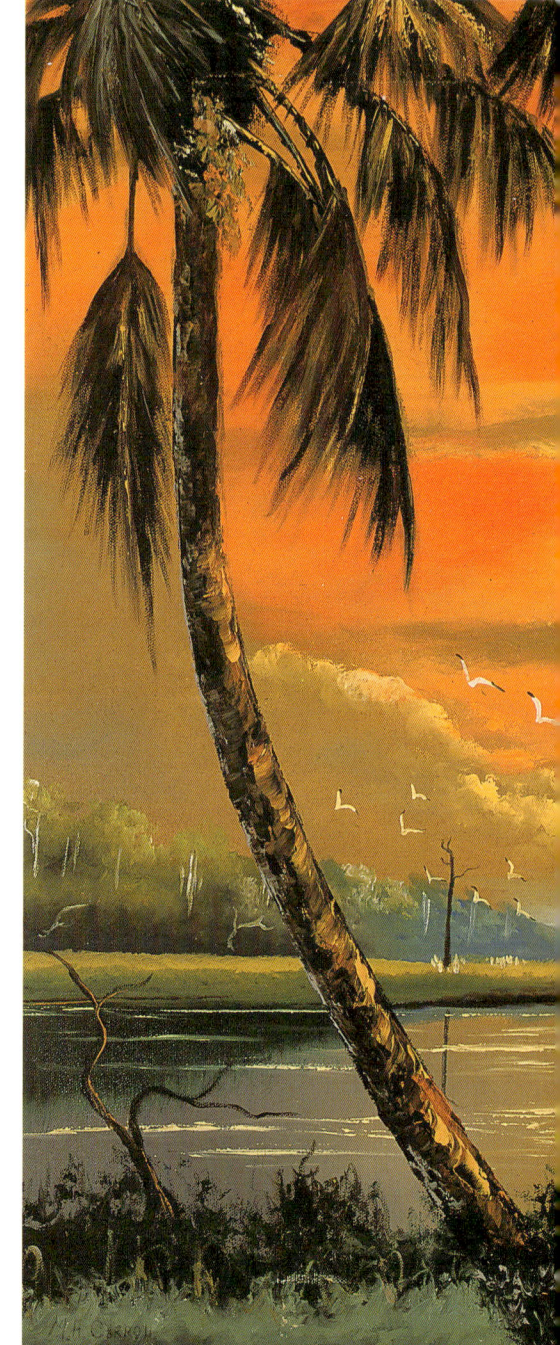

54. Mary Ann Carroll

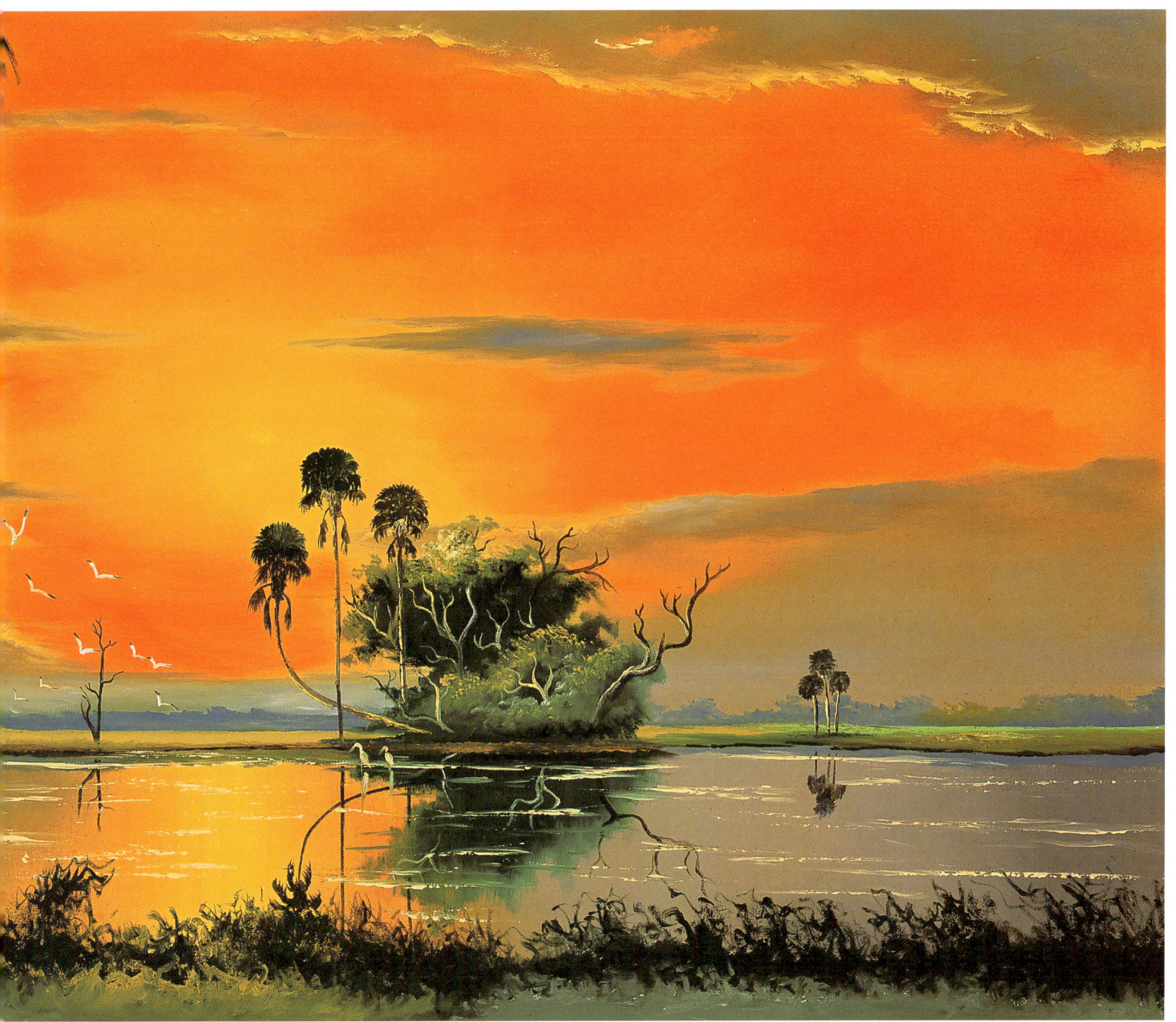

55. Roy McLendon

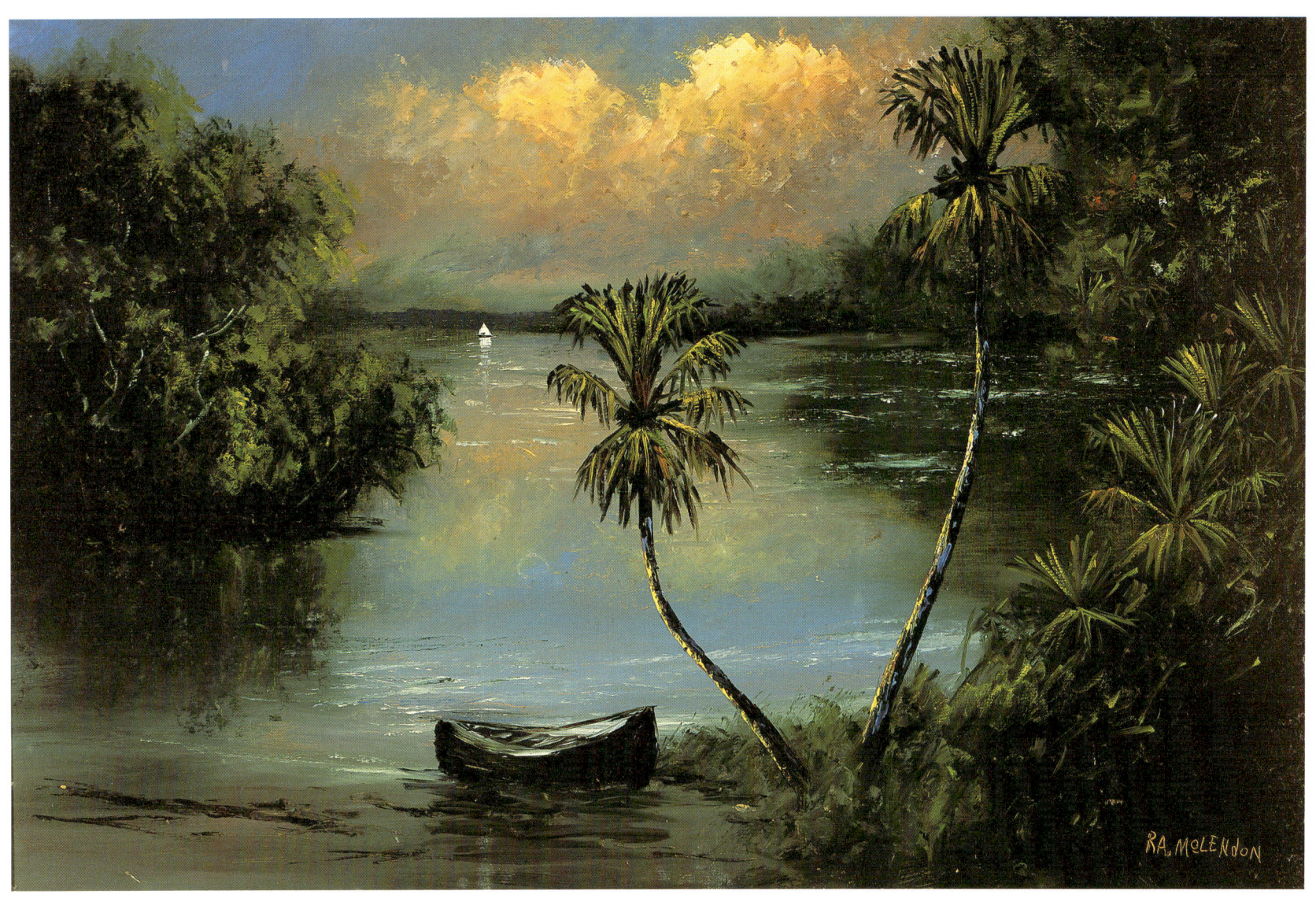

R.A. McLENDON

56. Johnny Daniels

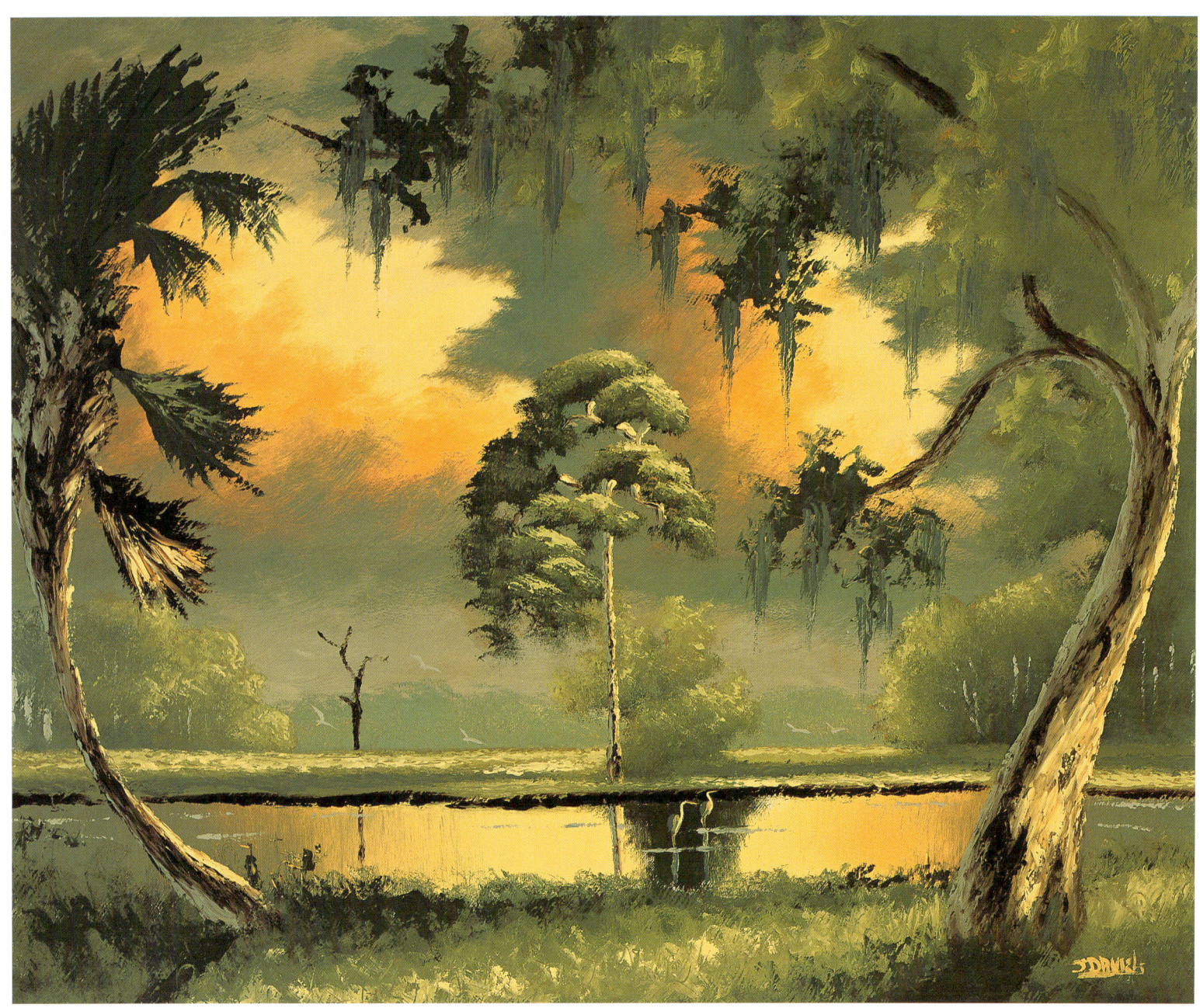

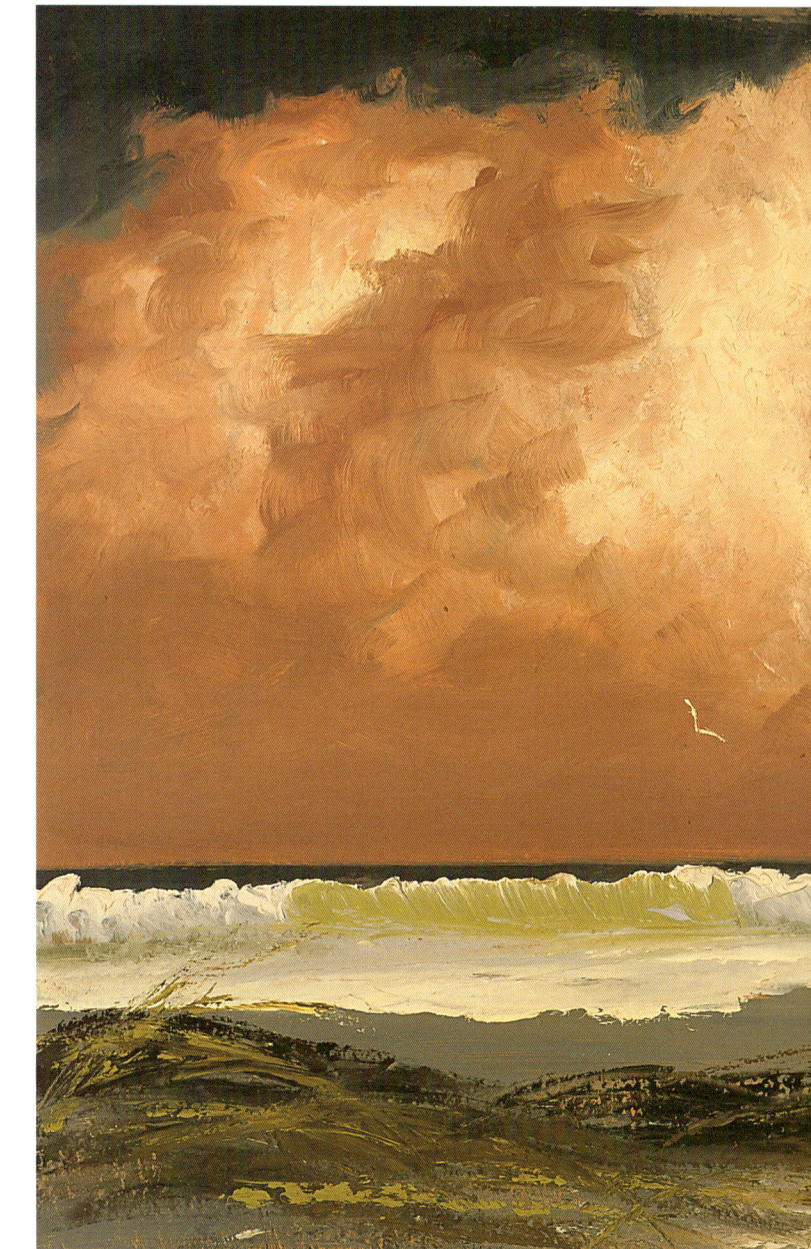

57. *Alfred Hair*

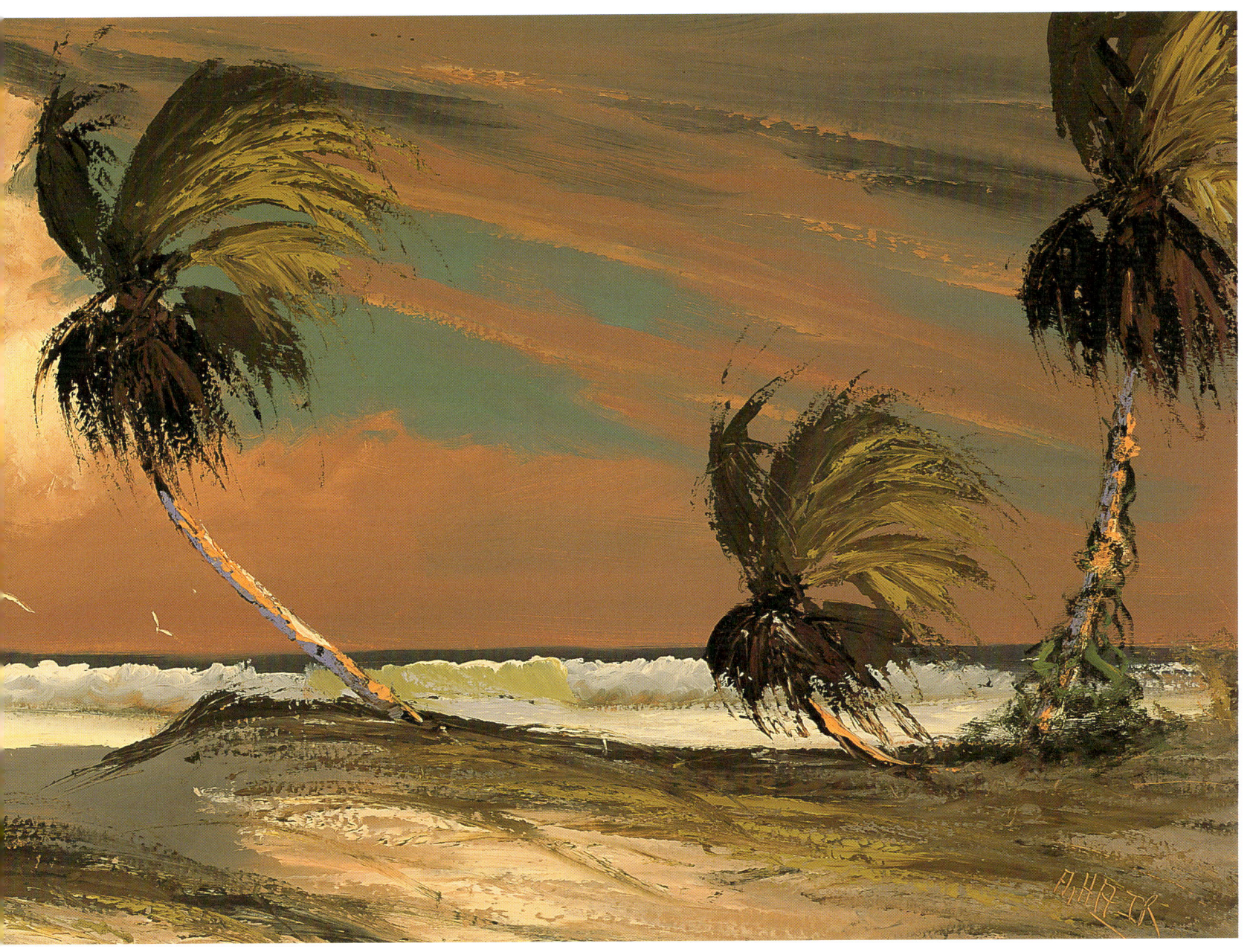

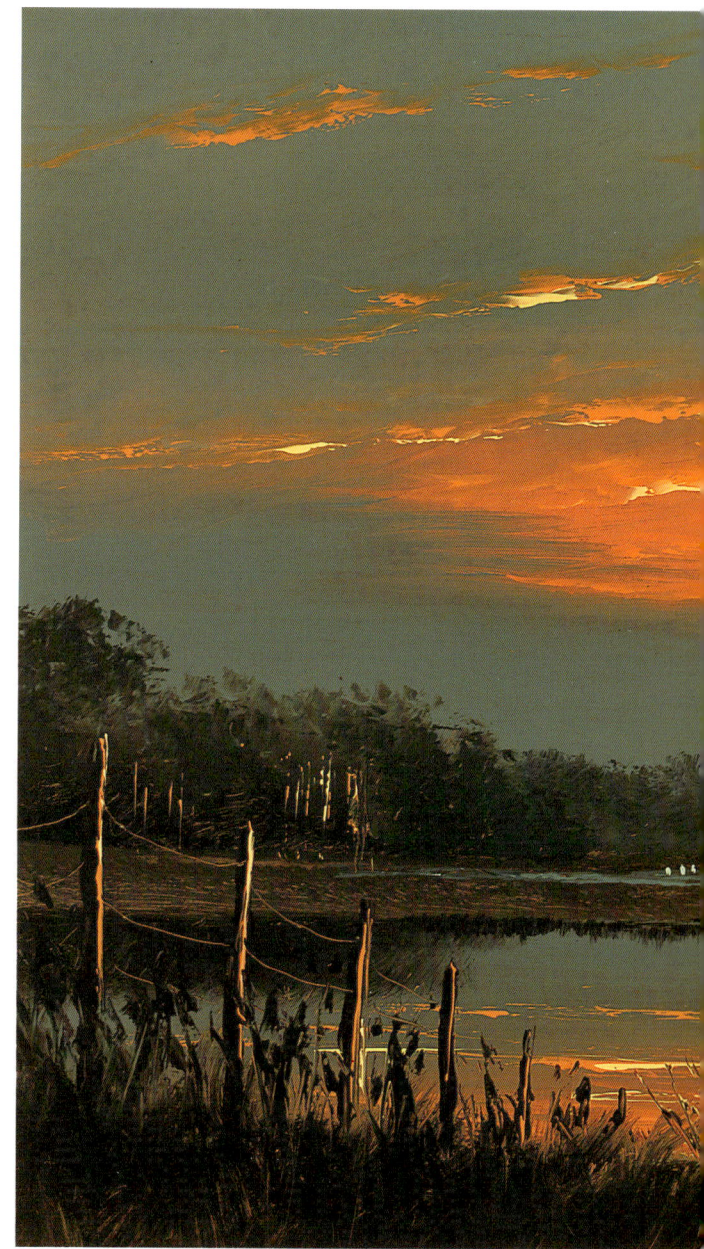

58. Harold Newton

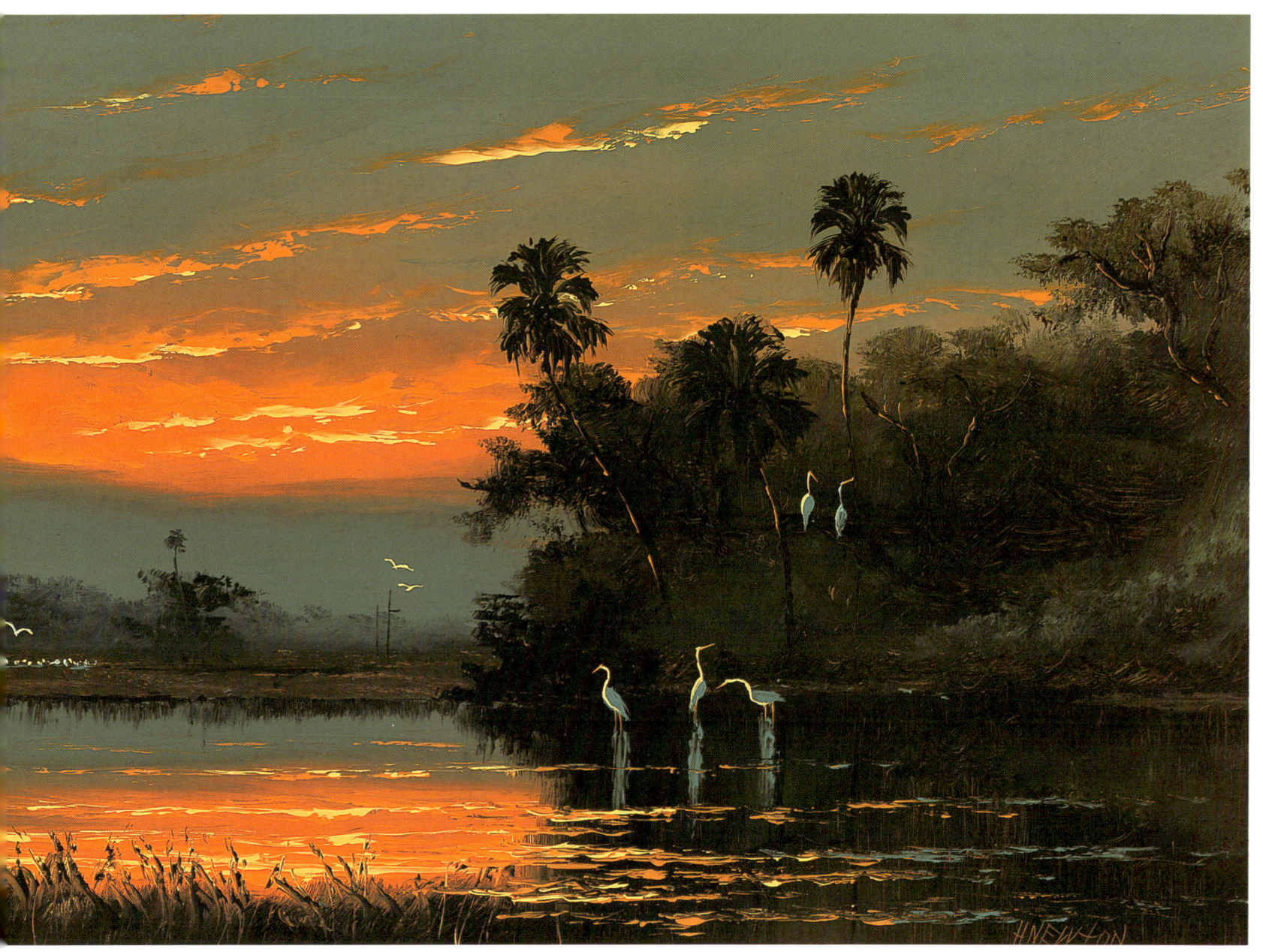

59. James Gibson

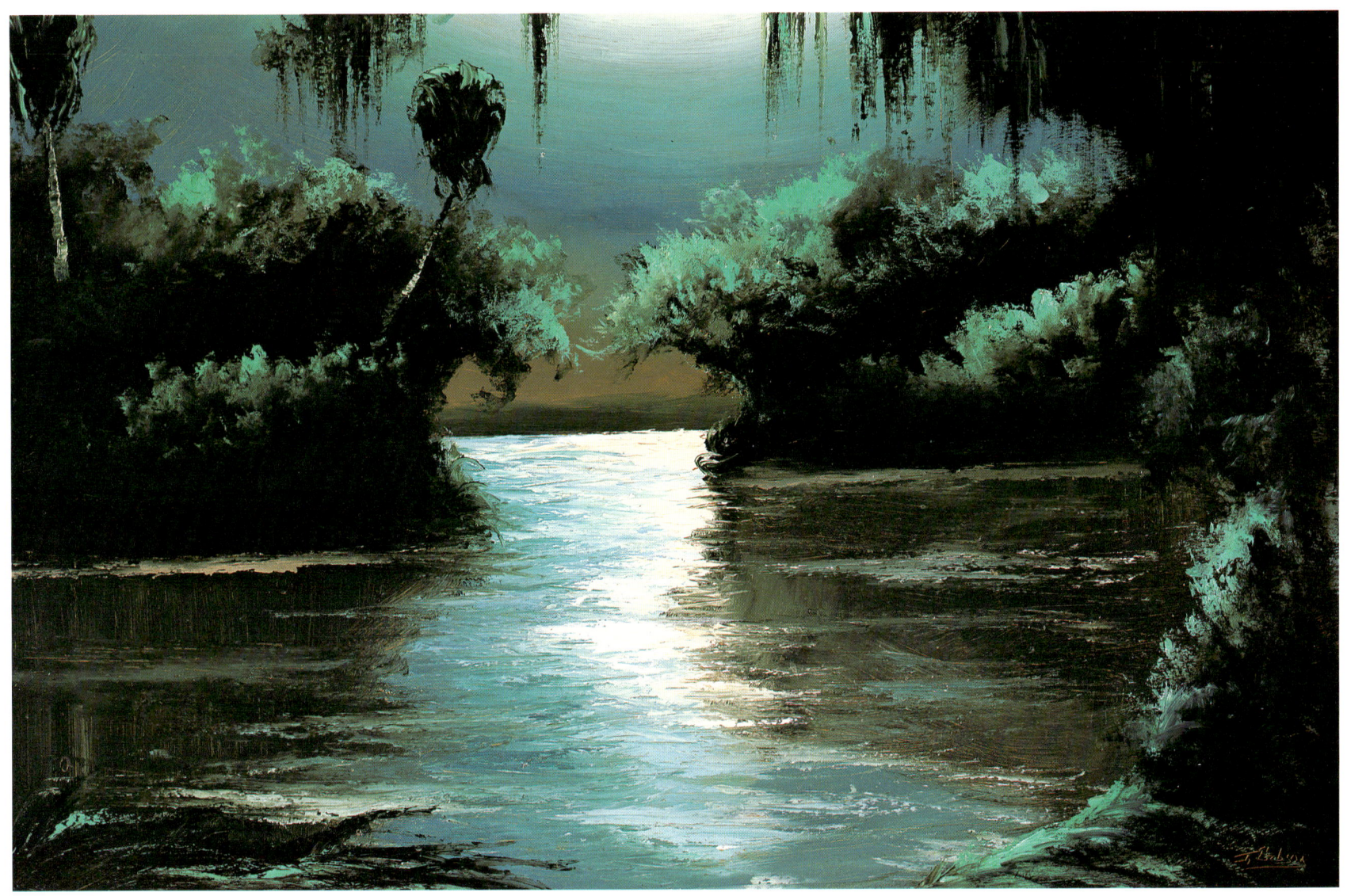

Notes

1. Preferring to cast a wide net, I have included all painters who fit the characteristics of the Highwaymen—young blacks from or associated with Ft. Pierce who painted in the shadow of Backus and sold their paintings on the streets. This is consistent with the sense of community that is central to the group. Jack Hempley and Purcell Dixon were the toughest to place; Dixon says that he never developed enough skill to be considered one of the Highwaymen, whereas Hempley pursued many activities other than painting. (He did possess the requisite speedy hands; in another of his jobs, as a barber, he offered his customers "a two-minute haircut or it's free.")

   Although I inquired widely, I could not learn much about H. Higgins, A. Nutting, or Bob Abbott, all of whom are rumored to have painted as Highwaymen. I saw two paintings by Abbott; one fit the general characteristics of High-waymen paintings but was terribly amateurish and otherwise lacked characteristics of the group. A George Buckner signature was painted out of the other one and Abbott's name flourished in its place! Johnny Wright was associated with the Ft. Pierce contingency but apparently, like others, made very few paintings. There isn't sufficient evidence to consider him a Highwayman.

   I also eliminated a few names that had circulated on the lists of collectors and other interested parties. For example, Tom Fresh turned out to be a Caucasian who had painted in Backus's studio. Lewis MacDaniels, although a landscape painter, is a friend of Robert Butler's son, and his art, as well as his age, differs significantly from that of the Highwaymen. Jimmy Stovall tried his hand at painting after having framed and sold paintings for Hair, but he opted for secure employment with the telephone company.

2. Although Hair painted on canvas board while studying with Backus, and occasionally afterward, he preferred to use Upson board, as Backus had done during lean times. Upson board became Hair's standard and would be the other Highwaymen's too. The 4' x 8' paper-based sheets were easily cut with a wallboard knife into waste-free formats: typically four 24" x 36" pieces—this being the Highwaymen's signature size—which were occasionally trimmed to 24" x 30" to accommodate particular wall spaces. The remaining 24" x 48" board was left as is or (more likely) cut into two 18" x 24" pieces with a 12" x 24" piece remaining, or in quarters to yield four 12" x 24" boards. The paintings were priced according to size: $35 for the largest, $25 for the standard, $20 for the medium size, and $12.50 for the smallest.

Upson board was manufactured both in linen and in matte (pebble-like) finishes, with linen being preferred because it resembled canvas, but either surface was used without much concern. The boards were primed with shellac, and, like Backus, the Highwaymen painted with oils and used palette knives for achieving surface effect and speed. Their paintings were not done with house paint, contrary to this erroneous myth, which is either a marketing gimmick by dealers or an inability to differentiate between the house paint used for the frames and the oil paint used for the paintings.

During the early 1980s the Highwaymen switched to Masonite because Upson board was becoming hard to find. (It didn't meet Florida's building code and was discontinued in 1991.) Also, consumers were requesting stretched canvas, so this became another popular painting surface.

3. Most of the existing literature on the Highwaymen is full of misinformation and was written by dealers primarily to create a market for the paintings. Even magazine and newspaper feature articles have contained numerous mistakes. My narrative focuses on the similarities of Newton's work to that of Backus and on the differences between their works and those of Hair and the other Highwaymen.

Personal interviews were conducted as follows: Hezekiah Baker, Ft. Pierce, September 13, 1998; Zanobia Jefferson, Ft. Pierce, September 13, 1998; Jim Fitch, Sebring, September 18, 1998; Jerry Johnson, Holly Hill, September 23, 1998; Sam and Roberta Vickers, Jacksonville, September 28, 1998; John Phillips, West Palm Beach, October 2, 1998; Don Brown, Ft. Pierce, October 4, 1998; Mary Ann Carroll, Ft. Pierce, October 4, 1998; Jim Murphy, Daytona Beach, October 14, 1998; James Gibson, October 17, 1998; Gary Libby, Daytona Beach, October 21, 1998; Livingston Roberts, Ft. Pierce, December 23, 1998; Charles Walker, Ft. Pierce, December 23, 1998; Curtis Arnett, Ft. Pierce, December 23, 1998; Johnny Daniels, Ft. Pierce, January 2, 1999; Gladys Bennett, Ft. Pierce, January 2, 1999; George Buckner, Gifford, January 2, 1999; Albert Black, Orlando, January 27, 1999; Isaac Knight, Ft. Pierce, January 29, 1999; Rodney Demps, Ft. Pierce, January 30, 1999; Jack Hempley, Ft. Pierce, February 4, 1999; Roy McLendon, Ft. Pierce, February 7, 1999; Tim Jacobs, Merritt Island, February 21, 1999; Alfonso Moran, Gifford, April 16, 1999; Mike Griffin, Bob Hommell, Merritt Island, April 24, 1999; Gray Brewer, Titusville, April 24, 1999; Ed Volonnino, Melbourne, April 30, 1999; Geoff Cook, Apopka, May 1, 1999; Robert Lewis, Merritt Island, May 4, 1999; Willie Reagan, Gifford, May 8, 1999; Trish Thompson, Port Orange, July 6, 1999; Purcell Dixon, Miami, July 10, 1999; Rudi Cleare, Merritt Island, July 11, 1999; Kelvin Hair, Ft. Pierce, August 2, 1999; Willie Pelt, Miami, August 3, 1999; Willie Williams, Ft. Pierce, September 15, 1999; John Maynor, Ft. Pierce, November 21, 1999; Henry Bosma, Vero Beach, January 28, 2000; Sylvester Wells, Cocoa, February 24, 2000; Charles Wheeler, Ft. Pierce, June 23, 2000.

I revisited or telephoned most of these people after our initial meeting. Other people I consulted (in telephone interviews only) include Bob Terry, Jr., Sam Newton, Robert Butler, and May Belle Mann. I became friendly with some of the collectors of Highwaymen paintings and have met many people who acquired paintings from the artists years ago and shared their ideas and recollections.

4. The backs of the frames were taped along the edges of the Upson boards with masking tape where they rested on the frames. (This was done as an effect, to imitate professional framers' use of kraft paper as a dust barrier.) The Highwaymen eventually phased out the practice because of the additional cost of the tape. The paintings were sold without picture-hanging wire stretched across the back, because this would have interfered with the stacking procedure and would have smeared the oils.

    Used or inexpensive frames took the place of crown molding when the artists could no longer obtain Upson boards. (Stretched canvas could not be used with the crown molding because it didn't have a recessed lip in which to secure a painting.) Newton apparently purchased used frames and used these along with crown molding, earlier and more often than did the other artists.

5. According to Don Brown, Backus assiduously studied volumes of arcane technique books—the bible being *The Art of Composition: A Simple Application of Dynamic Symmetry* (1926), by Michael Jacobs—in his efforts to ensure a classically correct rendition of the landscape.

6. Historian Michael Gannon writes in *Florida: A Short History* ([Gainesville: University Press of Florida, 1993], p. 130), that "no movement characterized Florida's political and social life in the 1960s as much as did civil rights for the state's long-neglected and much-abused African-American population."

    Mary Ann Carroll remembers that the death of Martin Luther King, Jr., drove a wedge between white and black Ft. Pierce. African-American residents commonly cite racism as being institutionalized in the town.

7. I had to contextualize the ideas and recollections of the painters and those associated with their story, but the perception of Alfred Hair was clear. He was widely beloved. People's eyes watered and they lowered their heads as they related their memories of him in reverent tones.

    Willie Williams, who opened Williams Department Store on Avenue E in 1951, outfitted most of the young men and women in the neighborhood. He recalls that Alfred came into his store the day before he was murdered and exclaimed, "I'm on my way to Miami—dress me!" Alfred and Williams selected "a yellow and blue casual sports outfit: blue pants, blue shirt, yellow coat, with black shoes." Williams adds: "He was some of the best . . ." Hair was going to move to Miami the day after his night on the town turned deadly. (His father lived in Hallandale, just north of Miami.)

    It would be pure speculation to consider the Highwaymen's fate had Hair lived and remained in Ft. Pierce, or if he had moved away. Nonetheless, it's interesting that he had planned to leave the region. While the Newtons worked the territory to the north of Ft. Pierce, Hair had gravitated southward to sell his paintings. "Alfred thought it would be a good place for his family and business," according to his sister Gladys Bennett. The pace of South Florida's growth must have appealed to him. He could have sold paintings singly and developed contracts for multiple paint-ings, says Roberts, as he had done with a popular furniture maker.

8. At this writing, Black is in prison on charges of grand theft (for extorting nearly a million dollars from a widow—though he and friends say that the verdict was unjust) and drug possession. In the Central Florida Reception Center, a penitentiary near Orlando, he is serving a twelve-year sentence that ends in 2007. He is a model inmate and allowed to paint murals on interior walls. He has produced more than 150 paintings that average 5 X 7 feet, and few, accord-ing to guards, took more than half an hour to complete!

9. The artists who continue to paint are evolving new directions and personal styles. This work deserves consideration.

10. Black says that at his request the artists he represented didn't sign some pieces, so that he would have an easier time selling them by claiming them as his own. He points out that he also scripted the "A" when he signed Hair's paint-ings, whereas Hair printed the letter, with a horizontal top line that converts an "H" into an "A." Black adds that Hair painted his name on those works with which he took more time but incised his signature when working fast. (With further regard to signatures, Newton crossed his "t" before scripting the vertical stem of the letter.)

    Hair signed "Freddie" to a few paintings. Roberts says that Hair painted the "Freddie" paintings for a business-man in West Palm Beach who intended to market them. He paid Hair just $100 for 300 paintings. They were too rushed, even for Hair, and he didn't want to be recognized as the artist. It is not clear whether Freddie was the name of the man who had commissioned the paintings or a nickname (for Alfred). Baker believes that the businessman's name was Freddie and that he wanted to take credit for the paintings. It has also been suggested that Hair signed "Freddie" on his very earliest paintings.

    Paintings signed "A. Hare" and "A. Hir" have also surfaced, but their attribution is uncertain. Some of the paint-ers speculate that they may have been the careless result of speed, but it is more likely that these were signed for Hair by one of his cohorts. The "A" in certain paintings signed "Hir" looks suspiciously like Black's.

    There are also some nicknames (like "Coffee," McLendon's childhood name). Mary Ann Carroll suggests that Hair may have signed made-up names on images that he found inferior to his usual standard. Or the painting may have been a group effort, with too many other artists adding elements to it for him to call it his own. (The paintings Carroll made prior to her marriage are signed with her maiden name, Snead. She doesn't remember the year she mar-ried, only that it was soon after beginning to paint.)

11. The idea that a work of art is more than the realistic depiction of objects and that an image can entice a viewer into dream/vision/escape is noted by Roger Shattuck in *The Banquet Years*. Discussing the French "primitive" painter Henri Rousseau, he comments that for Rousseau, a landscape "was not houses or mountains or a virgin forest, it was man walking in wonder among the trees."

Gary Monroe, professor of visual art at Daytona Beach Community College, is a documentary photographer with a long-time interest in "outsider" and vernacular art. His work has been recognized with numerous exhibitions and awards, including grants from the National Endowment for the Arts and the Fulbright Foundation, and he has been a popular lecturer for the Florida Humanities Council's Speakers Bureau. His photographs have been exhibited widely and published in *Cassadaga: The South's Oldest Spiritualist Community* (UPF, 2000), which he coedited, *Life in South Beach* (1989), and *Florida Dreams* (1993), among others. He lives in DeLand, Florida.